The Corporation in the Nineteenth-Century
American Imagination

EDINBURGH CRITICAL STUDIES IN LAW, LITERATURE AND THE HUMANITIES

Series Editor: William MacNeil, University of Queensland
Senior Deputy Editor: Shaun McVeigh, University of Melbourne
Deputy Editor: Daniel Hourigan, University of Southern Queensland

With a global reach, this innovative series critically reimagines the interdisciplinary relationship between legal and literary (or other aesthetic) texts through the most advanced conceptual frameworks and interpretive methods of contemporary theory available in the humanities and jurisprudence.

Visit the **Edinburgh Critical Studies in Law, Literature and the Humanities** website at http://edinburghuniversitypress.com/series-edinburgh-critical-studies-in-law-literature-and-the-humanities

The Corporation in the Nineteenth-Century American Imagination

Stefanie Mueller

EDINBURGH
University Press

Edinburgh University Press is one of the leading university presses in the UK. We publish academic books and journals in our selected subject areas across the humanities and social sciences, combining cutting-edge scholarship with high editorial and production values to produce academic works of lasting importance. For more information visit our website: edinburghuniversitypress.com

Edinburgh University Press Ltd.
The Tun—Holyrood Road
12(2f) Jackson's Entry
Edinburgh EH8 8PJ

Typeset in 11/13pt Adobe Garamond Pro
by Manila Typesetting Company, and
printed and bound in Great Britain

A CIP record for this book is available from the British Library

ISBN 978 1 3995 0500 0 (hardback)
ISBN 978 1 3995 0502 4 (webready PDF)
ISBN 978 1 3995 0503 1 (epub)

Contents

Figures

Acknowledgments

This book has been written in many places and with the encouragement and advice of many colleagues, friends, and sometimes strangers. I was supported by several institutions, among them my alma mater, Goethe University Frankfurt, which funded very early and hence very crucial research for this project, and the Alexander von Humboldt-Foundation, which made it possible for me to pursue a two-year post-doctoral fellowship at the University of California at Irvine. I want to thank the colleagues at the annual conferences of the Association for the Study of Law, Culture, and the Humanities, where I presented my work over the years. Special thanks go to Peter Schneck at the University of Osnabrück for his support and to Frank Kelleter and the John F. Kennedy Institute at Freie Universität Berlin, where I finished central parts of the manuscript.

Scholars whose encouragement, kindness, and knowledge supported me and my project in innumerable ways include Benjamin Betka, Birte Christ, Christian Kloeckner, Zuzanna Ładyga, and Katja Sarkowsky. Christa Buschendorf's guidance has been invaluable, and I can only hope that, in the future, I will have the opportunity to pass on what I have learned from her to other young researchers. Special thanks go to Brook Thomas, whose generous advice and foundational work on corporations in law and literature have helped this project to become reality. After all the travel, research, and exciting conversations with scholars, I have also had the fortune to have friends and family to come home to. I want to thank Mama, Sascha, Sarah, and Sonja for patience, laughter, and for all the cake. Finally, closest to my heart, this book is for Peter and for Linus, who took his first steps as I was completing this book.

Introduction: The Many and the One: Corporate Bodies and the Body Politic in US Law and Culture

In recent years, corporations and their role in democracies have received increasing attention not just from legal and cultural scholars but also from the public in the United States. Spectacular legal decisions, in particular *Citizens United* v. *Federal Election Commission* (2010), have contributed to this phenomenon and have raised questions about the legal status of corporations as subjects of rights and duties—in other words, as legal persons. In *Citizens United*, the US Supreme Court decided that corporations as legal persons are protected under the First Amendment of the Constitution and that they have the right to free speech. The ramifications of this decision raised concerns that touched the very meaning of democracy and citizenship in the United States. In the case of *Citizens United*, it was the idea of equal access and opportunity in the so-called "marketplace of ideas" that was deemed essential to a functioning democracy but in which corporations, by nature of their greater economic and social resources, appeared as larger-than-life actors, far more powerful than the individual citizen. In the mediation of this controversy which preceded, but mostly followed the Court's decision, David-versus-Goliath narratives and Frankenstein tropes abounded (335). Overwhelmingly, they conveyed the popular sense that the Court was not just adding to corporate power in the US but was essentially creating non-human actors whose power actively curtailed the rights of other citizens.

The present study is not about these twenty-first-century controversies, but rather about what preceded them. To fully understand the relationship between corporate power and democracy in the United States it is necessary to take a historical approach, one that equally recognizes the role of legal, economic, and popular discourses in the development of this relationship. To that end, this study presents a literary and cultural history of the corporation in the United States in the long nineteenth century. It shows how artists, lawyers and economists, fiction and nonfiction writers represented the corporate form's development: from its being understood as a creation of the law to a creature of the market. While the study proceeds chronologically—from the debates over banking corporations during the revolutionary period and their culmination in Andrew Jackson's Bank War in the 1830s, to the rise of large industrial corporations and the triumph of separate legal personhood in the 1930s—it also shows that this development from political to economic instrument was not inevitable, nor did it go unchallenged. The public origins of the corporation remained relevant to legal and cultural narratives about the role of corporations in democracies even as new combinations integrated entire industrial sectors at the end of the nineteenth century. Likewise, the collective nature of the corporation—the fact that it is a group of people acting together—never dropped out of sight for legal and literary writers, even as the corporation's legal individuality became more central to corporate rights and regulations.

Whereas classical studies of corporations and corporate culture in the United States (such as Alan Trachtenberg's *The Incorporation of American Culture* [1982]) have tended to see both primarily as phenomena of the marketplace and hence as shaped by economic discourses, this book argues that the legal as well as the popular imaginary also mediated the corporate form's transformation in the nineteenth century from a public tool meant to serve the common good to an instrument of private enterprise. While legal historians have long conceptualized this shift as the development from grant theory to natural entity theory, what has gone unstudied so far is how literature and culture contributed to this transformation of the corporation from a political actor to an economic actor—that is to say, how artists and writers, together with lawyers and economists, represented this transformation through narrative and metaphor. Based on the study of fictional as well as factual texts, this book shows how the corporation's public origins as well as its fundamentally collective nature continued to be relevant for much longer than previous scholarship has argued. In the process, it ultimately also urges us to question twenty-first-century narratives of corporate individuality and personhood.

The Private Corporation Aggregate

Today the corporation has become almost synonymous with the firm, the company, or the enterprise. When we think of corporations, we think of capitalist ventures. But the origins of the corporation, not just in the United States, are political and civic rather than purely economic.[1] In its most basic sense a

---

[1] I am using "political" here to emphasize its legal rather than economic characteristics and its public rather than private uses. My discussion thereby joins the work of Henry S. Turner, Joshua Barkan, and Philip J. Stern, who also advocate seeing the early corporation as a political entity.

corporation is a group of people who organize for some specific purpose, such as to form a town, and set down the rules by which to live together and to interact with people from outside their community. On a smaller scale, such citizens might decide to organize in order to open a school or build a bridge, for example; in other words, to contribute to the welfare and the common wealth of the community. Incorporation gives this body of people a separate legal existence, which is called "personhood." This legal fiction has its origins in Roman law, which distinguished between two forms of organization: associations and partnerships, so-called *societas*, and corporations, which were called *universitas* and from which our modern "university" derives its meaning. Even in Roman times, corporations (*universitas*) were legal persons while the other, contract-based forms were not. Incorporation thereby enabled a group to act as a single entity in law, to give itself rules and to enforce them, as well as to set the conditions of its existence more generally. The latter were often already part of the charter, which was granted by the sovereign; at first this was the English monarch and later the state legislatures. Such public corporations were dominant in the United States until the beginning of the nineteenth century, as James Willard Hurst notes:

> [A]lmost all of the business enterprises incorporated [in the US] in the formative generation starting in the 1780s were chartered for activities of some community interest—supplying transport, water, insurance, or banking facilities. That such public-interest undertakings practically monopolized the corporate form implied that incorporation was inherently of such public concern that the public authority must confer it. (15)

On account of their legal and political ties to the common wealth and public good, corporations were seen approvingly as "vehicles of public liberty"—towns, boroughs, fellowships—or more disapprovingly as *imperii in imperio*, such as in the famous statement by Thomas Hobbes (Speir 123): "Another infirmity of a Common-wealth is [. . .] the great number of corporations, which are as it were many lesser Common-wealths in the bowels of a greater, like worms in the entrails of a natural man" (Hobbes 230). As I will argue in more detail below, Americans recognized a structural kinship between the corporation and the body politic.

To emphasize the political beginnings of the corporation is not to downplay the extent to which they were used for economic gain but to broaden our understanding of how corporations structured and produced economic, political, and cultural practices. A case in point is the East India Company, one of the earliest and most powerful British trading companies. The East India Company was chartered to trade with Southeast Asia in 1600, and for this purpose it received extensive monopoly rights from Queen Elizabeth I.

By emphasizing the corporate form's political qualities, Philip J. Stern argues, analysis can move beyond the

> traditionally stark divisions between "trading" and "imperial" eras in Asia [. . .], pointing instead to a more continuous, gradual, and contingent story that envisions the evolution of empire as part of the transformation from early modern to modern forms of state, sovereignty, and political power. (7)

Taking a similar perspective, Joshua Barkan suggests that an analysis of the early modern corporation offers insights into a specific mode of governance that may well be specific to capitalism: "the corporation offered an image of sovereignty in a specifically liberal and decentralized mode" (19). Acknowledging the political dimension of the corporate form therefore opens new avenues into the early popular and legal imaginary and its impact on how Americans imagined power, self, and democracy under the conditions of an emerging market society.

In this respect, it is also important to remember that the development of the corporation in England and North America diverged significantly after US independence. In England, the Bubble Act of 1720 put a temporary stop to incorporations by requiring all joint-stock companies to obtain a royal charter. It had come on the heels of a stock-market crash so devastating that United States president Andrew Jackson would still refer to the South Sea Bubble when explaining why he disliked banks.[2] Receiving a charter for business purposes became so difficult after the Bubble Act that it forced not only English but also colonial entrepreneurs to "form [. . .] unincorporated joint-stock associations [. . .]. Many colonial 'companies' were, in fact, general partnerships" (Wright 22). In his *Wealth of Nations* (1776), Adam Smith would therefore treat corporations almost exclusively in terms of towns and guilds, and he would add to his critique of monopoly a critique of their impact on the individual's motivation, her self-interest. For Smith, corporations created so-called agency problems because, as Willard Hurst explains, they "must depend wholly on agents who could not be expected to display the sustained zeal for profit which moved individual proprietors" (48). However, while the development of the corporation and corporate law stalled in England, in the United States it accelerated after 1780.

---

[2] "Andrew Jackson [. . .] said more than a century later that ever since he read about the South Sea Bubble he had been afraid of banks" (Hammond 3).

In fact, by the end of the eighteenth century, the numbers of incorporation in the young nation had exploded.[3] "Between 1783 and 1801, 350 businesses were incorporated in the United States, a striking contrast to the approximately twelve corporations chartered in England during the entire eighteenth century" (Helfman 389).[4] Historians have long wondered about the reasons behind this "chartering spree" (Wright 25). Pauline Maier has suggested that Americans' enthusiasm for the corporate form can be seen as part of the early republic's "associational revolution" as described by Alexis de Tocqueville (McCarthy 2):

> They did so, Tocqueville suggested, for reasons tied to the nature of their society. In aristocratic communities, private associations were unnecessary because the followers and dependents of wealthy and powerful individuals were already bound together in "permanent and compulsory" associations. But in democratic nations, where citizens were "independent and feeble," they had to "learn voluntarily to help one another" or be "powerless."
> (Maier 58)

Moreover, she adds, Americans probably recognized the fundamental structural kinship between the republic and the corporation based on the similarity between constitutions and charters.

Whatever the reasons, the early history of the American corporation is a success story. "Americans did not invent the for-profit business corporation, but they did perfect the form—and far earlier than most believe—in the first half of the nineteenth century, surpassing the British and other precedents" (Wright 4). In fact, the first American treatise on corporation law, *Treatise on the Law of Private Corporations Aggregate* (1832) by Joseph K. Angell and Samuel Ames, starts from this very observation: that the history of the corporation in England has been mostly public (municipal, charitable, etc.) and that unincorporated forms, such as general partnerships and unincorporated joint-stock companies, dominate the private sector there. By contrast, Angell and Ames add, in the United States, "what is done here by the co-operation of

---

[3] Pauline Maier emphasizes that the immediate post-revolutionary period saw mostly public corporations, with the number of business incorporations increasing at the beginning of the 1790s. "Within a little over a decade after Independence, the fourteen incorporated cities and boroughs of late colonial North America had more than doubled: by 1789 about twenty previously unincorporated communities had been granted charters" (Maier 63).

[4] This estimate is based on the numbers provided by Oscar and Mary Handlin's important article "Origins of the American Business Corporation" (1945). For an even earlier inquiry see Joseph Stancliffe Davis's *Essays in the Earlier History of the Corporation* (1917).

several persons, is, in the greater number of instances, the result of a consolidation effected by an express act or charter of incorporation" (v). Consequently,
English law no longer adequately reflected the use that Americans made of
incorporation.

> While, therefore, we perceive the reason why so little attention has been
> devoted by English authors to the law of private corporations, we cannot
> but be impressed with a deep sense of the importance of this law in our own
> country. (Angell and Ames vi)

For Angell and Ames, the corporation in America is the private corporation aggregate: an instrument of private enterprise rather than public utility,
and a group entity rather than the (monarchical) *corporation sole*.

The case that provided the basic definition for the private corporation
aggregate at the beginning of the nineteenth century is *Trustees of Dartmouth
College* v. *Woodward* (1819),[5] in which John Marshall—the Court's chief
justice at the time—describes a corporation as "an artificial being, invisible,
intangible, and existing only in contemplation of law" (636). This definition
is familiar to even the most casual student of corporations in US history and
culture. Usually it is quoted alongside another Supreme Court decision, *Santa
Clara County* v. *Southern Pacific Railroad Company* (1886), as the beginning
of modern corporate personhood. In *Paternalism Incorporated* (2003), for
example, David Leverenz writes:

> In the *Dartmouth College* v. *Woodward* case of 1819, Chief Justice John
> Marshall incisively shifted the matrix by defining the corporation as an
> artificial person, created only in law. By 1886, when the Supreme Court
> applied several aspects of the Fourteenth Amendment to corporations, con-
> stitutional law was fine-tuning the similarities and differences between these
> artificial persons and human persons. (26)

Such shortcuts distort the legal and cultural development of the corporation, and they reflect a singular fascination with corporate personhood
that was not shared by nineteenth-century writers. That fascination says
more about our present moment than about the past. Instead of reading
Dartmouth as the beginning of corporate personhood, this study proceeds
from the premise that *Dartmouth* is culturally more significant as the beginning of the American corporation's privatization. By deciding that charters
are contracts within the meaning of the Constitution's Contract Clause, the

---

[5] Angell and Ames also draw on an English treatise, Stewart Kyd's 1793 *A Treatise on the Law
of Corporations*.

Court took the first step toward turning the corporation into a tool of private enterprise. Quoting Justice Joseph Story's concurring opinion in *Dartmouth*, Kent Newmyer explains,

> [Justice Joseph Story's] doctrine of public and private corporations[:] "Public corporations," he declared, were "such as exist for public political purposes only, such as towns, cities, parishes, and counties." Private corporations, the focus of his concern, were those whose foundations were private, that is, where the initial capital came from private individuals. "If, therefore, the foundation be private, though under the charter of government, the corporation is private, however extensive the uses may be to which it is devoted, either by the bounty of the founder, or the nature and objects of the institution." The uses or function of the corporation might even be public, but if the foundation was private so was the corporation, "as much so, indeed, as if the franchises were vested in a single person." (832)

Add to this precedent a movement for free incorporation that began to spread across the country by 1840 and that demanded that the corporation be made more democratic by making charters available upon application rather than through a special grant by the legislature. By the end of Reconstruction, jurists argued that corporations were a normal mode of doing business, essentially not much different from partnerships. By the end of the century, finally, the corporate form had become fully severed from the idea that it was bound to the common good; the form was flexible in purpose, capable of owning other corporations, and regulated according to a separate body of private corporation law. This gradual and by no means linear process is what this study calls the corporation's transformation from a political to an economic actor—or, to put it differently, from a creation of the law to a creation of the market.[6]

---

[6] To call the definitions of the different models of the corporation in the nineteenth century "untidy," as Tara Helfman has recently done, is almost an understatement (387). My study roughly follows Morton J. Horwitz's suggestion that there were three models available in the nineteenth century: artificial entity, contractual (or aggregate) model, and natural entity theory. They are important in that they represent different theories of the origin of the corporate entity and its rights. According to each, the corporation is either created by a sovereign grant, a contractual arrangement between private businessmen, or it constitutes a real entity, product of men's "natural" tendency to associate and to cooperate. However, this is not to suggest a progressive narrative in which one model superseded the other. A closer look at the recent and by now famous *Citizens United* decision, for example, reveals that all three models are still around; for an attentive reading see Stephens, "Are Corporations People? Corporate Personhood under the Constitution and International Law."

Of course, corporate personhood is part of this story. As we know it today, corporate personhood emerged at the turn of the twentieth century, and it drew legitimation from the idea that corporations are creations of the market rather than the law.[7] This so-called natural entity theory was based to some extent on European jurisprudence that the English scholar Frederic William Maitland and the American scholar Ernst Freund introduced to Anglo-Saxon jurisprudence.[8] In this sense, corporate personhood suggested that a corporation is independent of the state and independent of the natural members of the corporation, a subject of rights and duties. This view made sense at a time when, as legal historian Morton J. Horwitz has pointed out, the managerial revolution and the shift in corporate governance toward majority rule meant an internal restructuring of corporate organization that led toward the separation of ownership and operational control of property (see *1870–1960* 89). Yet for almost the entire nineteenth century, the corporation was significant as a group entity, and was perceived as such. While the relationship between its members was interpreted in different and not always consistent ways, the corporation was nonetheless a collective agent, an aggregate of individuals. Even as John Marshall pronounced the corporation "an artificial being, invisible, intangible, and existing only in contemplation of law" in 1819, he still considered it a representation of the members' aggregate rights as citizens.

The Corporation in the Nineteenth-Century American Imagination

Understanding the transformation of the corporation in the nineteenth century as its development from a creation of the law to a creation of the market, this book investigates the narrativization of the corporation, and specifically of corporate agency. That is to say, how did nineteenth-century Americans imagine corporations as acting in the world? Which narratives, tropes, and metaphors shaped and were shaped by this imagination? How did Americans make sense of corporations' growing influence in the marketplace? The book approaches these questions by way of a historical and interdisciplinary analysis that follows the legal, political, and cultural debates over corporations from the end of the eighteenth century to those at the beginning of the twentieth. It draws on a wide array of material—legal and economic treatises, court opinions, literary fictions, caricatures, business histories, and journalism—to understand how the legal as well as the popular imaginary mediated the corporate form's transformation in the nineteenth century. Accordingly,

---

[7] The corporation's reconceptualization was also part of a disciplinary shift, the emergence of legal realism. See for example Horwitz, *1870–1960* 85, and Hovenkamp, *The Opening of American Law* 106–7.

[8] See Horwitz, *1870–1960* 71–2, 101; and Turner 21–2.

each chapter introduces the reader to a set of legal, literary, and/or visual texts that negotiate the corporate form's transformation and its rise to prominence in US culture. Each chapter points out the narrative modes, genres, and metaphors that these texts employed, to what end they employed them, and how these are related to earlier (or later) instantiations of these forms.

My use of the term *imaginary* is based on the work of Winfried Fluck and Wolfgang Iser, who have argued that the imaginary is what allows literary fictions to be more than a mere mirror of reality. Essentially an act of transgression, the act of fictionalizing goes beyond the immediately available reality: "Whenever realities are transposed into the text, they turn into signs for something else. Thus they are made to outstrip their original determinacy" (Iser 3). In the process, the imaginary is given "an articulate gestalt" and some degree of determinacy (Iser 3). For Winfried Fluck in particular, this imaginary ultimately also transcends the individual through this process: as it engages with the real and is rendered determinate, the individual imaginary turns into a cultural imaginary. It is both a site of new meanings that seek to become socially recognized and hence real, and a repertoire of images, affects, and desires that continue to stimulate the individual imaginary into new manifestations (see Fluck 20–1). To study the corporation's transformation in the popular imaginary is therefore to outline and analyze the gestalt that the corporation is given in legal, economic, and cultural narratives throughout the long nineteenth century.

I use the term *popular imaginary* in my study to emphasize the fact that the rise of the business corporation was not a phenomenon with which only an established elite of writers were dealing in their work, nor one in which only such an elite audience was interested. In fact, as I show throughout this book, literary writers often employed more popular aesthetics, such as satirical and sentimental styles, to write about (business) corporations and other collective bodies. Consequently, the book also discusses texts that are less often studied in the context of economic or legal criticism, such as James Fenimore Cooper's *The Bravo* (1831), María Amparo Ruiz de Burton's *The Squatter and the Don* (1885), and Ida M. Tarbell's *The History of the Standard Oil Company* (1904). These texts are particularly valuable for an analysis of the corporation because they offer new perspectives that add complexity to our understanding of the subject and insights that have often been missing from standard accounts of the corporation in literature so far.[9]

---

[9] Scholars interested in corporations have tended to focus on well-known realist and naturalist works; for example, Walter Benn Michael's *The Gold Standard and the Logic of Naturalism* (1987) contains a chapter on Frank Norris's *The Octopus* (1901) and Josiah Royce's *The Feud of Oakfield Creek* (1887), while James Livingston's *Pragmatism and the Political Economy*

In this way, the book goes beyond previous studies that have tended to focus on the corporation in the second half of the nineteenth century and therefore on the form's rise to economic relevance. Instead, it joins more recent work that conceives of the corporation as political actor and draws on an interdisciplinary analysis of law and literature. Among these studies, Joshua Barkan's *Corporate Sovereignty: Law and Government under Capitalism* (2013), Henry S. Turner's *The Corporate Commonwealth: Pluralism and Political Fictions in England, 1516–1651* (2015), and Daniel Stout's *Corporate Romanticism: Liberalism, Justice and the Novel* (2016) stand out. The latter in particular, while it is dedicated to British literature, is similarly focused on the corporation as a collective body that joined other collectives in the literature of the Victorian age, and it thereby seeks to revise the widespread assumption of liberalism's easy triumph in the nineteenth century. In this respect, Christopher Newfield's 1996 *The Emerson Effect: Individualism and Submission in America* as well as Howard Horwitz's 1991 *By the Law of Nature: Form and Value in Nineteenth-Century America* have also been influential for the present study, as both investigate the legal and cultural narratives that shaped nineteenth-century notions of individualism in the United States.

Because of its collective nature, the corporation's narrativization has frequently been accompanied by the tensions and paradoxes that characterize the relationship between the one and the many in US culture. What becomes apparent in the pages that follow is that throughout the nineteenth century the corporation oscillated between two extremes. Specifically, corporations were either associated with monopolies and conspiracy, or with associations and cooperation.

The charge of conspiracy and monopoly originated partly in the corporation's common-law heritage and its association with the English Crown in the eighteenth century, and partly in how the form's use was increasingly committed to profit at the beginning of the nineteenth century. According to this view, corporations presented a special privilege that was a feature of feudal, not republican, societies, and they allowed a concentration of wealth that was likewise more characteristic of aristocracies than of democracies. But it was not only such cultural prejudice that associated corporations with the idea of wealthy elites conspiring against the people; it was also their specific legal structure, meaning the fact that individual identities were subsumed

---

of Cultural Revolution, 1850–1940 (1994) contains a chapter on Theodore Dreiser's *Sister Carrie* (1900). An exception is Brook Thomas's *American Literary Realism and the Failed Promise of Contract* (1997), which focuses on realist literature but deals with two little-known novels, David Graham Phillips's *The Cost* (1904) and Francis Lynde's *The Grafters* (1904).

in the corporate form so that, for example, foreign investors could take over US corporations and thus manipulate the economy. Nor was this a narrative specific to the young nation at the beginning of the nineteenth century, when recent political events certainly exacerbated the threat of foreign aristocracies and revolutions. By the late nineteenth century, the appearance of trusts and holding companies would raise similar fears over industrial combinations that would secretly seek to centralize and monopolize power in the marketplace. In María Amparo Ruiz de Burton's novel *The Squatter and the Don* (1885), for example, such corporate monopolies seek to put an end to state and national sovereignty, while twenty years later, Justice John Marshall Harlan, writing for the majority's anti-trust decision in *Northern Securities Company* v. *United States* (1904), still declared that "*[t]here is a potency in numbers when combined which the law cannot overlook*, where injury is the consequence" (341, emphasis in the original).

  At the same time, corporations were regarded more positively as part of the associational revolution that Alexis de Tocqueville praised in his *Democracy in America* (1835). For one thing, corporations allowed citizens to pool economic resources in a country without an aristocracy. As Kathleen D. McCarthy has shown in her 2005 study *American Creed: Philanthropy and the Rise of Civil Society, 1700–1865*, incorporation allowed the creation of hospitals, schools, and orphanages—and it afforded women control over property that, under the law of coverture, they did not usually possess. In this vein, corporations were portrayed approvingly as an expression of the associational spirit that defined US culture. In Washington Irving's *Astoria* (1836), for example, the narrator would explain that John Jacob Astor, while an able and successful individual merchant, had to incorporate in order to beat the British and Canadian fur-trading monopolies in the Northwest. In his dissent in the *Northern Securities* decision, Justice Oliver Wendell Holmes Jr. declared that Harlan's interpretation of anti-trust law, if sustained, "would make eternal the *bellum omnium contra omnes* and disintegrate society so far as it could into individual atoms" (*Northern Securities* v. *United States* 411). Both of these views expressed the idea that association and cooperation were phenomena essential to functioning societies and necessary for progress, and that corporations were only one manifestation of this phenomenon. As Theodore Sedgwick put it in 1835, "[a]ll the successful efforts of modern times are the result of association" (8).

  Seeing corporations first as legal and political in origin (rather than as primarily economic), and therefore as structurally related to the republic, also helps to understand this persistent double narrative of conspiracy and cooperation. Early modern theories of (state) sovereignty were corporate in nature and had—as Ernst Kantorowicz's *The King's Two Bodies: A Study in Medieval*

Political Theology demonstrates—a theological dimension. Regarding the latter, Kantorowicz argues that the corporation is a secularization of the *corpus mysticum*, Christ's mystical body, and therefore provided the means for imagining the sovereign body—first of the king, later of the republic—as enduring over time and beyond the lifespan of its individual members. As Henry S. Turner has pointed out, we see this most clearly in the concept of "the king as corporation sole," which is "a corporation of only one member, possessed of both a natural body and an invisible and immortal body politic" (11). The same duality also defines the corporation aggregate, which was first conceptualized in Roman law (*universitas*) and which we find frequently described as "body politic" and as "commonwealth" in early modern law and political theory. In each instance, corporate bodies are conceived as more than the sum of their parts, as consisting of mortal bodies as well as of a single immortal body, and they are understood as the basis of both private and public institutions. That is to say, a joint-stock company was as much a corporate body as a republic.[10] But as Hobbes's famous comment on corporations as parasites illustrates, based on this structural kinship, corporations were not only seen as extensions of the state's sovereign power but also as its potential rivals.

The corporation's cultural history therefore also takes us into debates over the place of groups in the American republic and over collectivity in US culture at large. The tension in the relationship between the one and the many is particularly evident with the onset of the privatization of the corporate form, which is also a process of democratization. As incorporation becomes available to the common man (and woman) through general incorporation statutes that replace the privilege of special charters in the 1830s and 1840s, the many-headed hydras that were a symbol of popular revolt in the eighteenth century turn into a symbol of passionate mobs threatening the republic— such as in James Fenimore Cooper's *The Bravo* (1831), in which the irrational masses in the street are presented as complementary to the "soulless corporation" of the state. But this concern over the influence of the anonymous masses in the republic also shapes the figure of the corporate agent as confidence man, as in the work of Nathaniel Hawthorne, Herman Melville, and John W. De Forest. In their literary fictions, corporate agents who are (in theory) acting not in their own interests but in the interest of their principals represent the increasing anonymity in an expanding national marketplace and the financialization of social bonds. As spiritual gain is replaced by material gain in the republic, these works figure the corporation as a symbol of the nation's moral decline.

---

[10] See Henry Turner's detailed discussion, pp. 10–23, in particular pp. 13–14.

Privatization therefore also raises the problem of—or rather, depends on—the positive redescription of corporate collectivity. Among the rhetorical sleights of hand that serve this purpose is the racialization of collectivity, which we find as early as the 1830s but which emerges with full force in the late nineteenth century. As Joel Pfister has discussed in detail in his study *Individuality Incorporated: Indians and the Multicultural Modern* (2004), for example, Native American tribal collectivity—in particular, the collective ownership of property—became the focus of the forced re-education that American Indian youths underwent in the Carlisle system, just as the Dawes Act of 1887 forced Native Americans into accepting the tenets of possessive individualism and simultaneously made land available to railroad corporations. In a similar vein, the stereotype of the "coolie" dominated the popular representation of the laborers who built the transcontinental railroads, Chinese immigrants in California in the 1870s; while African American freedmen, during and after Reconstruction, "were held to a standard of self-reliance that did not apply to the white business community," which is the topic of Charles W. Chesnutt's short story "The Partners" (Thomas, *Reconstruction* 206). In these and other cases, a compartmentalization took place that constructed racial otherness as the characteristic of *illegitimate* collectivity and thereby opened the discursive space for the white corporate elite, such as John D. Rockefeller, to declare that "[t]he day of combination is here to stay. Individualism has gone, never to return" (Nevins 622).[11]

As regards law and literature specifically, the analysis of the narrativization of the corporation and corporate agency shows that both ultimately construct the corporation as a problem of knowledge and perception. In literature, it is the challenge of representing an entity and its influence in the world that is (in Justice Marshall's words) an "intangible" and "invisible" being. To meet this challenge, literary writers availed themselves of the different generic modes offered by, for example, romance, satire, and the sentimental novel, and they drew on and developed the popular tropes that accompanied the rise of corporate power in the United States: the soulless corporation, the many-headed beast, or the octopus. As we will see, they also often drew on different temporal registers, associating the corporate form either with an outdated past or a progressive future. Conceiving of the corporation as of a problem of knowledge, the works of some literary writers, such as James Fenimore Cooper and María Amparo Ruiz de Burton, also explicitly strove to reveal what the law appeared to seek to conceal: to lift the corporate veil

---

[11] Statement made in a conversation with W. O. Inglis, who was assembling material for a biography in 1915. The material was incorporated into Allan Nevins's biography *John D. Rockefeller: The Heroic Age of American Enterprise* (1940).

and expose to their readers the collective nature of the corporate persona. Of course, the law did not simply seek to protect the corporate persona's integrity. Instead, nineteenth-century lawyers and judges frequently struggled over where the eye of the law should look: whether it should lift the corporate veil and regard the natural persons of which the corporation was composed in order to derive its judgment, or whether it should *not* look past the corporate name and hence its persona. A central question of these debates was the nature of the corporation itself: whether it must be considered an artificial creation—a product of the lawyer's art—or whether it must be considered natural, a product of the human habit of associating. In the twentieth and twenty-first centuries, these questions would become crucial in debates over corporate personhood and accountability.[12] As the following pages will show, in the nineteenth century, they were part of a larger discourse on the relationship between the one and the many.

---

[12] See Lisa Siraganian's *Modernism and the Meaning of Corporate Persons* (2020) for more on corporate personhood and liability in the twentieth century.

1

Narrating Monopoly and Empire: Austin, Irving, and the *Charles River Bridge* Case

In the popular imaginary of the late eighteenth and early nineteenth centuries, corporations were commonly associated with monopoly. There were at least two reasons for this: for one thing, some charters did indeed include "monopoly franchises, such as the right to build and operate a bridge over a particular body of water, or the right to enter an industry in which only chartered firms were legally authorized to operate, as was often the case in banking" (Hilt 41). But it was also the *special* charter that was necessary to incorporate such projects that encouraged this association. Even though, after US independence, the power to grant charters of incorporation rested with state legislatures rather than the English Crown, such charters were still a special legal privilege for those to whom they were granted, whether they included monopoly franchises or not; not every citizen was equally in a position to obtain such a charter. In addition, corporate and monopoly jurisprudence still relied heavily on the English common-law tradition, which was increasingly seen as an outdated and foreign body of law. During the Jacksonian era's push for equality in the political as well as the economic sphere, such special privileges and English traditions became the target of criticism.

Yet the young nation also needed capital and enterprise to grow its economy, and incorporation offered a powerful instrument for both. As Kent Newmyer notes, "By facilitating the accumulation of capital from a broad base without sacrificing centralized management, the corporation especially suited a country lacking consolidated wealth" (824). Hence, US law and economic policy regarded private investments largely "as an extension of state efforts to further economic growth," and there was no standing legal distinction "between private and public forms of investment" until the late eighteenth century (Horwitz, *1780–1860* 111). But by the beginning of the nineteenth century (and even more so during the Jacksonian era), such earlier "monopolistic strateg[ies]" were increasingly understood as an obstacle to economic growth (Horwitz, *1780–1860* 111). Moreover, English common law was largely "anti-competitive," which was partly an effect of "earlier feudal or mercantilist influences" (Horwitz, *1780–1860* 114) and partly due to the broad understanding of businesses such as mills, bakehouses, or malthouses as "public enterprises" (Horwitz, *1780–1860* 115). In addition there was the special case of franchises, such as ferries, which were exclusive privileges that had never been individual rights and were granted by the king or (which was practically the same) justified by "ancient usage" (Horwitz, *1780–1860* 115).

In the United States, by contrast, courts gradually began to acknowledge a changing economic environment as they introduced the distinction between corporations serving private interests and those serving public interests. In the *Dartmouth College* case (1819), Justice Joseph Story introduced a definition to distinguish between "private and public corporations" that would become central to the development of the private corporation aggregate (Horwitz, *1780–1860* 111). Essentially, Story suggested following the money: "If, therefore, the foundation be private, though under the charter of government, the corporation is private, however extensive the uses may be to which it is devoted, either by the bounty of the founder, or the nature and objects of the institution" (*Dartmouth* v. *Woodward* 669). The market revolution of the 1820s and 1830s accelerated this trend. In 1836, the decision in the *Charles River Bridge* case would prove to be a watershed moment, as it presented "the last great contest in America between two different models of economic development" (Horwitz, *1780–1860* 134).

At this point, the demand for general incorporation statutes which would abolish special charters and make incorporation available to the common man had already become widespread. The statutes and the increased availability of the form would contribute to the democratization of the corporation in the popular imaginary. Even though, as later chapters in this study will demonstrate, the association between corporations and monopoly would never entirely fade, incorporation's republican potential now came to the fore. Economic development and legal jurisprudence would contribute to a specific process, as they laid the groundwork for corporations to figure as instruments of private gain and enterprise rather than monopoly and feudalism. To understand the ideological and imaginative foundations of this shift, Chapter 1 looks at three literary texts and the legal and cultural debates from which they emerge: a business history, a US Supreme Court ruling, and a tale. All three deal with corporations and the problem of monopoly and competition, which all three translate into narratives about the past's legacies to the future. Washington Irving's *Astoria* (1836) revisits John Jacob Astor's attempt to establish a fur-trading monopoly in the Northwest between 1810 and 1812, while the case of *Charles River Bridge* v. *Warren Bridge* (1837) addresses a conflict between two bridges, one with ties to the colonial past and one incorporated in the early republic. William Austin's "Martha Gardner; or, Moral Re-Action" (1837) tells a fictional prehistory to *Charles River Bridge* v. *Warren Bridge* that reminds its readers of the values for which the American revolution was fought. In this manner, all three texts ultimately suggest that corporate monopoly and its origins in English common law are out of place in a thriving young republic. In the process, they need to find ways to narrativize the corporation: in terms of representing corporate agency as well as in terms of redefining it as a tool of enterprise and progress.

I. Washington Irving's *Astoria*

Washington Irving's *Astoria: or Anecdotes of an Enterprise Beyond the Rocky Mountains* (1836) is a business history and a romance of the West that was commissioned by John Jacob Astor. Irving and Astor had known each other for over twenty years by the time Astor made his request.[1] Irving was just completing *A Tour on the Prairies* (1835), a satirical account of frontier life that was based on his personal travels through so-called Indian Territory in 1832. While apparently fond of Astor and the idea of the project, Irving himself was too busy. In a letter written to his nephew Pierre Munro Irving in September 1834, he explained the situation into which the request had put him:

> The old gentleman has applied to me repeatedly in the matter, offering to furnish abundance of materials in letters, journals and verbal narratives, and to pay liberally for time and trouble. I have felt aware that a work might be written on the subject, full of curious and entertaining matter, comprising adventurous expeditions by sea and land, scenes beyond the Rocky Mountains, incidents and scenes illustrative of Indian character, and of that singular and but little known class, the traders and voyageurs of the Fur Companies. Still I am so much engrossed with other plans, that I have not time for the examination of papers, the digesting of various materials, etc., and have stood aloof from the undertaking, though still keeping the matter open. (Barry 133)

Irving wrote to his nephew with a business proposal: Pierre would "collate the various documents, collect verbal information, and reduce the whole to such form that I might be able to dress it up advantageously, and with little labor, for the press" (Barry 133). For that service, Pierre would eventually

---

[1] Antelyes writes that "[t]he two men probably first met about 1811, the very time that the events recorded in the book were taking place" (150).

receive $3,000 from Astor and $1,000 from Irving, while Irving himself would receive $4,000 from the publisher (see Ronda 976). With Pierre's help, Irving published *Astoria* in October 1836.

The subject of the book is Astor's fur-trading companies, the American Fur Company (AFC), which was incorporated in New York in 1808, and the Pacific Fur Company (PFC), a business association that was created specifically to establish a trading post at the mouth of the Columbia River and to secure the fur-trade monopoly in this region against British and Canadian competitors such as the Hudson Bay Company (HBC) and the North West Company (NWC). The PFC was a short-lived enterprise: created in 1810, it succeeded to establish Astoria, the company's main trading post and a fort, but was forced to hand it over to the NWC when the US government failed to send military protection during the War of 1812. As many critics have noted, despite the PFC's failure, the book is essentially an account of commercial imperialism or monopoly and empire. In the words of Irving's narrator, "[Astor] considered his projected establishment at the mouth of the Columbia as the emporium to an immense commerce; as a colony that would form the germ of a wide civilization" (*Astoria* 205). But in order to tell this story of national expansion and entrepreneurial vision, Irving's narrative had to negotiate his contemporaries' negative associations with monopoly and moneyed corporations.

In fact, what makes the text specifically valuable for this study is the way it rewrites the corporation so as to make it a symbol of republican enterprise. Because, while the story is set in the early 1810s, it was published in the 1830s, and therefore written for a Jacksonian readership who associated corporations with monopoly, and monopoly, in turn, with special privilege and the feudal past. In "What Is a Monopoly?" (1835), Thomas Sedgwick gives an example of this connection as he explains to his readers the difference between associations such as partnerships, which are based on private contract, and corporations, which are predominantly created through charters that were issued by the state legislatures:

> [W]hile partnerships can be formed by all persons [. . .], corporations can only obtain existence (with the exceptions which I shall hereafter state) by special grant from the Legislature. Charters of incorporation are therefore grants of privilege, to be exclusively enjoyed by the corporators. A charter of incorporation is therefore a grant of exclusive privilege, and every grant of exclusive privilege, strictly speaking, creates a monopoly [. . .]. [. . .] It must necessarily follow, to every person whose mind is cast in the republican mould [*sic*], [. . .] that the principle of corporate grants is wholly adverse to the genius of our institutions [. . .]. (13)

While representative of the contemporary rhetoric that associated corporations with monopoly and monopoly with "the English system" that remains like "gangrene [. . .] to taint the body politic," it is also important to note that the aim of Sedgwick's treatise is not to abolish corporations but to reform them (Sedgwick 13). As Chapter 3 will show in more detail, calls for general incorporation statutes (Sedgwick's "exceptions") would gain support during the 1830s and lead a growing number of states to make incorporation available to the general public in the 1840s. This trend was based on the insight that, as Sedgwick puts it, "[a]ll the successful efforts of modern times are the result of association" (8). Irving, too, tapped into this narrative to separate Astor's enterprise more distinctly from the negative connotations of monopoly.

For the narrative to portray Astor's enterprise as an emblem of the republic's commercial future, Irving first established its competitors, in particular the NWC, as quintessential monopolies by casting them as remnants of a feudal, even tribal British past. More significantly, however, he emphasized the dominance and power of Astor's private entrepreneurial vision, of which the AFC and PFC were the products. In addition, Irving's account of the PFC formally expresses the venture's associational nature by following Astor's agents and their adventures, which has garnered the text a reputation of lacking unity, as well as by exploring critically the challenges of delegation that a corporation posed for the entrepreneur.

A Chartered Enterprise: Monopoly and Empire in Astoria

While a much larger part of the book's action is devoted to the pursuits of the PFC and his agents, *Astoria*'s primary ideological investment is in the figure of John Jacob Astor. A successful merchant from Germany, Astor had already been in the fur business as an individual for several years before he conceived of the plan that would become the story of *Astoria*. In the 1790s, a treaty between Great Britain and the United States allowed direct trade relations between Canada and the US. A wealthy merchant, Astor initially continued to pursue the fur trade "on his own account" but he soon realized that his competitors were too powerful (Irving, *Astoria* 197). As the narrator explains, "With all his enterprise and resources however, he soon found the power and influence of the Michilimackinac (or Mackinaw) Company too great for him, having engrossed most of the trade within the American borders. A plan had to be devised to enable him to enter into successful competition" (Irving, *Astoria* 197). Despite his material and intellectual resources, Astor was no match for the trading companies that had already established a fur-trade monopoly in the Northwest. In order to be able to compete, Astor had to be more than a mere individual; he had to incorporate.

In its presentation of monopolies and corporations, *Astoria* goes to some lengths to stress that Astor was acting beyond mere self-interest and profit-seeking. "He was already wealthy beyond the ordinary desires of man," the narrator explains, "but he now aspired to that honorable fame which is awarded to men of similar scope of mind, who by their great commercial enterprises have enriched nations, peopled wildernesses and extended the bounds of empire" (Irving, *Astoria* 205). In a similar vein, the narrator repeatedly points out how Astor seeks the government's support for his project, insisting that Astor recognized the government's "wish [. . .] that the fur trade within its boundaries should be in the hands of American citizens," which the government itself had been "ineffectual" to realize (Irving, *Astoria* 197). It is with the government's support that Astor "obtained [. . .] a charter from the legislature of the state of New York, incorporating a company under the name of 'The American Fur Company' [in 1809]" (Irving, *Astoria* 197). In this way, the narrative weds Astor's corporate enterprise to the public's interests and the nation's future.

The special charters of incorporation, which state legislatures still predominantly issued in the early nineteenth century, were based on the logic of the sovereign grant and generally reserved for enterprises that had a public benefit. This did not mean, however, that they couldn't make a profit. Instead, as Naomi Lamoreaux explains, "the idea was that private citizens would be encouraged by the lure of profits to channel their savings into socially useful projects" ("Partnerships" 33). In exchange, such charters offered the company legal personhood as well as a selection of other privileges. However, among these, historians suggest, legal personhood seems to have been the primary incentive for incorporation, since a few of the other privileges—such as limited liability, for example—could be obtained through other business models as well.[2] As legal persons, corporations were capable "of suing and being sued, pleading and being impleaded, answering and being answered unto, defending and being defended, in all courts and places whatsoever, and in all manner of actions, suits, complaints, matters and causes whatsoever" (Porter 414). It meant having a common seal with which to authorize the corporation's actions in writing, and an existence beyond the presence (or lifetime) of the corporation's individual members—whether it was corporate perpetuity or, more commonly, a specified period of years, such as twenty-five in the case of Astor's American Fur Company. Finally, it meant property rights, as detailed in the AFC's charter, for example: "that they and their successors, by the name

[2] Through limited liability partnerships, for example. See Lamoreaux, "Partnerships, Corporations, and the Limits on Contractual Freedom in U.S. History: An Essay in Economics, Law, and Culture."

of the American Fur Company, shall in law be capable of buying, purchasing, holding, conveying and selling any lands, tenements, hereditaments, goods, wares and merchandise, or any real or personal estate whatsoever, for the use of the said company" (Porter 415). Yet, while they acted as a single entity in law, "a body politic and corporate," this was not to say that the law did not recognize the fact that a corporation was an association of individuals (Porter 415). The charter's reference to "John Jacob Astor, and such persons as shall hereafter be associated with him for that purpose, and their successors and assigns," as well as the document's consistent use of the third person plural, make that more than clear (Porter 414).

While the narrator admits the fact that Astor needed to incorporate to challenge the trade monopoly in the West, it also takes pains to portray the enterprise as a manifestation of Astor's ideal commercial vision. To preserve the force and purity of Astor's vision and motives, Irving's narrator insists that, despite what incorporation meant legally, "[Astor], in fact constituted the Company" (Irving, *Astoria* 197). The company's board of directors, the narrator explains, was "merely nominal," and most importantly, the corporation's capital was "furnished by himself" (Irving, *Astoria* 197). In fact, the narrator adds, "the whole business was conducted on his plans, and with his resources, but he preferred to do so under the imposing and formidable aspect of a corporation, rather than in his individual name" (Irving, *Astoria* 198). The narrator thereby reduces the corporate form to its persona, the mask or veil that it offered its members, as well as to its corporate agency. Even by the standards of the early nineteenth century, therefore, Astor's company was deemed a private corporation. And yet it becomes clear in the course of the narrative, and in particular when Irving addresses the reasons for Astoria's ultimate failure, that the *public* nature of the charter is still relevant, because it aligned the company's goals with those of the national government. As the charter's preamble declares, the company's contribution to the public good would be both imperial and commercial: "WHEREAS, such an establishment may be of *great public utility*, by serving to conciliate and secure the good will and affections of the Indian tribes toward the government and people of the United States, and may conduce to the peace and safety of our citizens inhabiting the territories bordering on the native Indian tribes" (Porter 414, my emphasis).

Scholarship on Irving's *Astoria* has often focused on the book's presentation of "US commercial imperialism" (LeMenager 685). This agenda is made explicit early on in *Astoria*, such as when the narrator explains that "[Astor] considered his projected establishment at the mouth of the Columbia as the emporium to an immense commerce; as a colony that would form the germ of a wide civilization; that would, in fact, carry the Americans across the

Rocky Mountains" (Irving 205). However, most scholars have also argued that the book does not tell a straightforward narrative of national mission. As David Watson puts it, "The history of Astoria is one of transnational corporate models, international investments, and agents who operate within a transnational model of imperialism in which loyalty to a particular nation-state is not a given" (11). While a "public utility," we may say, the corporation was also a tool of private enterprise and as such also acted independently of the nation-state's interests. It may even be said, as Peter Jaros and Jonathan Barkan have argued, that it installed and operated under its own form of "corporate sovereignty" (Jaros, "Irving's *Astoria*" 10; Barkan 20). As a result, the effects of Astoria's commercial imperialism are not straightforward, as Stephanie LeMenager has shown. Instead of a "clear cut narrativ[e] of progress," the Far West is presented as "resistant" and intractable, a site of "new and more sophisticated forms of savagery" that is increasingly slipping out of the US's reach (LeMenager 686, 585).

Some scholars, such as Watson and Jaros, have paid special attention to the "corporate model" at the center of *Astoria* (Watson 11). For Watson, the corporation in *Astoria* already presents a multinational actor productive of its own "hybrid, metonymic imperialism" (21), while Jaros draws attention to the difficulty of narrating the corporate model, in which he locates the origin of the book's "capacious literary form" ("Irving's *Astoria*" 4). Yet none have discussed the fact that, while the American Fur Company is a publicly chartered corporation, the Pacific Fur Company is an association based on private contract. This is not a small detail, however, even if the narrator admittedly does not dwell on it too much and often appears to treat the PFC as an extension of the AFC. We are simply told that, two years after the incorporation of the AFC, "On the 23rd of June, articles of agreement were entered into between Mr. Astor and [. . .] four gentlemen, acting for themselves and for the several persons who had already agreed to become, or should thereafter become, associated under the firm of The Pacific Fur Company" (Irving, *Astoria* 208). The arrangement had become necessary after Astor's original plan to cooperate with the NWC in order to avoid "detrimental" competition had been rejected by the NWC (Irving, *Astoria* 206). In his biography of Astor, Kenneth Porter explains that "[Astor] therefore decided that the best alternative was to associate with himself certain experienced members of that Company. To this end he made successful overtures to Alexander McKay, Donald McKenzie, and Duncan McDougall, all veteran Nor'Westers" (181). The association's purpose was the establishment of the trading post on the Pacific coast that would become Astoria and which is in large parts the subject of Irving's history. The agreement was long and detailed, specifying among other aspects the distribution of shares and the conditions under which the

PFC could be dissolved—both aspects that would prove crucial in the enterprise's final dramatic act.

Such unincorporated associations were not unusual during this period; quite the contrary. Unincorporated joint-stock associations and partnerships were much more common at the turn of the century than corporations because charters were not easy to obtain. "[I]n the simple late-eighteenth-century economy most business went on merely by private contract; the law never required that all business associations be chartered by the state" (Hurst 14). Special charters required that an enterprise benefited the general welfare and hence were predominantly issued for municipal and eleemosynary corporations as well as those enterprises that would help the economy grow, such as in the infrastructure sector, for example. Business corporations that operated on a smaller scale were regularly organized by private contract. In his essays on the early history of the corporation in the United States, Joseph Stancliffe Davis quotes from John Hector St. John de Crèvecoeur's description of the New England whaling industry to illustrate this practice: fishing and whaling industries were numerous. Usually, they were not joint-stock companies in the ordinary sense, but such as Crèvecoeur describes in his *Letters from an American Farmer*: "They have no wages; each draws a certain established share in partnership with the proprietor of the vessel; by which economy they are all proportionately concerned in the success of the enterprise, and all equally alert and vigilant" (qtd. in Davis 92).

As unincorporated association, the PFC is to some extent removed from the odium of monopoly that was often attached to business corporations in the popular imaginary of the Jacksonian period. Because it was based on private contract it was even more of an expression of the American spirit of enterprise that Irving evokes so frequently throughout *Astoria*. It also implies the spirit of association noted by Alexis de Tocqueville and which even Thomas Sedgwick conceded was fundamental to the nation: "All the successful efforts of modern times are the result of association. Our Declaration of Independence was made by the *United* Thirteen Colonies" (8, italics in the original).[3] The narrative of *Astoria* translates this difference by establishing a strong contrast between the North West Company and the Pacific Fur Company, in which the NWC is associated with monopoly and the feudal past while the PFC (and by extension even the AFC) is associated with competition and the republican future.[4] In fact, in its portrayal of the enterprise and

---

[3] See Butterfield for a discussion of corporations as voluntary associations during the first three decades of the nineteenth century.

[4] In the words of Peter Antelyes, whose *Tales of Adventurous Enterprise* (1990) provides a foundational assessment of *Astoria*, "Where [Astor's] company seeks the expansion of a

the corporation, *Astoria* is astonishingly pro-commerce—and in this regard it is quite different from William Austin's presentation of corporate monopoly in "Martha Gardner; or, Moral Re-Action" (1837) or James Fenimore Cooper's *The Bravo* (1831).

Despite the fact that the American Fur Company seeks a monopoly in the fur trade as much as the Mackinaw or the North West Company, it is the latter that is consistently presented as "the corporate villain in the drama that seeks monopoly" (Antelyes 181). As noted earlier, in this respect Irving's narrative draws on the association of monopoly with special privilege, feudalism, and the past, which in turn only serves to characterize the AFC more strongly as democratic, republican, and progressive. This binary is presented early on in the book, beginning with a short history of the NWC. By "amalgamation with a rival company in 1787[,] [. . .] the famous "North West Company" [was created] which for a time held a lordly sway over the wintry lakes and boundless forests of the Canadas, almost equal to that of the East India Company over the voluptuous climes and magnificent realms of the Orient" (Irving, *Astoria* 188–9). While it does not hold a monopoly based on a royal grant as the East India Company or the Hudson Bay Company did, it is consistently portrayed in terms that evoke feudal societies. "Most of the clerks", the narrator tells us, for instance, "were young men of good families, from the highlands of Scotland," and while that serves initially as an indicator of a thrifty, persevering character, it takes on an almost tribal quality later in the narrative (Irving, *Astoria* 190). For example, during their visit to Hawaii, former NWC employee McDougall and the other agents that travel with him on the *Tonquin* dress in traditional Scottish kilts when they meet Tamaahmaah, the islands' king. "Knowing the effect of show and dress upon men in savage life and wishing to make a favorable impression as the *Eris* or chiefs of the great American Fur Company, some of them appeared in highland plaids and Kelts to the great admiration of the natives" (Irving, *Astoria* 235). Even though they use their personal connection to a feudal past to the company's advantage in this instance, the narrator also notes the foreignness of the agents, such as when they take to speaking "Gaelic" among themselves aboard the *Tonquin*, much to the dismay of the American captain (Irving, *Astoria* 239).

competitive marketplace, [the NWC] seeks only monopoly; where his brings mobility within a fixed social structure, theirs brings only stasis and hierarchy. Generally, the British commercial system is described as feudal, essentially antithetical to the marketplace envisioned by the Americans" (181).

This ancient Scottish heritage is also stressed by the narrator in his account of the NWC, such as when he describes the place of the Company's annual meeting, Fort William. "Here, in an immense wooden building, was the Great Council Hall, as also the banqueting chamber, decorated with Indian arms and accoutrements and the trophies of the Fur trade" (Irving, *Astoria* 192). Irving thus sets up a scene reminiscent of the world portrayed in the novels of Walter Scott, and one that is distinctly in the past: "for the feudal state of Fort William is at an end; [. . .] the lords of the lakes and forests have passed away; and the hospitable magnates of Montreal—where are they!" (Irving, *Astoria* 193). The progress of history means that the time is ripe for a republican company to take over, but as the reader soon learns, while the glorious days of the generous chiefs at Fort William are over, the feudal structure of the Company itself has survived, as it continues to hold its sway over the territory "by right of possession" (Irving, *Astoria* 203).

In his study of Irving's Western narratives, which include *A Tour of the Prairies* (1835), *Astoria* (1836) and *The Adventures of Captain Bonneville* (1837), Peter Antelyes explains that, with regard to its celebration of Astor's commercial vision, *Astoria* is different from Irving's earlier, satirical and critical works, in particular *A Tour of the Prairies*. Antelyes suggests that we should read *Astoria* as "a romance of economic idealism" and as a "prophetic" narrative (160, 170) that is both "a celebration and a warning" (149). In its pro-commercial romance mode, the text revels in what it stages as the grandeur of Astor's entrepreneurial vision and presents the reader with a narrative of the ideal commercial society, in which self-interest serves the general interest: "the heroes pursue a goal of economic expansion against villains who obstruct that goal; and each event realizes the causes of self-interest and the common good, and the effects of mobility and hierarchy, the joining of the self to the community and the severing of ties between them" (Antelyes 161). This ideal "balance of self-interest and communal obligation," which centrally defines the ideology of civic republicanism, would gradually be replaced by the pursuit of purely selfish, profit-oriented goals, and thereby jeopardize the American mission itself (Antelyes 163). *Astoria*'s "warning" therefore consisted in its account of (and explanation for) the enterprise's failure and in the analogy it impresses upon the reader between Astoria and America: "In this sense, Irving's maturational history of the Astorian expedition is a narrative model of how the culture should 'read' its current economic expansion in the context of all American history" (Antelyes 170). Reading the failures of the past as a cautionary tale as well as a lesson for future success was therefore a central element of Irving's narrative project. We will see that it played out its temporal logic on several levels.

Corporate Villains Within and Without: Agency and Astoria's Failure

Early reviewers and scholars have commented on what they perceive as *Astoria*'s lack of formal unity. As Peter Jaros observes, "[i]t regularly elicits frustration and distaste in the manner of Hugh Egan's succinct assessment: '*Astoria* does not possess the unity Irving thinks it does'" ("Irving's *Astoria*" 2). On first sight, this appears to be a consequence of the writing process itself, which is more accurately defined as a process of assemblage: *Astoria* is based on letters, journals, and papers that Irving and his nephew Pierre Munro Irving received from John Jacob Astor, as well as first-hand accounts written by the association's members. It is as much a business history as a romance of the West. On the one hand, it follows John Jacob Astor, "the master spirit," who remains in New York City; on the other, the association that travels on land and by sea to the mouth of the Columbia River (Irving, *Astoria* 475). As it attempts to incorporate those various sources and the voices that they represent, the narrative sometimes appears to lose sight of its main purpose and to digress too much. However, for Peter Jaros, this narrative "excursivity" is not so much digression as it is a formal manifestation of *Astoria*'s imperial design: "While the world *Astoria* pictures looks formless and lawless from the perspective of territorial, national sovereignty, it is structured by the excursive patterns of exploration, trade, and narrative to which nomadic corporate capitalism gives rise" ("Irving's *Astoria*" 14).

It is also possible to understand *Astoria*'s form as a response to the challenge of scale that the narrativization of the corporation posed for Irving. In his preface, Irving writes:

> The work I here present to the public is necessarily of a rambling and somewhat disjointed nature, comprising various expeditions and adventures by land and sea. The facts, however, will prove to be linked and banded together by one grand scheme, devised and conducted by a master spirit; one set of characters, also, continues throughout, appearing occasionally, though sometimes at long intervals, and the whole enterprise winds up by a regular catastrophe; so that the work, without any labored attempt at artificial construction, actually possesses much of that unity so much sought after in works of fiction, and considered so important to the interest of every history. (*Astoria* 181)

Both romance and history, the narrative needs to negotiate between two scales: the individual's expansive long-term vision and the association's local short-term pursuits. Irving's response to this challenge is to cut his narrator free from generic constraints and let him move back and forth both temporally (through analepses and prolepses) as well as spatially (from New York

City to Astoria, from the Hawaiian Islands to China). This narrative mode also allows Irving to present the full complexity of causes that lead to Astoria's failure, among them agency problems.

Much of the book follows the history of the association as its members attempt to execute Astor's vision. Two expeditions leave for the Columbia River, one by land and one by sea; they are led, respectively, by Astor's "chief agent," Wilson Price Hunt, a US citizen, and by Duncan McDougall, his "proxy" in Hunt's absence, a Canadian and former employee of the NWC (Irving, *Astoria* 210, 208). Both pursue the association's primary goal—to establish Astoria, a trading post at the mouth of the Columbia River—in which McDougall succeeds in April 1811, after an eventful journey by sea. Hence, while Astor is throughout presented as "the master spirit" who plans, finances, and orchestrates the enterprise from his offices in New York City as well as the "father" of the "the embryo establishment" that the partners name after him, he can only act through his agents and has to rely on them to realize his vision (Irving, *Astoria* 252). Yet it gradually becomes clear that, while they are overall experienced and capable, they are lesser men in spirit. To some extent, therefore, as Irving's narrator follows their adventures, the narrative becomes one of the challenges of delegation.

To understand these challenges and how they are central to a narrative of corporate organization and agency in the first decades of the nineteenth century, we need to take a brief look at the law that governed principal-agent relationships. The increasing significance of these relationships was a sign of the expansion of the marketplace in the United States during this period. In his *Commentaries on the Law of Agency*, which were written in the 1830s, Justice Joseph Story explains that it was "the expanded intercourse of modern society," characterized by "the exigencies of trade and commerce," for example, and "the necessity of transacting business at the same time in various and remote places," which required the skilled "aid and assistance and labors of many persons" (*Commentaries* 2). Agents were such persons, acting in the principal's name and (most importantly) in the principal's interest. "Indeed, for most practical purposes, a party dealing with an agent, who is acting within the scope of his authority and employment, is to be considered as dealing with the principal himself" (Story, *Commentaries* 153). In the course of the nineteenth century, it would be the law of agency that afforded corporate organizations to grow and the corporation to act beyond state and national limits.

Even though it was therefore a central component in the modernization of the corporate form, the law of agency was initially based on much older laws and customs. When Story compiled this body of laws for his *Commentaries*, for example, he drew on the laws that regulated the relationships between master and servant. Hence, a closer look at the law of agency reveals the intensely personal terms on which it is premised. This is evident, for example, from the fact that agencies are rarely created by contract, which Story throughout calls a "solemn instrument":

> An agency may be created by the express words or acts of the principal, or may be implied from his conduct and acquiescence. So, also, the nature and extent of the authority of an agent may be expressly given by a solemn or an unsolemn instrument, or may be implied or inferred from circumstances. (*Commentaries* 50).

Not having fixed the scope of the authority in writing, the principal must thoroughly trust his agent, given that he can be held liable for the latter's deeds. Likewise, such trust between principal and agent was the basis for third parties to treat an agent as a "proxy" or representative of the principal—which was, after all, the agent's central purpose.

While Irving's narrator eventually singles out Hunt and McDougall as representative of the best and the worst of Astor's agents, it is significant that the blame for the enterprise's failure is not pinned on any agent individually. Rather, as Antelyes puts it, "all the participants together create the disaster" (174–5). In fact, the narrative suggests that their collective failure is due to the fact that they are lesser men than Astor: they are the instruments with which to execute his vision, but they "were not imbued with his own spirit" (Irving, *Astoria* 595). As a result, when they are faced with difficult choices, they end up making several bad decisions with disastrous consequences for the company.

Throughout *Astoria*, such bad decisions often stem from an agent taking too much or too little risk—a balanced assessment of which emerges as a key characteristic of a great entrepreneur like Astor. For example, the captain of the *Tonquin*, the ship that takes McDougall and three other partners to the Columbia River, dies when an attempt to trade with a group of Native Americans goes horribly wrong. Despite his sympathies for Captain Thorn, the narrator is unequivocal about the reasons for this disaster: he did not follow Astor's lead and took too great risks with the Native Americans. "It is a catastrophe that shows the importance in all enterprises of moment, to keep in mind the general instructions of the sagacious heads which devise them" (Irving, *Astoria* 271). While loyal and acting in Astor's interest, Astor's "chief agent" Hunt eventually proves too cautious: "[C]onflicting questions perplexed and agitated [Hunt's] mind, and gave rise to much anxious reflection, for he was a conscientious man that seems ever to have aimed at a faithful discharge of his duties" (Irving, *Astoria* 572). When he decides not to return to Astoria, but to ensure the safe passage of his ship to the Asian markets,

Hunt inadvertently seals Astoria's fate. "So essential it is for an agent in any great and complicated undertaking," the narrator muses in the book's final pages, "to execute faithfully and to the letter, the part marked out for him by the master mind which has concerted the whole" (Irving, *Astoria* 595).

What is more devastating, however, is that the agents eventually succumb to self-interest. That agents do not act in their own but in their principal's interest is the key principle of the agent-principal relationship. Eventually, however, this is precisely what begins to emerge as a central weakness of the association, as its members increasingly act out of selfish motives. As Antelyes points out, this shift in the agents' loyalties and motivations toward self-interest initiates the enterprise's failure, as Astor's ideal economic vision of a union of private enterprise and national welfare is corrupted and degenerates into "mere acquisitiveness" (Antelyes 161). This is most clearly visible in the decision-making process that eventually leads the association to abandon Astoria to the British. In the winter of 1812, as the situation at Astoria grows difficult, McDougall and McKenzie give themselves over to gloom and desperation, "foreboding nothing but evil" (Irving, *Astoria* 550). When an agent of the NWC informs the partners of Britain's declaration of war and the expected arrival of an "armed" company ship with the express orders of capturing Astoria, McDougall and McKenzie "gave up all hope of maintaining their post at Astoria" (Irving, *Astoria* 551). Despite some evidence that the whole enterprise was not only still economically viable, but that it would also have been possible to defend Astoria, McDougall and McKenzie invoke their right—per the agreement—to "dissolve the concern, if before the period of five years, it should be found unprofitable" (Irving, *Astoria* 560). McDougall, being not only a former employee but also related to "one of the principal characters of the North West Company," returns to the NWC after the association has handed Astoria over to the British (Irving, *Astoria* 581).

Just as the corporation's internal problems arise from agents who are downright sabotaging the enterprise, such as McDougall, but also from people who are simply less capable than Astor, such as Hunt, so does *Astoria* present external pressures as both actively and passively contributing to the company's demise. This includes not only the First Nations tribes who oppose the traders and trading posts, and the NWC, which actively seeks to beat its competitor. The corporation's failure is ultimately also due to the lack of support from the US government, which the narrator explains in the following passage.

> In a word, Astoria might have realized the anticipations of Mr. Astor, so well understood and appreciated by Mr. Jefferson, in gradually becoming a commercial empire beyond the mountains, peopled by "free and independent Americans, and linked with us by ties of blood and interest."

We repeat, therefore, our sincere regret that our government should have neglected the overture of Mr. Astor, and suffered the moment to pass by, when full possession of this region might have been taken quietly, as a matter of course, and a military post established, without dispute, at Astoria. Our statesmen have become sensible, when too late, of the importance of this measure. Bills have repeatedly been brought into Congress for the purpose, but without success; and our rightful possessions on that coast, as well as our trade on the Pacific, have no rallying point protected by the national flag, and by a military force. (Irving, *Astoria* 596)

The narrator's criticism of the US government's unwillingness to support Astoria by sending the military, for example, and protecting it against the British troops, is a critique of the government's ultimate lack of national and imperial vision. But it also suggests that, just as the corporate agents' self-interested pursuits compromise the enterprise's commercial idealism, so does the government's lack of support suggest a failure to acknowledge the corporation's significance for the general interest and welfare as defined in its charter. In this regard, Irving once more employs what Antelyes calls a "prophetic" mode (170), a "warning" (149), in that *Astoria* seems to suggest that here is a lesson from the past and a legacy which the United States need to acknowledge if they want commercial and national expansion in the future.

In fact, as the next chapter will further demonstrate, associating American corporations with the future and progress, as opposed to monopoly and a British feudal past, is a recurrent theme in narratives that seek to democratize and ultimately legitimize the corporate form. In *Astoria*, establishing this cultural as well as temporal contrast between the PFC and its British-Canadian competitors is one way in which the narrative seeks to democratize the form in the popular imaginary; finding a literary form that represents the enterprise as an associational and collective one, and as such as an expression of the young republic's highest values, is another. Future chapters will show that for writers like Irving, who are trying to tell stories of corporate power, it is a central challenge to narrate corporate agency and to negotiate scale: on the one hand there is the portrayal of an ideal figure of the entrepreneur, who provides the enterprise with vision as well as with formal unity; and on the other, there are the numerous agents through which the corporate enterprise acts in the world. In *Astoria*, one of the effects of this double structure is that the purity of Astor's vision can remain intact even as its execution is compromised. By the end of the nineteenth century, this neat separation will have become less tenable, as questions of responsibility and accountability in corporate business become more significant for writers.

The next section of this chapter continues to explore the corporation and the problems of monopoly and competition during the market revolution by turning to a landmark case in monopoly jurisprudence, the *Charles River Bridge* case. What *Astoria* and the narrative contained in the justices' opinions in *Charles River Bridge* v. *Warren Bridge* have in common is how they employ contrasting temporalities to convey one type of corporation as a vehicle of progress and another as a remnant of the past. As shown in the chapter's final section on a tale that was inspired by the case, the *Charles River Bridge* case thereby also captured a cultural moment of transition and the anxieties attending this shift: while corporations promised stability and long-term security for some, others saw them merely as vehicles of the nation's entrepreneurial spirit.

II. Vested Rights or Competition: the *Charles River Bridge* Case

The *Charles River Bridge* case, which was decided by the US Supreme Court in early 1837, would significantly contribute to the legal foundations of the private business corporation in the nineteenth century. It was among the first cases to address not just monopoly, but more specifically monopoly and transportation.[5] Legal historian Carl B. Swisher explains that during this period,

> transportation problems were perhaps the most critical of all those the American people had to face. Sailing vessels, steamboats, turnpikes, canals, railroads, all these were subjects of constant occupation. A year and a half before the Taney Court heard argument in the case, the first railroad train had come puffing into the heart of Washington, [. . .] thereby rendering largely obsolete the once profitable stagecoach lines between Washington and Baltimore. (74)

It also presented the first case in which an American court had to adapt the English common-law tradition on monopoly to American conditions. American judges tended to "rel[y] on the common law's list of enterprises historically recognized as prerogatives of the crown" because they lacked, as

---

[5] While its central question consisted in whether the charter implied the exclusive privilege of collecting tolls for crossing the Charles River until 1855, it also spawned a host of more technical questions. For example, there was the question of jurisdiction, because whether the federal court had jurisdiction in the first place depended on whether the conflict did indeed qualify as a violation of contract and thereby would come under the Constitution's Contract Clause. There were also more immediate and complex questions of the interpretation of charters and grants; for example, whether the charter should be constructed against the grantor, as had been the rule in English common law, or whether the grantor forewent all control over what had been granted.

Herbert Hovenkamp points out, a "usable model for natural monopoly," and hence were at a loss "when a business that had always been competitive—a common right—changed because technology and the market changed" (*Enterprise & Law* 114). As Chapter 4 is going to show, the problem of new technology and competition also connects the *Charles River Bridge* case with the *Slaughterhouse Cases* of 1873.

From the start, the story of the two bridges is one of progress and improvement. Initially, Harvard College had received a colonial charter for a ferry across the Charles River. Later, in 1785, the legislature of Massachusetts had granted a charter for the incorporation of a bridge to replace the ferry, a cumbersome mode of traveling. The bridge had received a charter for forty years, which was shortly afterwards extended to seventy years. It included the privilege to collect tolls during this period as a way of compensating the proprietors for the expenses of building and maintaining the bridge. The College, moreover, had been compensated for the loss of income through the ferry service by granting it an annuity from the bridge's tolls. In 1828—forty-three years after the Charles River Bridge had been erected, but before its charter had run out—the people of Charlestown and Boston demanded a new bridge.[6] Warren Bridge was subsequently incorporated, though under very different conditions than the first bridge. The Warren Bridge corporation's charter was good for a maximum of six years or until the original building costs had been earned through tolls, thereafter to become free of charge and property of the commonwealth. For a variety of reasons, Warren Bridge was a huge success. Without any traffic and thus without any income, Charles River Bridge soon had to close down permanently.[7]

---

[6] In addition to requesting a toll-free bridge, there was also a technological aspect to this demand. "The petitioners contended that the draw of the Charles River Bridge obstructed travel; [and] that the access avenues to the bridge were narrow [. . .]"; though Stanley I. Kutler, author of the only in-depth historical study of the case, also notes that the proprietors of the Charles River Bridge soon offered to improve access to the bridge, albeit to no avail (Kutler 19).

[7] The case has a protracted timeline. In 1828, the plaintiffs had taken their complaint to the Massachusetts supreme court, and in 1831, they appealed the state court's decision in the US Supreme Court under Chief Justice John Marshall. But "absences and vacancies prevented a decision by the Marshall Court," and it was not until 1837 that the case was decided (Kutler 3). By then, John Marshall had died and had been replaced by President Jackson's former attorney general (1831–3) and secretary of the treasury (1833–4) Roger B. Taney, who would be known to later generations mostly for his opinion in the *Dred Scott* case. By then, the Warren Bridge corporation had recouped its expenses and the bridge had become free and the property of the state of Massachusetts.

In the course of their arguments, the two parties in *Charles River Bridge* v. *Warren Bridge* championed very different narratives about property and progress. In the Charles River Bridge corporation's argument, property's security is essential for the republic; in the Warren Bridge corporation's view, property's claim to special protection represents an obstacle to national development. On one side, Whigs like Daniel Webster and Joseph Story stood for the old order and the firm belief that security of property and stability of laws are necessary preconditions for the country's prosperity. This was the position of the Marshall Court in *Fletcher* v. *Peck*, which had given rise to the doctrine of "vested rights" and was driven by the belief that property had to be protected from "the excesses of democratic control" (Alexander 194). On the other side, Democrats like Chief Justice Roger B. Taney represented faith in progress and in the benefit of competition for the public good. As Gregory Alexander puts it, "the Taney Court understood entrepreneurship as a force for undermining hierarchical privileges and opening up opportunities for the broader community" (206). A look at the ruling and the arguments presented by the lawyers reveals that those narratives draw on two different temporal registers. One is geared toward the preservation and continuation of past values into the future, while the other seeks to foster change and not to be burdened by the past. Similar to *Astoria*, those narratives therefore integrate the corporation into their specific temporal registers.

As we have seen, it was not unusual for the Charles River Bridge corporation to be associated with the feudal past by way of monopoly. What is surprising instead is the degree to which the Charles River Bridge's lawyers contributed to that association. In their arguments, Warren Dutton and Daniel Webster sought to establish continuity between the original charter for a ferry and the bridge's charter, to invoke the special status of ferries in the English common-law tradition. As a result, they aligned the Charles River Bridge corporation more closely with that body of law that, as Thomas Sedgwick had argued, was like "gangrene" to "the body politic" (13). A ferry, *Black's Law Dictionary* explains, "is treated as a franchise, and defined as the exclusive right to carry passengers and freight across a river, lake or arm of the sea, or to connect a continuous line of road leading from one side of the water to the other." A franchise, the plaintiffs' attorneys argued, is essentially different from a monopoly. A monopoly, Dutton explained, consists in the exclusive enjoyment of "a natural right" common to all, "and as such is justly odious" (*Charles River Bridge* v. *Warren Bridge* 451). While he conceded that a monopoly curtails the common rights of all, he maintained that a franchise has never been a common right in the first place, but a special property of the state. It is something that the state temporarily takes from its sovereign powers and grants to the corporation, such as the franchise of a ferry. Hence,

Daniel Webster demanded that the proprietors of Charles River Bridge be compensated for the loss of their property, their franchise, because by granting the same franchise to another bridge, the legislature had deprived them of it. Claiming the status of a ferry suggested that the grant of exclusive privileges was implied *by default* and did not need to be made explicit (as it is, indeed, nowhere to be found in the charter). In addition to the continuity which they sought to establish between the Charles River Bridge corporation and a royal grant from colonial times, it was their repeated invocation of the English common law that allowed the Warren Bridge lawyers to invoke the threat of special privilege in turn. They rejected Dutton's attempt to emphasize some sort of continuity with "medieval common law" and its static conception of property in favor of a dynamic and progressive young nation that seeks to forge its own law, "instead of [forging it] in kings' bench, or the exchequer" (Horwitz, *1780–1860* 115; *Charles River Bridge* v. *Warren Bridge* 484). Simon Greenleaf, John Davis's co-counsel for Warren Bridge, is even more explicit in his interpretation of the ruling's implications.

> Let it not be said that, in the American tribunals, the presumption and intendment of law is, that a state will not redeem its pledges any further than it is compelled by judicial coercion [. . .]. [. . .] But proclaim to Europe, and we shall hear its reverberations, in tones louder than the thundering echoes of this capitol; with the bitter taunt, that while the unit monarch of the old world, is the dignified representative of national honor; the monarch-multitude of the new is but the very incarnation of perfidy. (*Charles River Bridge* v. *Warren Bridge* 473)

Greenleaf's distinction between "the unit monarch" (the king) and "the monarch-multitude" (the people) suggests that the position vis-à-vis the common law is evident in the passages above. The invocations of feudalism must also be read, at least to some degree, in a changing understanding of the nature and function of the common law in the US at the time.

This change is the emergence of an understanding of law as an instrument of social change in the nineteenth century. In the previous century, "the common law was conceived of as a body of essentially fixed doctrine to be applied in order to achieve a fair result between private litigants in individual cases" (Horwitz, *1780–1860* 1). The shift toward regarding the law as a tool of social change and toward a more active role for judges was intrinsically connected with the influence of "the beginnings of a modern conception of sovereignty" (Horwitz, *1780–1860* 17). To the degree that Americans began to conceive of their Constitution as an expression of popular will, the common law's natural-law foundations no longer served to give it legitimacy. As Morton J. Horwitz explains, "This definition of the basis of obligation in terms of popular will was a far cry from the eighteenth-century conception of obligation derived from the inherent rightness or justice of law" (*1780–1860* 19). Reconciling the common law and the principle of popular sovereignty, Horwitz adds, "became the central task of judges and jurists at the turn of the century" (*1780–1860* 20). What made it increasingly unsuited for American conditions were "the feudal origins of English law" (Horwitz, *1780–1860* 20).

This is particularly evident in the area of property. American judges and legal scholars recognized that the static conception of property that was characteristic of the English common law was increasingly out of sync with the dynamic and progressive conditions of a young nation. Referring to the *Charles River Bridge* case as an example, Morton J. Horwitz writes that "the spirit of development was undermining traditional notions of property" (*1780–1860* 132). This recognition also entailed the gradual divestment of the "anticompetitive doctrines" contained in the English common law that sought to protect property against "injurious competition" (Horwitz, *1780– 1860* 114). Horwitz observes that it was "the public nature of an enterprise" that legitimized such protections: "Even at the beginning of the nineteenth century English courts still enforced the rule of medieval common law, that no market or fair could be established within seven miles of each other. Just as markets were regarded as franchises, since they were originally established by grants from the king, so too were ferries, and the same exclusionary policy prevailed" (*1780–1860* 115). Finally, the degree to which courts found different, more dynamic conditions in America also included the corporation. While the common-law tradition conceived of the corporation as a public instrument, committed to serving the public interest, Americans were already beginning to use the corporation for private gain.

By rejecting the Charles River Bridge's claim to vested rights and exclusive privileges, the Court's decision reflects this changing understanding of corporations, competition, and development. "The object and the end of all government, is to promote the happiness and prosperity of the community by which it is established; [. . .] and in a country like ours, free, active and enterprising, continually advancing in numbers and wealth; new channels of communication are daily found necessary both for travel and trade; and are essential to the comfort, convenience, and prosperity of the people" (*Charles River Bridge* v. *Warren Bridge* 422). In contrast, Joseph Story's dissenting opinion presents the law's power to secure property for long periods of time, or to put it differently, to secure the continuation of vested rights into the future, as a necessary counterbalance to the uncertainty of that future. Hence, risk features centrally in Story's explanation for the need for stable laws and long timespans (the epitome of which would be corporate perpetuity). Story argued that the hazards of investing in public utility projects are enough to keep investors away even without adding the threat of legal insecurity when it comes to their property.

In his pursuit of this argument, Story relied on personal memory to evoke the risky conditions under which the proprietors of the Charles River Bridge undertook their enterprise. With great detail and a certain degree of gloom, he describes the past as a place of instability and insecurity, both politically and technologically. He calls it "that period of general bankruptcy, and distress and difficulty," and recounts that

> [t]he constitution of the United States was not only not then in existence, but it was not then even dreamed of. The union of the states was crumbling into ruins, under the old confederation. [. . .] I would even now put it to the common sense of every man, whether, if the constitution of the United States had not been adopted, the charter would have been worth a forty years' purchase of the tolls.

> This is not all. It is well known, historically, that this was the very first bridge ever constructed in New England, over navigable tide waters so near the sea. The rigours of our climate, the dangers from sudden thaws and freezing, and the obstructions from ice in a rapid current, were deemed by many persons to be insuperable obstacles to the success of such a project. It was believed, that the bridge would scarcely stand a single severe winter. And I myself am old enough to know, that in regard to other arms of the sea, at much later periods, the same doubts have had a strong and depressing influence upon public enterprises. (*Charles River Bridge* v. *Warren Bridge* 609–10)

Under such difficult conditions, granting charters for forty and even seventy years seems only appropriate because they safeguard the enterprises against the vicissitudes and hazards of time. In fact, by emphasizing the time of incorporation as a moment before the United States was "even dreamed of," Story suggested that the corporation contributed to the building of the commonwealth of Massachusetts.

Story's argument thereby portrays the corporation as an institution capable of providing secure and stable, because long-term, property relations. With a theoretical lifespan that exceeds that of humans, the corporation can hold and manage property in a manner that is independent of human frailties, whether personal or social. For Peter Dobkin Hall, the period following the *Dartmouth College* case witnessed a "struggle to erect a rock-like legal foundation to save wealth, learning, and respectability from the shifting sands of public favor" (114). Republicans found this rock-like foundation, he suggests, in the private corporation as protected by the Contract Clause.

Robert Ferguson has shown that this logic informs Joseph Story's reasoning in the famous *Girard* case, which was decided a few years after *Charles River Bridge* and which concerned the last will of Stephen Girard, a successful Philadelphia banker, who had left a substantial part of his wealth to the city with the provision that they use it to establish an orphanage. Represented in court by Daniel Webster, too, Girard's heirs had contested the will. When the Court ruled in favor of the city of Philadelphia, it fell to Story to write the majority opinion. Reading Story's opinion in the context of contemporary republican fears over lost connections with the founding generation and the material expression of this loss of connection in a transformation of property law (inheritance), Ferguson observes that for Story,

> [s]omething beyond traditional institutions had to supply the continuity between increasingly separated generations of Americans, and that something was going to be corporate power. [. . .] The *Girard* decision went to great lengths not just to find the necessary power to support Girard's bequest to the corporation of Philadelphia but to merge that power with the force of individual human rights. "It is now held," wrote Story, "that where the corporation has a legal capacity to take real or personal estate, there it may take it and hold it upon trust, in the same manner and to the same extent as a private person may do." (248)

In fact, Chapter 3 of this study shows how the corporation, with Story's support, is declared a citizen for the purposes of determining jurisdiction in the year of the *Girard* decision. The temporal dimension that informs Story's dissent in the *Charles River Bridge* case already contains the idea that corporations provide stability in a changing world that is defined by the short-term temporal regime of commerce and the unpredictable shifts of public favor.

For Roger Taney and the defendants' attorneys, however, what is at stake in the *Charles River Bridge* case is that the past is threatening to take the future hostage. The time of progress is characterized by acceleration, and the development of the nation requires more flexible property arrangements. Moreover, in their narrative, and particularly in the occasionally ironic comments of attorney John Davis, the state is not weak and helpless without corporations, but wields its sovereign powers to encourage competition and "improvements." In a famous passage, Taney rejects the idea that the state signs away its franchise indefinitely or that it hands it over to the corporation without retaining any form of control. To do so would contradict the very idea of government, Taney explains.

> The continued existence of a government would be of no great value, if by implications and presumptions, it was disarmed of the powers necessary to

accomplish the ends of its creation; and the functions it was designed to perform, transferred to the hands of privileged corporations. (*Charles River Bridge* v. *Warren Bridge* 548)

As legal scholars such as Gregory Alexander and William J. Novak have shown, Taney's view of the state's sovereign power over corporations expressed the common-law vision of the well-regulated society in which the *salus populi*, the welfare of the people, reigns supreme. This maxim legitimated the regulation of public safety, public economy, public space, public morals, and public health. As Novak explains,

> Public regulation—the power of the state to restrict individual liberty and property for the common welfare—colored all facets of early American development. It was the central component of a reigning theory and practice of governance committed to the pursuit of the people's welfare and happiness in a well-ordered society. (2)

Hence, the state as committed to the welfare of the people is also the state that is committed to "improvements," and in particular to technological progress. To accept the Charles River Bridge's argument that it had an exclusive franchise and that, though its technology (for example, the width of the bridge) was outdated, it should not have to give up its profits for a fitter competitor—to accept such an argument, Taney maintains, would be to literally collapse the opposition between past and future. He writes:

> Let it once be understood that such charters carry with them these implied contracts, and give this unknown and undefined property in a line of travelling; and you will soon find the old turnpike corporations awakening from their sleep, and calling upon this Court to put down the improvements which have taken their place. The millions of property which have been invested in rail roads and canals, upon lines of travel which had been before occupied by turnpike corporations, will be put in jeopardy. We shall be thrown back to the improvements of the last century, and obliged to stand still, until the claims of the old turnpike corporations shall be satisfied; and they shall consent to permit these states to avail themselves of the lights of modern science, and to partake of the benefit of those improvements which are now adding to the wealth and prosperity, and the convenience and comfort, of every other part of the civilized world. (*Charles River Bridge* v. *Warren Bridge* 552–3)

The temporal dimension of Taney's narrative is made explicit here: it is the nightmare of a past that catches up with the present and prevents progress into the future. Instead of accelerating its development, the nation would "stand still" (*Charles River Bridge* v. *Warren Bridge* 553).

In retrospect, the *Charles River Bridge* case appears to mark a period in which the corporation was still perceived as a fundamentally public, political institution in the service of the community, while already beginning to become more widely employed as a private economic tool in the service of individuals. "Taney's opinion," writes Alexander, "was filled with the rhetoric of the rights of the community, not the market; of politics, not economics" (209). It is in this vein that the Court would continue to assert its control over the corporation: because it maintained a belief in the priority of the public good over individual interests, and because it saw commerce and entrepreneurship as democratizing forces. Yet, somewhat paradoxically, the Jacksonians' crusade against vested rights and their belief in competition as an instrument of progress and development also presented a crucial step toward modernizing the corporate form and accelerated the emergence of the private business corporation.

With regard to the popular imaginary, moreover, the *Charles River Bridge* case is also relevant for how it develops the themes of property and propriety and of self-interest and general interest that already informed Irving's characterization of corporate businesses in *Astoria*. This chapter's final section turns to the tale that was inspired by the *Charles River Bridge* case: William Austin's "Martha Gardner; or, Moral Re-Action" (1837), which is set in Massachusetts in 1785 and tells the story of an old widow's resistance to the newly incorporated Charles River Bridge and its relentless pursuit of her property. Its heroine is an embodiment of revolutionary values and of private virtue that can ultimately outlast even a powerful (and theoretically immortal) corporation. In doing so, Austin's tale suggests that Americans should rely on their values and virtues rather than on institutional structures and social hierarchies for stability and guidance in tumultuous times.

III. "Martha Gardner"

In the same year that the Supreme Court decided the *Charles River Bridge* case, the lawyer and Democrat William Austin published "Martha Gardner; or, Moral Re-Action," in which he revisited the legal conflict by way of a literary fiction. Austin "had been a classmate of Joseph Story at Harvard" and was better known for "Peter Rugg, the Missing Man"—a story that, as Brook Thomas notes, "[Nathaniel] Hawthorne loved" (*Cross-Examinations* 51). Surprisingly, instead of retelling the contemporary conflict that the lawsuit had just settled, Austin set the basic narrative in 1785, the year in which the Charles River Bridge was chartered, and pitched "the Great

Corporation" against a "poor widow" (566). In this way, the story appears to shift the focus from monopoly's effect on the republic and national progress toward its effect on the private citizen and common (wo)man. By contrasting the corporation's ruthlessness in pursuing its goal to dispossess Martha Gardner with her quiet virtue, the story strongly suggests that corporate monopoly is undemocratic and that it is, in fact, anathema to the values for which Americans fought in the Revolutionary War. In this respect, Austin's short story is much more critical of corporations than *Astoria*, which imagines a new and progressive corporation. But like *Astoria*, "Martha Gardner" employs a "prophetic" mode, and it does so to draw attention to the temporal implications of corporate property that the *Charles River Bridge* case had so powerfully brought to light.

Austin's story sets up the conflict between two vastly unequal opponents. Martha lives in a "cottage between Boston and Charlestown, on the Charlestown shore," which she inherited from Sir Francis Willoughby, who first settled Charlestown (Austin 565). In fact, Martha is from the start strongly associated with the founding of the commonwealth of Massachusetts as well as with the founding of the republic, because her family, we are told, gave its name to "Bunker Hill" (Austin 566). She is beloved by the community, which purchases "sweetmeats, nuts, and apples at the shop of Martha Gardner" and has strong emotional connections to the land (Austin 565). It is this land that the "Charles River Bridge, the greatest enterprise of that day" covets (Austin 566). The corporation takes Martha to court over her land, which they "fancy [. . .] was their corporate property," apparently because the bridge is directly adjacent to Martha's home on the river's shore (Austin 566). Three times the corporation takes Martha Gardner to court, and while Martha appears to prevail each time, it also becomes clear that the legal battle and her anxiety over losing her home hasten her to the grave. Shortly before her final appearance in court and amid a storm that threatens to destroy the bridge, Martha utters a prophecy in which she predicts that, while the corporation may defeat her, it will ultimately not prevail. A footnote by the author tells the reader about the Supreme Court's decision in the *Charles River Bridge* case, suggesting that Martha's prophecy had finally come true.

That the conflict is one of significantly unequal opponents is particularly apparent in their unequal command over two key resources: money and time. For example, as "a poor widow," Martha lacks the financial resources to go to court (Austin 566). In fact, the narrator portrays lawsuits as an aristocratic sport, an entertainment for the rich and powerful, and in this way, the corporation is once more cast as a remnant of feudalism. To make this point, the narrator gives an example from the French Court of a "French officer" who is involved in a hundred lawsuits during peacetime because he is bored. "When he was summoned before Louis 15th as a public nuisance, the king ordered him to drop them all; but he, falling on his knees, entreated that he might retain half a dozen of them for his diversion, otherwise he should die with languor during the long peace" (Austin 566). This anecdote also underlines the martial aspect of the lawsuit into which "the richest corporation in New England" draws Martha, but more importantly, by giving an example from the French aristocracy, it emphasizes that privileges of any kind are undemocratic and un-American (Austin 566). Moreover, Martha is ill equipped to fight a corporation because she is mortal, unlike the corporation. In the course of the story, the corporation "summons" Martha thrice to court, to which Martha exclaims: "This may be a sport to them, but it is death to me. I have but a short lease of all worldly things" (Austin 570). The corporation, the story suggests, can outlast the individual and is therefore not only more powerful economically, but also temporally. While it did not command corporate perpetuity, the Charles River Bridge's charter granted it seventy years—a lifetime beyond the lifespans of its individual members.

In fact, the narrative does acknowledge the fact that the corporation consists of individuals, but the corporation is not embodied in any individual, whether a "master spirit" like Astor or a group of agents. Instead, "Martha Gardner" attempts to evoke the corporation's superhuman properties: its longevity, its near omnipotence, and ultimately, its soullessness. In this vein, the narrator explains:

> The metaphysicians distribute man into three parts—the animal, the intellectual, and the moral. Which of these is most likely to prevail in a Corporation? The Corporation of Charles River Bridge was composed of many men, in that day, well remembered now for their private and public worth. Less than five of them would have redeemed Niniveh. But, unhappily, the animal and intellectual part of Corporations generally govern the body, and conscience is a non-corporate word. (Austin 572)

The passage describes the corporation as an entity different from the shareholders in their individual capacities, an entity that can be compared to "man" and found lacking. As the next chapter shows, this lack of consciousness was associated with the idea of the corporation as pursuing selfish goals rather than the general interest—it was expressed in the trope of the *soulless corporation*. While Austin does not employ this trope explicitly, the narrator's comment that "conscience is a non-corporate word," as well as his reference to Plato's parable of the many-headed beast, strongly suggest that contemporary readers would have understood his description in this way.[8] In Plato's *Republic*, the many-headed beast is an important element in the parable of the human soul, justice, and tyranny. The question that Socrates and Glaucon are discussing in Book Nine (588b ff.) is whether the unjust are living a more satisfied life than the just. In order to settle this question, Socrates asks Glaucon to "mol[d] an image of the soul in speech"; that is, to imagine the following metaphor:

> "Well then, mold a single idea for a many-colored, many-headed beast that has a ring of heads of tame and savage beasts and can change them and make all of them grow from itself. [. . .] Now, then, mold another single idea for a lion, and a single one for a human being. Let the first be by far the greatest, and the second, second in size." "That's easier," [Glaucon] said, "and the molding is done." "Well, then, join them—they are three—in one, so that in some way they grow naturally together with each other." "They are joined," he said. "Then mold about them on the outside an image of one—that of the human being—so that to the man who's not able to see what's inside, but sees only the outer shell, it looks like one animal, a human being."

In this image the human soul consists of reason, spirit and appetites, with the latter represented by the many-headed beast. Depending on whether man feeds the savage heads or the tame, they grow stronger and rule over his soul. Of course, the corporation possesses only two out of three components of man's soul, which is why the corporation's characterization also suggests a variation on the theme of soullessness that was common during this period. Unlike the virtuous citizen, the corporation is ruled only by calculating reason and appetites, and in place of virtuous interiority we find a many-headed monster.

Given that Austin's portrait of corporate monopoly is more focused on exploring its superindividual and superhuman properties, the narrative also has to find a way to narrate corporate agency beyond embodying it in individual agents. Accordingly, the corporation is presented as speaking through the law and through writing (rather than through an agent): "the Great Corporation appeared to Martha in the shape of a summons, commanding

---

[8] The narrator refers to Plato in a different context: "I have heard it observed, that many ages past a man by the name of Plato, being in the dark, guessed a great deal about the immortality of the soul" (Austin 568).

her to appear at Court, and submit to a new trial in the form of a review" (Austin 570). It also begins to haunt Martha in her dreams:

> "When I lay my head on my pillow, the Corporation appears to me in all its terrors; when I sleep—no, I do not sleep—when I dream, I dream of the Corporation; and when I awake, there stands the great Corporation of Charles River Bridge against Martha Gardner. They, seemingly almighty, and I, nothing." (Austin 568)

The corporation's influence is thus portrayed as powerful yet indirect and invisible. It is rather "metaphysical" in the way that treatise writers, judges, and attorneys would often describe the fictional entity of the corporate person at the beginning of the nineteenth century.[9] In this respect, moreover, Austin employs conventions of the romance that are closer to those developed by Nathaniel Hawthorne than Washington Irving.

In his "Preface" to *The House of the Seven Gables*, Hawthorne defines his own romance as distinct from the novel on account of its recourse to "the Marvellous": romance does not "aim at a very minute fidelity," but seeks "the truth of the human heart" (*House* 3). Similarly, throughout "Martha Gardner," the narrator observes events and appearances that display "a tinge of the marvellous," such as the reappearance of an "old wooden post" or Martha's prophecy at the end of the tale, in which she predicts the demise of the corporation (Austin 567, 568). In addition, Brook Thomas has noted the similarities between the plots of "Martha Gardner" and *The House of the Seven Gables*, from the little shop that the old widow keeps in her cottage to the sub-plot involving a lost deed (see *Cross-Examinations* 52). In its exploration of temporal registers and its use of a "prophetic" mode, however, "Martha Gardner" does share striking similarities to *Astoria*, as well as the *Charles River Bridge* case.

Similar to those two texts, "Martha Gardner" associates the corporation with the feudal past and warns of this past as trying to claim the republic's future. This is not only apparent in its earlier alignment of the corporation with the French nobility, but also in how it does not pitch one corporation against another (which could be a more progressive corporation, as is the case of the AFC in *Astoria*) but against an individual who is likewise associated with the past. The past with which Martha Gardner is associated by virtue of her family heritage ("Her family name was Bunker, whence came Bunker

---

[9] In the introduction to his *Treatise*, Stewart Kyd famously rejects the idea that a corporation is "a mere metaphysical being" (15).

Hill," 566) is that of the American Revolution. But while Martha represents the values of the Revolution, she makes no claim on the present in the way that the corporation does. Instead, the story's emphasis on her frailty, on how she is simply trying to live out her last days peacefully, and the fact that she does not have an heir, strongly suggests that she is ready to pass on. Her legacy is a prophecy and a warning of the dangers that corporate monopolies present to the republic.

Setting his literary fiction in the year of the real Charles River Bridge corporation's chartering and having Martha prophesy the people's eventual triumph over its monopoly therefore allows Austin to establish a moment of contact between the (revolutionary) past and the Jacksonian present. In her prophecy, Martha declares that

> [t]he traveler shall shun it, and shall pass another way to the great city; and they of the great city shall shun it, and pass another way; and they of the Great Corporation shall avoid it—turn from it, and pass another way. It shall disappear in all its glory, as the great highway of the North, and still remain visible, as an everlasting monument. (Austin 573)

Through its use of prophecy and the theme of inheritance, Austin's story casts corporate monopoly as an obstacle to national progress and development in a manner strikingly similar to Irving's warning in *Astoria*—though as we have seen, Irving was ultimately less worried about corporate monopoly per se than about his country failing to seize the opportunities offered by private enterprise through incorporation. Reminiscent of Chief Justice Taney's concern that the feudal past in the shape of corporate monopoly is trying to take the future hostage, Austin's story turns to Martha Gardner as an embodiment not only of revolutionary values but also of private virtue. As the next chapter shows, "Martha Gardner" thereby provides a connection not only between the "prophetic" modes and temporal registers of corporate monopoly, but also the fear of conspiracy and corruption and the rise of a many-headed beast, whether a soulless corporation or a soulless public.

2

The Soulless Corporation:
Cooper and the Decline of the Republic

In the popular imaginary of the late eighteenth and early nineteenth centuries, corporations were not only associated with monopoly, but also with conspiracy and corruption. When the narrator in "Martha Gardner" exclaims that "conscience is a non-corporate word," he is alluding to what was at the time a well-known trope, the soulless corporation (Austin 572), and hence, implicitly, to the transformation of the corporation at the beginning of the nineteenth century from a public tool that serves the general interest to a private instrument that serves selfish purposes. On the one hand, this trope emerged from a republican tradition that was increasingly under pressure as the nation experienced the democratization of both political and economic spheres: the market revolution and the expansion of the franchise under Andrew Jackson. From that perspective, the corporation became an emblem of selfish pursuits, and none more than the banks or so-called moneyed corporations. For Democrats, such as the author James Fenimore Cooper, soulless corporations presented a political elite corrupted by wealth, and their corrupt designs were hidden precisely by the incorporated entity and what the law called the corporate veil. In this way the corporation became associated not only with monopoly privileges and the corruption that followed from a privileged pursuit of selfish goals, but also with conspiracy. For Whigs, on the other hand, these selfish goals were attached to an older nightmare of irrational mobs in the streets, a collective body cut loose from its sovereign head: the many-headed beast of the plebeian masses.

To understand corporations' association with conspiracy and corruption in the popular imaginary during this period, this chapter begins with a brief look at the key beliefs of civic republicanism. Then it turns to the controversies over central banking from the eighteenth century to the Jacksonian era, as well as to the controversy surrounding President Andrew Jackson's veto over the rechartering of the Second Bank. By reviewing these controversies and how they activated the popular trope of the soulless corporation, the chapter shows that it was the legal form itself, the specific organizational structure of corporations, to which fears of conspiracy and corruption attached: its collective nature, its investment structure, and its increasing dedication to financial pursuits. The chapter's middle section presents a detailed analysis of James Fenimore Cooper's *The Bravo* (1831), today one of Cooper's lesser-known and certainly less studied works. Set in eighteenth-century Venice, it tells a jeremiadic tale of republican decline and oligarchical conspiracies that follows several characters as they attempt to protect themselves and their loved ones from the city's corporate government, which is the "soulless corporation" at the center of all the text's plots (Cooper, *The Bravo* 138). What makes Cooper's romance particularly valuable is how it activates not only the trope of the soulless corporation but also (at least implicitly) the trope of the many-headed beast in its portrayal of the irrational, plebeian mob as a threat that is complementary to the calculating and unscrupulous corporate elite. To fully understand the connection between corporations and the trope of the many-headed beast, the chapter's final section explores some of the caricatures that accompanied Andrew Jackson's struggle with the Second Bank. What these literary, political, and visual texts make evident is that the corporation's increasing democratization (defined here as the spread of general incorporation laws and thus increased availability of the form) evoked a register of republican fears that is different from, yet inextricably related to, the fear of a feudal past holding the nation back. If Irving, Austin, and Taney presented corporate monopoly and its origins in English common law as out of place in a thriving young republic, Cooper's text in particular reveals the degree to which the corporation's collective nature could also evoke the fear of the many, whether conspiring elites or irrational plebeian mobs. Moreover, in contrast to Irving's *Astoria*, Cooper's romance is much more concerned with the effect of corporate power on the individual: how corporate agents become subsumed and ultimately corrupted as their actions are guided no longer by the general interest but by the special interest of the corporate body.

I. Selfish Pursuits: Civic Republicanism and Moneyed Corporations

The city of Venice, the setting of Cooper's *The Bravo*, held a special place in republican ideology. It was considered a model republic, as it represented "[a] commonwealth [that] was [an] immortally serene, because perfectly balanced, combination of the three elements of monarchy, aristocracy, and democracy" (Pocock 102). Published in 1832, *A Treatise on the Law of Private Corporations*

Aggregate by Joseph Angell and Samuel Ames highlights this republican and civic promise of incorporation:

> In all the countries which had been provinces of the Roman empire, the municipal establishments of the Romans retained some vestiges of those elective forms, and of that local administration which had been bestowed on them by the civilizing policy of those renowned conquerors. These remains of Roman government, though they were not sufficiently striking to attact [*sic*] the observation of the petty tyrants in whose territory they were situated, yet, beyond doubt, they contributed to prepare the people for more valuable privileges in better times. (12)

Municipal corporations, Angell and Ames suggest here, served as training grounds for a republican future: Italian city-states like Venice had a history of incorporation that expressed their "passion for liberty" and that not only trained their citizens in self-government but also instilled in them the moral virtue that was deemed necessary for the maintenance of a republic (Angell and Ames 12–13).

This moral virtue was a core tenet of civic republicanism, which drew on sources from classical antiquity as well as from the English Commonwealth writers. In twentieth-century scholarship, civic republicanism first became a subject in the scholarship of Bernard Bailyn, Gordon Wood, and J. G. A. Pocock, who sought an alternative to Louis Hartz's *The Liberal Tradition* (1955). At the center of republicanism stood the ideal of the public good (*res publica*), which, as Gordon Wood argues, meant that individual interests were sacrificed for the commonwealth and virtue consisted of the surrender of self-interest to the general interest. Pocock's study, on the other hand, gave the common good a more active character by locating it in the "civic" sphere (hence civic humanism or civic republicanism) and in the values of personality, property, and independence. Common to all interpretations is the basic assumption that the republican tradition rests on the promise of public virtue and the threat of corruption. Understood as more than the sum of individual interests, the public good required virtuous citizens for its realization and support. For citizens to be virtuous, it was imperative that they be free of external influence, such as the government's. For this independence, private property (and hence its protection) provided a crucial foundation. Instead of merely a market commodity, property was therefore understood as *propriety*, the basis for social order. In this respect, private property was not exempt from state regulation either. As Gregory Alexander explains:

> The concept of the common weal [. . .] was understood to have substantive meaning. The common law maxim *salus populi suprema est lex* (the welfare

of the people is the supreme law) had real content. The public good was not understood as simply whatever the market produces, for the market was viewed as a realm in which individuals were too vulnerable to the temptation to act out of narrow self-interest rather than, as proprietarian principles required, for the purpose of maintaining the properly ordered society. (2)

From this point of view, corruption would ensue wherever independence was compromised. For example, corruption was a threat when one government branch depended on the other, when private citizens depended on the government, or when the pursuit of wealth and luxury led to "moral decay in the life of the citizenry" (Speir 123).

Jacksonians had ample opportunity to see American citizens and organizations turn to such dangerous pursuit of wealth and luxury, of course. After all, theirs was the age of what Charles Sellers has called "the market revolution." But on an even more foundational level, the first decades of the nineteenth century witnessed what Gordon S. Wood has described as the "end of classical politics": as the system of checks and balances replaced the former model of interdependent groups, it left the individual at liberty to pursue her particular interests.[1] In other words, while the pursuit of the common good and general interest had been a priority and the foundation of the republican state, the political system was now such that it no longer required or even supported such submission to the common good, thereby allowing Americans to pursue their self-interests. The trope of the soulless corporation registers "the partial shift from republicanism to liberalism" in this period, as it highlighted what was most monstrous about the corporation: its singular commitment to selfish purposes (Pocock 523). In Pocock's words: "If men no longer enjoyed the conditions thought necessary to make them capable of perceiving the common good, all that each man was capable of perceiving was his own particular interest" (522).

To explain the origin of the soulless corporation, scholars often turn to *The Case of Sutton's Hospital* (1612), in which Sir Edward Coke writes that corporations "may not commit treason, nor be outlawed, nor excommunicate [*sic*], for they have no souls" (Coke 303). Angell and Ames, too, include Coke's definition in their 1832 treatise and note that, "[i]t is reported by Lord Coke, that C. Baron Manwood demonstrated that corporations have no soul by the following curious syllogism: 'None can create souls, but God; but a corporation is created by the King; therefore, a corporation can have no

---

[1]   "In place of individual self-sacrifice for the good of the state as the bond holding the republican fabric together, the Americans began putting an increasing emphasis on what they called 'public opinion' as the basis of all governments" (Wood 612).

soul'" (4). However, the reasons why the idea of soullessness was associated so strongly with corporations were probably more complex. A look at the debates over banking and financial speculation in the 1830s suggests that soullessness referred to the kind of self-interested behavior that was becoming more common in the emergent market society and that violated the ideas of civic republicanism in which Americans were still trained to view their country.[2]

Nevertheless, while soullessness was therefore a charge that originated in a republican rhetoric of corruption and virtue, it may have attached itself so powerfully to the corporation not only on account of the organizations' increasing commitment to profit (at least in the popular perception) but also because the assumption was that the corporations' fundamentally collective nature exacerbated this tendency. As the narrator in *The Bravo* puts it, the problem is "the selfishness of all corporations, in which the responsibility of the individual, while his acts are professedly submitted to the temporizing expedients of a collective interest, is lost in the subdivision of numbers" (Cooper 146). In other words, while (true) republics had a moderating influence on their citizens' passions, by holding them publicly accountable, corporations—even though deceptively similar in that the individual "professedly submit[s] to the temporizing expedients of a collective interest"—fueled such passions by allowing individual accountability to be lost in "numbers."

II. Central Banking, 1786 to 1836

In the popular imaginary, banking corporations presented the epitome of the soulless corporation, even though they did serve a public function by making money and credit available. Their association with the concentration of wealth, exacerbated by the "special privilege" of incorporation, made them seem exclusively dedicated to the economic benefit of their shareholders. In this regard we can see a distinct US rhetoric take shape in the debates over central banking in the eighteenth and early nineteenth centuries, that adapted an older republican rhetoric to New World concerns over the corrupting influence of wealth and commerce. As Bray Hammond has observed, for example, the Jacksonians still took recourse to an agrarian tradition when they expressed their distrust of banks, despite their commercial bend: "The phraseology of idealism was adapted to money-making [. . .]. Though their cause was a sophisticated one of enterpriser against capitalist, of banker against regulation, and of Wall Street against Chestnut, the language was the same as

---

[2] For instance, during the debates over the tariff in December of 1836, we find reference to "heartless and soulless speculators," and even in *The Bravo* the term is used almost synonymously with selfishness (United States Congress 1154).

if they were all back on the farm" (328). This rhetoric contributed to the formation of a popular imaginary of corporate power and agency in the United States that would survive into the twentieth century. While Andrew Jackson's veto of the rechartering of the Second Bank of the United States in 1832 is in many ways an excellent illustration of this imaginary, I will briefly review three previous debates that attended the incorporation of central banks: the Bank of North America (1786), the (First) Bank of the United States (1790), and the Second Bank of the United States (1816). In this way I show that anti-corporate rhetoric not only highlighted the structural kinship between corporation and republic that Cooper explores in *The Bravo*, but also which fears attached to specific formal features of the corporation.

Many of the republican fears over centralization of power emerge in the debates over the (First) Bank of North America in the spring of 1786. The Bank was incorporated on December 31, 1781, at a time when the colonies urgently needed money to finance the War of Independence, and the Bank's most immediate purpose was to "provid[e] the Congress with the funds to stay in existence" (Kaplan 11). But after only three years in business, in the spring of 1785, the Bank's opponents successfully campaigned to repeal its charter. In the subsequent debates over the rechartering of the Bank, it is possible to identify three main motifs, the first of which was the fear of "influence," whether by the corporation on the government or vice versa. For example, the house committee report, based on which the charter had been repealed, stated in its conclusions about the Bank of North America that, "We have nothing [. . .] in our free and equal government, capable of balancing the influence which the bank must create" (Carey 57). Connected to this motif was a second one: moral corruption and specifically greed. Representing the agrarian position was William Findley, who declared that "[t]his institution, having no principle but that of avarice, which dries and shrivels up all the manly, all the generous feelings of the human soul, will never be varied in its object and if continued will accomplish its end, viz., to engross all the wealth, power and influence of the state" (Carey 66). Findley's comment suggests that the charge of corruption was based on the corporation as a specific form of organization. Ian Speir makes a similar observation and explains that the Bank's critics considered the problem of greed as "institutional"; he adds that "[t]he bank, like any corporation, had to be run according to its 'natural principles'—profit-making for its shareholders—and it would seek to attain this end regardless of the costs to the public" (138).

A third and particularly powerful motif in the debates was the threat to democracy by foreign elites. This motif was also the one that, as Bray Hammond has remarked, was most clearly connected to the corporate form, specifically to its private investment structure (56). The committee report, for example, stated that "[f]oreigners will doubtless be more and more induced to become stockholders, until the time may arrive, when this engine of power may become subject to foreign influence. This country may be agitated with the politics of European courts, and the good people of America reduced once more to a state of subordination and dependence upon some one or other of the European powers" (Carey 56). Like a Trojan horse, this passage suggests, the private nature of the corporation would allow foreign aristocrats to enter and undermine American democratic institutions. At the same time, opponents of the Bank rejected the idea that foreign stockholders could prosper from American resources. Thomas Paine, for example, argued that such reasoning was short-sighted: "As for the absurd condemnation of foreign investment in the bank's stock, Paine said the enemies of the bank 'must have forgotten which side of the Atlantic they were on,' for their arguments would be true if the situation were the other way round [sic] and Americans were putting their money in foreign banks" (qtd. in Hammond 60). Nonetheless, the threat of foreign investments would prove to be an enduring motif in the debates over (banking) corporations.[3]

Many of these fears also accompanied the debates over Alexander Hamilton's proposal for the Bank of the United States in 1790. His plan for a national bank was modeled after the Bank of England and, like the Bank of North America before it, it would operate from Philadelphia, which was then the nation's financial capital. To the fear of the concentration of too much power in too few hands and the fear of foreign subversion was added the fear of an infringement on the rights of individual states. Thomas Jefferson and James Madison specifically questioned Congress's right to charter a corporation in the first place. Madison pointed out that this right had been on the table during the Convention in 1787, that he himself had proposed it, but that it had been rejected. Thus, it had not become part of the Constitution. Related to this objection was a special concern raised by the proposed charter's inclusion of the right to open branch offices in other states.[4] To grant the corporation a charter, Thomas Jefferson argued, would "communicate to

---

[3] In the end, the charter was restored and the Bank continued business for fourteen more years. Parts of the BNA survive in Wells Fargo today; see Ian Speir, "Corporations, the Original Understanding, and the Problem of Power."

[4] Thomas Jefferson specifically rejected the idea that the right to incorporate was implied by the Constitution's "general phrase" about the government's power "to make all laws *necessary* and proper for carrying into execution the enumerated powers" (Clarke and Hall 92, emphasis in the original). While Hamilton argued in favor of a broad construction of this provision (what would come to be known as the "doctrine of implied powers"), Jefferson maintained that the government could collect taxes, etc. without incorporating a bank—it was not "*necessary*" in this regard.

them a power to make laws paramount to the laws of the States" (Clarke and Hall 91). The Bank's branches would interfere with the sovereign rights of the individual states and would constitute a kind of foreign influence. Quoting Jefferson, Richard E. Ellis explains: "The bank would be a monopoly, and in its operation would violate in various ways the rights of the states which were protected by the Tenth Amendment, which provided that 'all powers not delegated to the United States nor prohibited by it to the states, are reserved to the states, or to the people'" (35).

It was not until 1816, when the Second Bank of the United States had opened its doors on Chestnut Street in Philadelphia, that the issue of the Bank's constitutionality and its relationship to the states was settled. As historians have pointed out, the First and Second Banks operated within very different financial environments: by 1816 the number of state-chartered banks had grown significantly, and those banks felt threatened by the national bank and its local branches.[5] Some states, such as Ohio and Kentucky, retaliated by levying taxes on the Bank, which the latter refused to pay. "Six states heavily taxed branches of the Bank, and fourteen passed stay laws to prevent the Bank from collecting its debts" (Remini, *Bank War* 28). The resulting lawsuit, *McCulloch* v. *Maryland* (1819), addressed the question of the legitimacy of state taxation of the Bank's branches. Timing was important because Pennsylvania was preparing a debate over whether to tax the Bank's branch in Pittsburgh, and a decision in the affirmative would have further strengthened states like Ohio and Kentucky in their course. The Court ruled in favor of the Bank and thereby seemed to settle the question of constitutionality and of federal incorporation once and for all. As for the states' rights, Edward Kaplan notes, "The decision was also important because it did question state sovereignty, and declared that national law superseded state law whenever the two conflicted" (72). Since its decision, Richard E. Ellis notes, "it has become the foundational statement for a strong and active central government and the broadening of its powers" (11).

The so-called Bank War is usually said to have begun in 1829 with Jackson's first address to Congress, in which he openly criticized the Second Bank, and to have ended in 1836, when the Bank's charter ran out and the nation was poised on the brink of yet another financial panic. Given the importance of this period in American politics and in economic history, it is not surprising that historians have extensively studied the Bank War and that their interpretations have varied over the years. Progressive historians like

---

[5]   Edward Kaplan writes that, "The maximum number of branches at any one time was twenty-five in 1830" (57).

Arthur Schlesinger Jr. have seen Andrew Jackson as the representative of the common man and the conflict over the Bank as a class conflict; "consensus school" historians like Richard Hofstadter and, in his wake, Bray Hammond, have rejected the idea of a class conflict in favor of a struggle between two capitalist elites (between Chestnut Street and Wall Street). Later-generation historians like Marvin Meyers and Robert Remini have focused more on the role of Andrew Jackson and his personality, while Charles Sellers's 1991 *The Market Revolution: Jacksonian America, 1815–1846* once again framed the conflict in terms of a struggle between social classes.[6] In a recent article, Stephen Mihm concludes that it is probably more accurate to say that all those factors contributed to what happened during Jackson's second term. In Mihm's words, "The Bank War was a long, protracted conflict involving many factions, personalities, and motives. On occasion, it was a conflict between different regions of the country, or more often, different classes: rich and poor as well as the rich and those who wished to be rich. And at other times the conflict mutated simply because of the clash of personalities between Jackson and Biddle" ("Fog" 368). In effect, the Bank War resulted in a stronger government, or more specifically, in a more powerful executive branch.

What historians of all schools generally agree on is the size and significance of the Second Bank of the United States. Bray Hammond writes that in 1823, the year Nicholas Biddle took over, "[t]he Bank was the largest corporation in America, and one of the largest in the whole world" (292). Robert Remini notes that, "[b]y 1828, the Bank was a financial colossus" (*Bank War* 39). The key differences between the First and the Second Bank were a higher capitalization (the Second Bank received $35 rather than $10 million, due to the war effort) as well as the fact that "the president of the United States was now given the power, with the consent of Congress, to name five of the twenty-five directors instead of their all being elected by the stockholders, as was the case with the [First Bank of the United States]" (R. E. Ellis 42). Otherwise, the Second Bank was what Mihm calls a "reincarnation of the old one" ("Fog" 354): it was chartered for twenty years and had the same public-private ownership ratio (20 percent to 80 percent).[7] During his presidency, Biddle turned the Bank into a regulatory agency: between 1823 and 1828, the Bank "prospered, proved innovative, and was run conservatively. [. . .] It performed central banking activities such as regulating the money supply and the expansion of credit" (Kaplan 93). Accordingly, a majority of American

---

[6] For a detailed discussion of those approaches see Mihm, "The Fog of War."

[7] Another significant difference, which Remini notes: "the government received a bonus of $1.5 million for granting the charter" (*Bank War* 27).

citizens supported the Bank until 1833/4,[8] when Biddle began to actively retaliate against Jackson's policies by curtailing credit, for example (Remini, *Bank War* 40, 45). Located in Philadelphia like its predecessors, the Bank moved into newly built quarters on Chestnut Street in 1824. "[T]he Greek Temple," as critics called it (Remini, *Bank War* 40), had been designed by William Strickland and "was patterned after the Parthenon" (Hammond 299). In this regard, the building was not an exception. Hammond notes, "If not Greek in pattern, bank architecture [in the US] was at least classic" (300).

The Bank War was conducted in the rhetoric of the older debates of national banks, and in a larger sense, it was a financial and political struggle over centralized power. An important theme throughout was conspiracy, which—as we have seen—the republican tradition attached to corporate bodies by way of their association with wealth and privilege, as well as the structural kinship to the commonwealth. Moreover, as the examples of the debates over the Bank of North America and the First Bank of the United States illustrate, Americans also harbored the fear of foreign subversion. They believed that British investors, hidden among the corporation's numerous shareholders, would try to influence American politics. (Note that the charter of Astor's American Fur Company, for example, declares that all shareholders must be US citizens.) In the specific context of the Bank War, it was the rumor that some of the Second Bank's branches had campaigned for John Quincy Adams that brought the theme of conspiracy center stage in the conflict. While its beginning is usually dated with Jackson's first critique of the Bank as president of the United States, evidence suggests that the conflict's political dimension began with these rumors, which Jackson must have heard about by January 1830. As Robert Remini notes, Jackson truly believed that the Bank presented a concentration of power dangerous to the republic and such rumors seemed to confirm his greatest fears (Remini, *Bank War* 44).[9] Roger Taney—soon to be Jackson's secretary of the treasury, and a future chief justice who would preside over the *Charles River Bridge* case—also feared that the Bank would "influence elections" (Remini, *Bank War* 45, 49–50). Stephen Mihm and other historians note that Biddle investigated the charge but could not find any evidence for it.

Yet even Jackson's critique of the Bank did not, at first, preclude a compromise. In his second message to Congress in December 1830, Jackson suggested that the Bank simply become a branch of the Treasury, and thus a

---

[8]   Edward Kaplan likewise notes, "By the end of February 1834, public opinion had turned against the Second Bank and became very pro-Jackson" (142).

[9]   In the message to the cabinet about the removal of the deposits, he calls the Second Bank "a vast electioneering engine" (Richardson 1234).

part of the government; a year later, in December 1831, he was ready to drop the conflict if Biddle agreed to some slight moderations of the charter (Remini, *Bank War* 73). The reason for his change of mood was the fact that Jackson feared that the Bank issue could cost him re-election. Given this opportunity to put the conflict to rest, historians agree that Biddle committed a blunder by submitting the request for an early rechartering of the Bank instead.[10] He was advised to do so by National Republican leaders, among them presidential candidate Henry Clay, which Stephen Mihm interprets as a self-serving move: "[H]e wanted Jackson to veto the bill, which would help deliver Pennsylvania—and the election—to Clay" ("Fog" 358). As it turned out, however, Jackson not only successfully vetoed the renewal of the charter but also made the Bank a central issue of his campaign in 1832, and while this may not have swayed the masses in his favor, it did not keep them from re-electing him (Remini, *Bank War* 45).

While not all historians are quite as damning in their estimate of Jackson's veto message as Bray Hammond—who has described the text as "legalistic, demagogic, and full of sham" (405)—most of them agree that the question of constitutionality, such as would usually warrant a presidential veto, is comparatively small in this case.[11] In the veto's most famous passage, the President deplores that the Bank's charter was a special privilege only granted to the wealthy: "It is to be regretted that the rich and powerful too often bend the acts of government to their selfish purposes" (Remini, *Age* 80). Retelling the conflict of power in terms of a class struggle would prove to be an effective move because, as Stephen Mihm points out, "[i]t turned the Bank War into a struggle between the haves and have-nots, but made the latter category so capacious that it could include anyone who wasn't a director or stockholder of the Bank of the United States. The enemies of the Bank could be farmers, mechanics, laborers, but also bankers, businessmen, and entrepreneurs" ("Fog" 361). Casting Jackson as their representative, the President himself thus became the quintessential common man.

By contrast, the President's (and, therefore, the people's) enemy in this narrative is a corporation. While the veto uses the same language of privilege, monopoly, and tyranny that had characterized the earlier debates over central banking, it attaches its criticism even more specifically to the Bank's corporate properties. For example, the veto begins by suggesting that the Bank be turned into "a Branch of the Treasury Department," because as a corporation

---

[10] Biddle requested the renewal for the charter on January 6, 1832. It passed both houses of Congress before Jackson vetoed the renewal in July.

[11] In addition to Jackson, the veto message was written by Roger Taney, Amos Kendall, Andrew J. Donelson and Levi Woodbury (Remini, *Bank War* 81).

it has "stockholders" and therefore, for example, can tempt or sway the masses into investments (Remini, *Age* 72). The veto continues that "[t]he proposed substitute would have few officers and no stockholders, make no loans, have no debtors, build no houses, rent no lands or houses[,] make no donations, and would be entirely destitute of the influence which arises from the hopes, fears and avarice of thousands" (Remini, *Age* 74). This motif of corruption is predictably tied to the fear of foreign conspiracy, such as when the veto cautions that "much of its stock is owned by foreigners, through the management of which an avenue is opened to a foreign influence in the most vital concern of the Republic" (Remini, *Age* 74).

Even more fundamentally, the veto maintains that incorporation itself makes the Bank unconstitutional, beginning with the fact that the Constitution did not grant the federal government the power to incorporate. As it is, the argument continues, the Bank's charter violates the sovereignty of the states and, to add insult to injury, "strengthens the General Government" (Remini, *Age* 74). While the veto portrays the corporation as an illegitimate (because unconstitutional) tool of the federal government, it also portrays it as a rival sovereign,[12] an *imperium in imperio*: "But if we yield to the Federal Government this power, it is one which ought not to be exercised—Because if it puts the community, at large and their property at the mercy of a corporation which will in the end pursue its own interest" (Remini, *Age* 76). In the final paragraphs of the veto, the usurpation of power becomes concrete in the image of a shadow government: "When such Bank shall have been a short time in operation and its Branches planted in the respective States, it can and probably will control the election, and through them the politics of the country" (Remini, *Age* 77).

During the election campaign of 1832, the Democratic Party focused on the veto and saw its worst fears confirmed when Biddle began to pour money into an anti-Jackson campaign (Remini, *Bank War* 98–101). But Biddle's strategy backfired. He had the veto message reprinted and distributed because he assumed that it would mobilize the people against Jackson, but the veto and its rich-against-poor message proved popular. While this suggests that the Bank War was a class conflict, Stephen Mihm highlights its paradoxical outcome: "If the Bank War was a class conflict, then, it was most unusual: the working people won in the short run, yet they unwittingly ushered in a system that primarily benefits elite bankers, entrepreneurs, and speculators" ("Fog" 369). In this context, the emergence of a third party, the first of its kind in

---

[12] Remini also makes this observation: "this extragovernmental 'power in the State'" (*Bank War* 81).

the US, the Anti-Masons, is also sometimes cited as a sign of the democratizing forces at work during this period, though historians like Remini point out that anti-masonry was local as it originated in New York and in a special constellation of bank and government (the Albany Regency) under which farmers and laborers suffered (see Remini, *Bank War* 89, 150–2.).

In the fall of 1833, Jackson proceeded to prematurely close the Second Bank by removing all government deposits and having them distributed into state banks. To do so, Jackson first had to fire and replace Treasury secretary William J. Duane with Taney because of the former's resistance against the measure. By distributing public funds across the nation, Jackson was hoping to disperse the concentration of power he so feared.[13] In March 1834, the Senate (where the Whig Party had a majority) issued a censure, to which Jackson promptly responded with a "Protest," written mostly by members of his Cabinet such as Taney. The "Protest" responds to the critique of his dismissal of Duane by formulating Jackson's idea of the presidential office (as well as conspiratorial fears over corporations):

> The President is the direct representative of the American people, but the secretaries are not. If the Secretary of the Treasury be independent of the President in the execution of the laws, then is there no direct responsibility to the people in that important branch of this Government to which is committed the care of the national finances. And it is in the power of the Bank of the United States, or any other corporation, body of men, or individuals, if a Secretary shall be found to accord with them in opinion or can be induced in practice to promote their views, to control through him the whole action of the Government (so far it is exercised by his Department) in defiance of the Chief Magistrate elected by the people and responsible to them . . . (Remini, *Age* 115–16, ellipsis in the original)

Jackson's understanding of his office, the idea that he was the direct representative of the people, was not only new, but it was also not covered by the Constitution. Yet it stuck. As Robert Remini explains, "No longer was the chief executive the head of a coordinate branch of the government, responsible to Congress; henceforth he was the spokesman and leader of the American people, the formulator of national policy" (*Age* 111). Stephen Mihm concurs that "Jackson used the Bank War to turn his office into a bully pulpit.

---

[13] This effective increase of the power of banking corporations is the great irony of Jackson's policies. "Claiming sole statutory authority for deciding, [Duane] bombarded the President with warnings that banking's 'loose corporations' were 'so partial in their operations, and so liable to be perverted, as to affect seriously the morals, impair the earnings, and endanger the liberties of the people'" (Sellers 335).

The presidency has never been the same" ("Fog" 364). It is important to emphasize the somewhat paradoxical dynamic that developed during Jackson's active opposition to the Bank. As he proceeded to break up and disperse what he considered a monopoly of power and a centralized body that rivalled the influence of the government, he fashioned his office in decidedly undemocratic ways that would reverberate far beyond his personal lifespan.

III. James Fenimore Cooper's *The Bravo*

An early scene in James Fenimore Cooper's *The Bravo* (1831) illustrates the way in which the romance tells the story of Venice as that of a "soulless corporation" (Cooper, *The Bravo* 138). In the palace-like home of one of the republic's senators, Gradenigo, the narrative presents a series of nighttime audiences. Taking place without any witnesses, in a room with hidden doors opening to secret passageways, the scene emphasizes one of the most important qualities of the Venetian government as depicted in the novel: its conspiratorial secrecy. In the course of the interviews, Gradenigo rejects an old fisherman's request that his juvenile grandson may be spared life on the galleys and thereby reveals another crucial characteristic of the government: its imperative of expediency. At the end of the scene in which Gradenigo has displayed all the facets of a Venetian politician, the narrator observes, "A senator, [Gradenigo] stood in relation to the state as a director of a moneyed institution is proverbially placed in respect to his corporation; an agent of its collective measures, removed from the responsibilities of the man" (Cooper, *The Bravo* 91). In *The Bravo*, a republic has gone bad, and Cooper's metaphor for the body politic that it has become is the "soulless corporation."

Looking at the context in which James Fenimore Cooper conceived of and wrote *The Bravo*, critics often suggest that the novel seeks to draw attention to the dangers that the English and French republics faced in the 1820s and 1830s.[14] Cooper and his family had arrived in Paris in 1826 and stayed

[14] Looking for Cooper's inspiration for *The Bravo*, Robert S. Levine argues that, while living in Europe, Cooper could have learned about the US-American Antimasonic discourse. This was about the struggle of farmers and laborers against the Albany Regency in New York that was portrayed as a feudalistic conspiracy of bankers and politicians against the common man. The death of William Morgan, a New York stonemason who had prepared the publication of a book containing all the secrets of the lodge in 1826, had fueled this fear. Levine argues, "The similarities suggest that Antimasonic discourse, which Cooper knew of primarily through newspaper reports, may have influenced his thinking on the European revolutions and guided him toward simple explanations for rather more complex phenomena" (73). For Levine, this connection would also contribute to our understanding of the novel's gothic elements: the masonic power of the corporation is literalized in the Venetian palazzos. Yet, as this chapter will show, the association of moneyed corporations

in Europe until 1833, thus witnessing the early years of the July monarchy. During this period, Cooper also traveled through Europe, including a visit to Venice, and he developed a friendship with General Lafayette, whom he had met during the latter's visit to the US in 1824. Cooper also intervened in the European debate over republican forms of government and specifically in the so-called Finance Controversy (stoked by reactionary claims that the republican form of government was particularly expensive) by penning an open letter to General Lafayette in 1831 and by publishing "Notions of the Americans" (1828), in which he portrayed "America as model republic" (Levine 69). Moreover, Cooper published a European trilogy during this period, beginning with *The Bravo* (1831), followed by *The Heidenmauer* (1832) and *The Headsman* (1833). The European settings allowed Cooper to write extensively about the dangers facing republics, the American included.[15]

The Bravo follows several characters as they attempt and for the most part fail to protect themselves and their loved ones from Venice's corporate government, the "soulless corporation": the nobleman Don Camillo wants to marry the heiress Violetta, a ward of the state, while the old fisherman Antonio attempts to rescue his juvenile grandson from military duty by appealing first to Senator Gradenigo (his foster brother) and then directly to the doge (Cooper, *The Bravo* 138). Their stories are connected through Jacopo, a mysterious and brooding young man who has a reputation for being the state's assassin (a bravo), but who turns out to be another victim of the state: Jacopo's father was innocently incarcerated, and Jacopo has agreed to serve as the state's titular assassin and thereby as its scapegoat, should the state reconsider the prison sentence. After his friend Antonio has been secretly executed, Jacopo realizes that his father will never become free, and he agrees to assist Don Camillo in getting Violetta out of Venice. While he succeeds in this endeavor, it is too late to save himself, and the novel ends with Jacopo's beheading in front of an approving crowd of commoners and fishermen who have been led to believe that it was Jacopo, rather than the state, who killed Antonio.

---

with conspiracy not only had a much longer and rhetorically richer history. It was also going through its latest iteration at the time that Cooper was writing and publishing *The Bravo*: in the conflict between President Andrew Jackson and the Second Bank of the United States, the most powerful American corporation of its day.

[15] "Good republican that he was, he believed the fate of all republics to be intertwined and precarious" (Levine 71). See Loveland for Cooper's rejection of the Monroe Doctrine. Politically, Cooper was a Democrat, though as Marvin Meyers has put it, "[r]eading Cooper as a straight Jacksonian author would require a rude forcing of the texts" (59).

Yet while Jacopo's story is full of secrets and surprising twists, and even though he is the titular hero of the tale, the novel is not really about him. Rather, as Cooper explained a few years after the publication of *The Bravo*, the novel's protagonist is the Venice corporation. With the events in Europe and with what he perceived as his countrymen's misguided sense of security in mind, Cooper had determined to write a series of novels set in Europe that would illustrate the corrupting influences that he thought threatened republics everywhere. Writing *The Bravo*, the first of the trilogy, he realized that "[i]n effecting such an object, [. . .] the government of Venice, strictly speaking, became the hero of the tale. Still it was necessary to have human agents" (*American Democrat* 277). In other words, Cooper set out to narrativize the corporation and to show his readers how a collective entity acts in the world: to make corporate agency visible and readable.

The most obvious strategy by which he achieves this goal, and one that is familiar to us from Irving's *Astoria*, is to show the reader corporate agents in action. Hence the narrative introduces the reader to senators, such as Gradenigo and Soranzo, who are part of the mysterious Council of Three; and to the doge, who is the nominal head of the Venetian republic. Yet, throughout, the narrator also insists that these are merely agents and therefore only tools through which the corporation acts as their principal. They have interiorized the corporation's central guiding principle, "expediency," and subordinate all acts and decisions to it (Cooper, *The Bravo* 138). When, for instance, Senator Gradenigo is approached by his elderly foster brother, the humble fisherman Antonio, with the request to help Antonio save his juvenile and innocent grandson from military service until he is of a proper age, Gradenigo quickly stifles a brief feeling of compassion and refuses to help. "The soulless, practised, and specious reasoning of the state," the narrator subsequently observes, "had long since deadened every feeling in the senator [. . .]" (Cooper, *The Bravo* 62). The doge, too, cannot but feel a modicum of sympathy for Jacopo's cause, when the latter's fiancée applies to the prince for a pardon on his behalf. However, despite being the head of government, the doge is powerless to stop the execution. In fact, Cooper goes to some length to show that corporate agents are tools that are dispensable, as when, out of the blue, Gradenigo is replaced by a young, new senator, Paolo Soranzo. Soranzo, in turn, rapidly transforms from a man of sympathy to another man of expediency, which culminates in a scene where he returns home to his wife and children only to realize that "[f]or the first time, in his life, he entered [his home] with a distrust of himself" (Cooper, *The Bravo* 329). While these agents have been corrupted by the "system" into which they have let themselves become incorporated, the novel suggests that we should look beyond individual agents (Cooper, *The Bravo* 231).

One of the strategies in which the novel conveys the corporation's power beyond embodiment in individual agents is the architectural and topographical structure of Venice, the corporation's urban manifestation. Observed carefully, the gothic cityscape itself alerts us to the presence of corporate power, such as when the narrator describes Gradenigo's home: "It was a residence of more than common gloom, possessing all the solemn but stately magnificence which then characterized the private dwellings of the patricians in that city of riches and pride" (Cooper, *The Bravo* 66). Venice emerges as a city that, while it may appear gay and stately, singularly lends itself to the business of secrecy and conspiracy. "It is a fault in most descriptions [. . .] that while the stranger hears so much of the canals of Venice, but little is said of her streets: [. . .] narrow, paved, commodious, but noiseless passages" (Cooper, *The Bravo* 25). Forever celebrating carnival, the theme of obscurity also includes the citizens who don masks after nightfall. While the government presents this custom as a boon ("A mask is sacred in Venice. [. . .] Such are the high privileges of liberty"), the novel insists that a society of masked individuals is a society that fosters irresponsible and selfish behaviors (Cooper, *The Bravo* 99). With their identities concealed by masks, citizens simply vanish among the crowds and cannot be held accountable for their deeds.

While this is the setting in which corporate agency is made visible, to narrate how the corporation acts in the world, Cooper employs the metaphor of the *machine*, when he refers to "the peculiar machinery of the state" (Cooper, *The Bravo* 127). Strikingly, the operation of this machine is repeatedly characterized as noiseless. Its silent influence reaches everywhere:

> Though Venice at that hour was so gay in her squares, the rest of the town was silent as the grave. A city, in which the hoof of horse or the rolling of wheels is never heard, necessarily possesses a gloomy character; but the peculiar form of the government, and the long training of the people in habits of caution, weighed on the spirits of the gay. (Cooper, *The Bravo* 43)

This noiselessness strongly suggests that "the peculiar machinery of the state" is an engine without an operator. No mastermind operates its levers; no human principal is ultimately revealed as its source of agency, as is the case in Irving's *Astoria*. It is in this noiseless operation that Cooper comes closest to presenting his tale's real protagonist in direct action, without the intermediary use of agents. To some extent, this is even the case in the tribunal scenes. Even though the scenes present senators deciding on the fate of Antonio and Jacopo, most of the agents are mute. Hidden behind masks and robes, they communicate with their secretary through hand signals, while their presence and power are conveyed mostly by "a deep and impressive silence" (Cooper, *The Bravo* 132).

That this silent operation in the world is also brutally efficient is nowhere more apparent than in the scenes depicting Jacopo's and Antonio's executions. Antonio, the fisherman who is Senator Gradenigo's foster brother and who had begged for his grandson's life, is killed by drowning in the Canale Orfano. Even though there is no question that he was executed, the actual event appears devoid of any human agency. After the gondola of the state has retrieved the monk who took Antonio's confession, the latter appears to have simply fallen off his boat:

> The officer released the person of the monk, who passed quickly beneath the canopy, and he turned to cast a hasty glance at the features of the fisherman. The rubbing of a rope was audible, and the anchor of Antonio was lifted by a sudden jerk. A heavy plashing of the water followed, and the two boats shot away together, obedient to a violent effort of the crew. The gondola of the state exhibited its usual number of gondoliers bending to their toil, with its dark and hearse-like canopy, but that of the fisherman was empty! (Cooper, *The Bravo* 179)

Antonio's execution occurs between the sounds of the rope and the water, couched in gerund and passive constructions that convey agency without identifying its source.[16] This is not, however, a failure of the narrator's ability to identify the principal and source of the action. Instead, this is precisely the nature of the power of the corporation, which ultimately transcends the individual.

Mechanical metaphors play an increasingly important role in the development of the corporate form in the course of the nineteenth century. In fact, mechanical rather than bodily analogies in discussions of political communities had not been available for long. From the late seventeenth century to the early eighteenth century, a view of the political system as the machine of state or as a political machine developed, which was influenced by the work of René Descartes, Isaac Newton, and Montesquieu. "[F]or the mechanisation of political thought, Montesquieu's *The Spirit of Laws* (1748) was particularly influential, arguing that political systems—not unlike human beings—should be understood as machines set in motion by 'springs' such as virtue" (Ihalainen 8). Mechanical analogies received special pertinence, moreover, during the War of Independence, when the British parliament, in discussion of the kingdom's relationship to the colonies, recognized the limits of body metaphors in its implications of disease and decay. Mechanical analogies such

---

[16] "The emphasis on the mechanics of the capsizing, coupled with our remote perspective on Antonio's 'heavy plashing,' convey the impersonal efficiency of the Venetian 'soulless corporation'" (Levine 88).

as those used by Montesquieu offered a way to conceptualize the political system as a balance between different forces, driven by internal rather than external impulses (see Ihalainen 34–6.). The clockwork as a quintessential example of this type of metaphor also implied regularity and transparency to contemporaries (see Böckenförde 558). Yet in *The Bravo*, the "machinery of the state" is not transparent per se but requires the mediation of the narrator.

In the extensive commentary passages that characterize the narration in *The Bravo*, Cooper chooses a narrative mode that tries to establish distance from the immediate action and to render it more abstract. Cooper himself defines this mode of narration as "scale," and it is a mode that tries to connect macro- with micro-level occurrences, to connect the system with its agents. After one such commentary, for example, the narrator explains that he must return from the government-protagonist to the "human agents": "Treating, as we are, of the vices of the Venetian system, our pen, however, has run truant with its subject, since the application of the moral must be made on the familiar scale suited to the incidents of our story" (Cooper, *The Bravo* 275). The presumably grander scale of "the peculiar machinery of the state" (Cooper, *The Bravo* 127) thus gives way to a smaller-scale exploration of the system's impact on its agents.

When the narrator returns to the actions of individuals, they are import-ant as a representative of the agent-position available in a corporate system. The threat of corruption looms obviously large, as it would in any tale in the republican tradition. However, what makes this threat specific to the novel's corporate setting is its impact on subjectivity. In *The Bravo*, corruption becomes manifest in the gap between person and position, as is illustrated by the stories of Gradenigo and Soranzo. Cooper suggests that the corporation accelerates the kind of interiorization of virtue that Pocock ascribes to American society, as it replaces equality of opportunity with equality of condition:

> When men had been differentiated and had expressed their virtue in the act of deferring to one another's virtue, the individual had known himself through the respect shown by his fellows for the qualities publicly recog-nized in him; but once men were, or it was held that they ought to be, all alike, his only means of self-discovery lay in conforming to everybody else's notion of what he ought to be and was. (537–8)

From a classical republican perspective, therefore, the soulless corpora-tion may not deprive its agents of their souls; instead, it encourages them to compartmentalize, by fostering in them a high regard for their own interest and a disregard for the common good. Indeed, assuming an almost sociolog-ical perspective, Cooper suggests that a republican system produces virtuous citizens, so, if corruption abounds, it must be read as a symptom of a system that has already declined. Moreover, even though the narrator praises public opinion throughout as a tool of accountability that is central to the health of a republic, he is highly critical of what is called "the masses" and "the mob." Like the corporation, the mob is part of Venice's "factitious system" and a symptom of its "natural tendency to dissolution" (Cooper, *The Bravo* 250). It is also anther group entity, and the representation of its agency (or rather lack thereof) further illuminates Cooper's portrait of corporate agency and power.

The Soulless Public

As cities such as New York began to grow rapidly in the 1820s and 1830s, contemporary Americans became fascinated with urban crowds. To some extent, *The Bravo*'s urban setting and the narrator's panoramic perspectives can be said to cater to this fascination. Yet ultimately the novel is more interested in presenting the violence and terror of which crowds, or rather mobs, are capable. Following eighteenth-century conventions of describing crowds of commoners as fickle, irrational masses that can easily be manipulated, the novel thereby balances its portrait of the corporation as a collective that is guided only by expedience with a portrait of the plebeian multitude as guided by passion. While critical of both, Cooper ultimately judges their power and agency differently.

Two scenes are central to this comparison. In the first scene, Antonio has unexpectedly won the regatta on the day of the *Festa della Sensa*. The old fisherman had joined the race against young and popular gondoliers, not for private gain but because he had hoped that a victory in the race would sway the doge in favor of liberating his grandson. He is not a professional gondolier but an old man whose body is scarred from fighting in the Venetian army. Thus, Antonio is representative of the poorest and commonest members of the state, although they do not identify themselves with him. Instead, he is an object of derision at the start of the regatta: "[T]hough of all the competitors perhaps the one whose motive most hallowed his ambition, he was held to be the only proper subject of mirth" (Cooper, *The Bravo* 103). Yet, once Antonio has won the race, popular feeling turns in his favor:

> Then there arose a general shout among the living mass, which bore on high the name of Antonio, as if they celebrated the success of some conqueror. All feeling of contempt was lost in the influence of his triumph. The fishermen of the Lagunes, who so lately had loaded their aged companion with contumely, shouted for his glory, with a zeal that manifested the violence of the transition from mortification to pride [. . .]. (Cooper, *The Bravo* 112–13)

Just as their derision and contempt had been disproportionate to Antonio's perceived social transgression, so the crowd's transition to pride is marked by hyperbole, by "violence." In the course of the novel, the civic crowd, or "multitude" as it is often called, is repeatedly characterized by its tendency to yield to impulses and the concomitant susceptibility to manipulation.

The second scene ensues after the fishermen have discovered Antonio's corpse and they carry him to the palace of the doge to ask for justice. The narrator's description of the fishermen not only continues in the condescending vein, as evidenced by the quotations above, but also impresses upon the reader the very real risk of a riot, which prompts government (unbeknownst to the crowd) to have the military on alert.

> But the rioters were unequal to any estimate of their own force, and had little aptitude in measuring their accidental advantages. They acted solely on impulse. [. . .] When the body [of Antonio] was found [. . .], they yielded to passion, [. . .] without any other definite object than a simple indulgence of feeling. (Cooper, *The Bravo* 251)

In this passage, as in others, the multitude is all passion, all impulse, but no purpose. Though a many-headed multitude, the crowd is practically headless, and when one of the senators suggests that Antonio could have been killed by the bravo Jacopo, the crowd eagerly seizes on this simple but evidently satisfying explanation. This pretense will then serve as the official reason for Jacopo's execution.

With its emphasis on its potential for violence and its general irrationality, the depiction of the crowd belongs to the pre-revolutionary imaginary. In her reading of such depictions in early modern texts, Monika Fludernik characterizes such accusations as two-pronged: "confusion (lack of a single aim) and dishonorable motives (lack of disinterested virtuous intentions)" (702). While a supporter of Jackson, Ross J. Pudaloff argues that "the valorization of a culture politically democratic and socially aristocratic" was for Cooper "the proper business of an American literature" (712). Even Levine, who is generally unwilling to accept the idea that Cooper was a "lifelong conservative," admits that by the late 1830s the latter may still have displayed a habitual suspicion of corporations, but his true fear lay elsewhere (96). Quoting from *The American Democrat*, Levine reports: "[B]y the end of the text he declares that, though aristocrats may pose a threat to the republic, equally dangerous, and just as iniquitous, are the democratic masses: 'The publick, every where, is proverbially soulless'" (100).

Nonetheless, Cooper's extended and quite detailed crowd scenes also serve a more specific purpose than simple crowd-bashing (though it clearly serves that purpose as well). The crowd scenes present yet another way for Cooper to narrate corporate influence and power. On one level, this is shown to be a systemic influence, encoded in the social order—the "artificial condition"—produced by the corporate regime: the commoners of Venice, in particular the fishermen, are dependent on the more powerful classes of Venice, "constantly subject [. . .] to the degrading influence of a superior presence" (Cooper, *The Bravo* 251, 109). On another level, it is the result of the corporation's direct operation on the citizenry, as when "[a]gents of the police [have] been active in preparing the public mind" for Jacopo's execution (Cooper, *The Bravo* 353). As with law, literature can also be put to corrupt uses. In *The Bravo*, storytellers are employed by the state to spread what we would call propaganda today:

> Here the improvisatore, secretly employed by a politic and mysterious government, recounted, with a rapid utterance, and in language suited to the popular ear, [. . .] the ancient triumphs of the republic; while, there, a ballad-singer chaunted to the greedy crowd, the glory and justice of San Marco. Shouts of approbation succeeded each happy allusion to national renown, and bravos, loud and oft-repeated, were the reward of the agents of the police, whenever they most administered to the self-delusion and vanity of their audience. (Cooper, *The Bravo* 90)

Throughout the novel, the narrator's description of the common men and women of Venice is quite as scathing as his description of the "soulless corporation": ruled by their passions and selfishness, the crowds are easily manipulated by the corporate government.

However, Cooper also makes clear that there is a difference between the agency of the corporation and that of the plebeian multitude. While the threat of their violence looms large, the multitude lacks unity and therefore, ultimately, also agency. Unlike the corporation, it is precisely not ruled by expedience. This difference also translates into the aestheticization of their respective power: whereas corporate agency and influence are marked by silence, the multitude's irrational disorder is marked by noise. Antonio, for example, at first feels "the stings of so many unlicensed tongues" as the crowd hurls insults at him, yet he later becomes the object of their pride as they "shouted for his glory" and "[t]en thousand voices were lifted, in proclaiming his skill" (Cooper, *The Bravo* 108, 113). Only occasionally does the crowd fall silent, as when the influence of the Church achieves order and the fishermen form a funeral procession for Antonio:

> The swarthy, expressive faces of the fishermen gleamed with satisfaction, for in the midst of the rude turmoil, they all retained a deep and rooted respect

for the offices of the church in which they had been educated. Silence was quickly obtained, and the boats moved on with greater order than before. (Cooper, *The Bravo* 253)

While the noise often consists of cries and shouts, with occasional though anonymous questions and expressions, it can lose even this modicum of articulateness and descend into an oceanic "murmur" (Cooper, *The Bravo* 353).

In Jacopo's execution scene, both agencies are displayed: a mechanical and active one and an organic and passive one. As Jacopo's fiancée, Gelsomina, tries to convince the crowd of his innocence, "[a] common murmur drowned her voice" (Cooper, *The Bravo* 357). With Jacopo's head already on the block, his friends momentarily believe the corporation has changed its mind:

> "Ha! There is a sign from the palace!" shouted the Carmelite, stretching his arms, as if to grasp a boon. The clarions sounded, and another wave stirred the multitude. Gelsomina uttered a cry of delight, and turned to throw herself upon the bosom of the reprieved. The ax glittered before her eyes, and the head of Jacopo rolled upon the stones, to meet her. A general movement in the living mass denoted the end. (Cooper, *The Bravo* 357)

The preverbal murmur drowns Gelsomina's individual voice, just as the "living mass," stirring like a "wave," makes it impossible to identify individuals in the crowd. Both the corporate and the plebeian multitude ultimately contribute to Jacopo's destruction, though the latter's contribution weighs more heavily because Jacopo—the central node in a network of characters, and a selfless, noble individual throughout the story—may have been their only hope for leadership. As they watch and condone his beheading, they remain without a head themselves: "Each lived for himself, while the state of Venice held its vicious sway" (Cooper, *The Bravo* 358).

IV. King Andrew and the Many-Headed Beast: Picturing Jackson's Bank War

The connection that *The Bravo* establishes between corporations and crowds is not unique to Cooper's novel. In caricatures from the period we frequently find monarchical figures as emblems of feudal and tyrannical power, as well as monstrous figurations of corporate power that highlight collectivity and superhuman properties such as longevity. In particular with regard to the latter, such images draw on an eighteenth-century tradition of picturing the masses that suggests that corporate power was seen as a serious threat precisely because it did not rest and was not embodied in a single individual.

The caricatures that depict the Bank War in the 1830s highlight the different kinds of power, and hence the different types of danger, that the War's protagonists present. For example, in a caricature published in the fall of 1833,[17] when Jackson was preparing to have the federal deposits removed, he is "King Andrew the First" (Fig. 2.1). Clad in regal attire, he stands alone in front of a throne, the veto message in one hand, a scepter in the other. In tatters under his feet we see the Constitution and the coat of arms of Pennsylvania, the Second Bank's home state. In front of him lies a book titled *Judiciary of the U States*. At the top of the print are the words, "Born to Command." What had raised particular concerns among Jackson's opponents was his rejection of the Supreme Court's ruling in *McCulloch*.[18] In his response to the veto message, Daniel Webster denounced Jackson as making "a claim to despotic power," and this motif would eventually carry over into depictions of Jackson as a monarch (Remini, *Age* 93). While the caricature is somewhat generic in its identification of any kind of illegitimate power with royalty, the irony of Jackson—the self-styled common man's representative—as king is, of course, strong. (The choice of "Whigs" for the name of the new opposition party a year later followed the same strategy.) Moreover, it is the solitude of the figure, the fact that the throne room is empty except for him, that is remarkable. Nobody has handed him the crown or aides him in his endeavors; the image implies that Jackson does it all by himself.

While Jackson's assumption of power was portrayed as despotic by his opponents, corporate power (and by extension the corporation itself) was pictured as non-human and specifically *animalistic*. Opposition newspapers, for example, called the state banks that received the deposits Jackson's "'pet' banks" (Remini, *Bank War* 125). The most prevalent visual metaphor of corporate power was the many-headed beast or hydra. In a print titled "Political Quixotism: The Diplomatic Hercules attacking the Political Hydra,"[19] for example, Jackson is in what appears to be his bedroom and fighting a monster

[17] The Library of Congress provides the following information: "The print is dated a year earlier by Weitenkampf and related to Jackson's controversial veto of Congress's bill to recharter the Bank in July 1832. However, the charge, implicit in the print, of Jackson's exceeding the President's constitutional power, was most widely advanced in connection not with the veto but with the 1833 removal order, on which the President was strongly criticized for acting without congressional approval."

[18] In *Aggressive Nationalism*, Richard E. Ellis maintains that "Jackson's famous veto of the bill rechartering the 2BUS in 1832 was, on its most basic level, a response to John Marshall's decision in *McCulloch* v. *Maryland*" (11).

[19] Above and below the capital letters further titles are added, so that the full title would read: "Political Quixotism[,] Shewing the consequences of sleeping in patent magic spectacles. The diplomatic Hercules[,] attacking the political hydra[.] From a very big picter in the Jinerals Bed-Room, draw'd off from Nater by Zek Downing, Historical Painter to Uncle Jack & Jineral Jackson."

BORN TO COMMAND.

OF VETO MEMORY.

HAD I BEEN CONSULTED.

KING ANDREW THE FIRST.

Figure 2.1 "King Andrew the First," New York, 1833. Library of Congress, Prints and Photographs Division, Washington, DC.

with nine heads, several tails, fierce claws and teeth (Fig. 2.2). This nightmarish scene is probably from 1833, the year in which Jackson proceeded to make an end of the Second Bank for good. By battling the mythical hydra, Jackson is placed in the role of Hercules. In the classical tradition, one of the twelve labors of Hercules is to fight the Hydra of Lerna. The hydra is one of several monsters born from the same parents; others include the Sphinx and Cerberus (Linebaugh 2). The hydra's most significant power is its ability to regenerate: whenever Hercules lops off one of its heads, it is replaced by

Figure 2.2 Ezra Bisbee, "Political Quixotism," New York, 1833. Library of Congress, Prints and Photographs Division, Washington, DC.

twice the number. By adding the qualifier "quixotic," the caricatures thus emphasize the impression that the hydra represents a near impossible task, but also that Jackson's struggle is less heroic than foolish. It also suggests that this enemy, like Don Quixote's windmills, is imaginary; just like Major Jack Downing, a popular fictional character invented by journalist Seba Smith,[20] who observes that Jackson is merely having a nightmare.

This delusional quality is also present in other works by Ezra Bisbee that satirize Jacksonian politics, though sometimes as visionary or prophetic element. In his in-depth analysis of the representation of mobs in nineteenth-century art, Ross Barrett has read the work not only of Bisbee but also of

[20] A fictional character that Smith invented for his newspaper, the *Portland Courier* (Maine), the Major allowed Smith to satirize the conduct of the Maine legislature without seeming partisan. The character was so popular that Smith soon had him report from Washington, where the Major became a friend and assistant to the President. The Major's popularity also meant that the character was often plagiarized. His letters were published as *Letters of Major Jack Downing of the Downingville Militia*. For a study of the function of fictional characters in American newspapers see Welford D. Taylor's *The Newsprint Mask*.

Hudson River School painters such as Thomas Cole against the backdrop of classical republican fears of crowds and the tradition of the jeremiad in America. This "prophetic framework," Barrett argues, "reshapes the meanings of the depicted turmoil," in that it serves "to affirm the orderly precepts of hierarchical republicanism" (31). Bisbee's "Political Hydra" presents a more complex affirmation of classical republicanism, in that it mocks a Jacksonian (and in fact revolutionary) reinterpretation of the Hercules myth in which the hydra has come to represent aristocratic and monopolistic conspiracy, whereas it was formerly a symbol of plebeian crowds.

The story of Hercules fighting the hydra has a long history as a political trope that scholars have traced back to the sixteenth century. In this political mythology, Hercules is the symbol of power, order, and development, as Peter Linebaugh and Marcus Rediker explain. "The classically educated architects of the Atlantic economy found in Hercules [. . .] a symbol of power and order. For inspiration they looked to the Greeks, for whom Hercules was a unifier of the centralized territorial state, and to the Romans, for whom he signified vast imperial ambition. The labors of Hercules symbolized economic development" (Linebaugh 2). The trope was also familiar to the founding fathers, who used Hercules as a symbol of progress. John Adams, for example, "proposed in 1776 that 'The Judgment of Hercules' be the seal for the new United States of America" (Linebaugh 2). The allusion to the Herculean effort to establish order and promote development throws into higher relief the designations of the heads of the Jacksonian hydra: the heads are labeled "U.S. Bank," "Deposits," "Bribery," "Pensions," "[. . .] of the People," and "Corruption of the [. . .]." In this way, the hydra appears to represent an overwhelming disorder and an obstacle to progress.

But the hydra also carried other connotations that are more manifest in a second caricature, published three years later. "General Jackson Slaying the Many-Headed Monster" depicts Jackson (on the left) raising a stick labeled "VETO"; Major Jack Downing on the right; the head of Nicholas Biddle at the center;[21] and a much smaller vice president, Martin Van Buren, in the background (Fig. 2.3). The "many-headed monster" is somewhat more snake-like, and in contrast to the previous image its heads are human, complete with top hats. Each head, including the largest in the center, carries the name of a state, which suggests that they are meant to represent the Bank's branch offices. In his speech bubble, Jackson accordingly refers to them as Biddle's "four and twenty satellites." Significantly, Biddle's top hat carries the

---

[21] Helen P. Trimpi briefly notes that "in several pro-Jackson prints, the Devil is used to caricature 'Nick' Biddle in Jackson's battles with the United States Bank" (37). See Chapter 3 of this study.

GENERAL JACKSON SLAYING THE MANY HEADED MONSTER.

Figure 2.3 Henry R. Robinson, "General Jackson Slaying the Many-Headed Monster," 1836. Library of Congress Prints and Photographs Division, Washington, DC.

inscription "Penn.," suggesting that the occasion for the caricature may have been Biddle's successful bid for a state charter in Pennsylvania that allowed the Bank to survive in a new format beyond 1836. Like the mythical hydra, the corporation had thus displayed exceptional powers of regeneration. At the same time, the hydra's human heads also suggest two very different embodiments of power: the General, like the monarch, is an individual, though he personifies the sovereign state, whereas the hydra represents a reproducing and therefore possibly immortal multitude.

This multitudinousness is further qualified by the animal chosen to represent it. Though recognizably the hydra of Jackson's rhetoric, it is also referred to as a snake. In Plato's parable of the human soul, for example, the many-headed beast is also depicted as "snake-like" and "licentious" (590a, b). While Biddle (on account of his first name) was sometimes depicted as the devil, in the 1836 caricature, explicit reference is made to a viper. The caricature itself, through Jackson and the Major, refers to it as a snake. Jackson speaks of it as "venomous" and the Major speaks of a viper: "How now you nasty varmint, be you imperishable? I swan Gineral that are beats all I reckon, that's the horrible wiper wot wommits wenemous heads I guess . . ." The Major is referring to the mythical belief that the female viper bites off her mate's head during copulation. In the Middle Ages the viper was known as "the most villainous kind of beast, and particularly because it is the cunningest of all species when it feels the lust for coition" (T. H. White 170). Its violent habits of procreation—the male's head is bitten off, and the female dies when giving birth—made it a symbol for lust and passion that did not stop short of unions outside its own species. As a twelfth-century bestiary puts it, "[The viper] decides to have a bastard union with the sea eel (Murena) and makes ready for this unnatural copulation. Having gone down to the seashore and made its presence known with a wolf-whistle, it calls the Murena out of the waters for a conjugal embrace" (T. H. White 170). Through its use of the viper, the caricature therefore suggests that the Bank's rechartering as a Pennsylvania state bank is a "cunning" move of procreation outside its species, and it suggests a lustful, passionate quality.

Yet there is at least one more symbolic dimension to the many-headed monster that is relevant here: its representation of a multitude or group. Renaissance representations of the crowd as many-headed monster can be found, for example, in Shakespeare's *Coriolanus*, whose protagonists express "contempt for the 'giddy,' 'rude' and 'ragged' multitude" (Kokkinakis 83).[22] Scholars of the representation of English crowds in the seventeenth and eighteenth centuries generally agree that such depictions drew on a classical tradition that portrayed plebeian crowds as inevitably irrational and potentially dangerous.[23] Yiannis Kokkinakis points out that references to the monstrous multitude increased in the decades leading up to the English Civil War. As the crowds' demands for political participation became more insistent, their perceived headless irrationality became more threatening to what was still considered a natural social order. In their study of the history of labor in the Atlantic world, Linebaugh and Rediker explain, for example, that the same rulers that identified with Hercules "found in the many-headed hydra an

[22] See C. A. Patrides, "'The Beast with Many Heads': Renaissance Views on the Multitude."

[23] In *Crowds and Popular Politics in Early Modern England*, for example, John Walter writes, "Tutored by the politics of the state and the preachings of the Church, many gentlemen regarded the people as fickle and irrational: the many-headed monster. This view of the people mingled fear as well as contempt. History, as well as their readings about the plebs in the ancient world prescribed by their classical education, warned them that the people were capable of challenging their rule" (182). Christopher Hill explains that in Stuart and Tudor England, the common opinion among the ruling elite was that "'[the] people' were fickle, unstable, incapable of rational thought: the headless multitude, the many-headed monster" (181).

antithetical symbol of disorder and resistance, a powerful threat to the building of state, empire, and capitalism" (2).

As suggested earlier, the late eighteenth-century revolutions in America and France led to a reinterpretation of the myth. For example, Thomas Paine interpreted Hercules as a symbol of the common man and the hydra as the aristocracy (Kokkinakis 84).[24] Similarly, in a 1793 French allegory of "the defeat of federalism" represented by the Girondins, a giant Hercules triumphs over a slain monster (Hunt 96). Described by historian Lynn Hunt, the image shows the people as Hercules, who "gather[s] the fasces, symbol of unity, in one hand," while towering over a monster that is half-human and half-snake (97). In its revised revolutionary version, the myth thus individualizes the multitude in the single figure of Hercules, while its representation of the aristocracy as hydra multiplies the threat it poses.[25] But, as Hans Blumenberg argues, a culture's work on myth is never finished. Hence, while the caricatures of Jackson and the Second Bank are generally drawn in the revisionary spirit, they also mock it: Jackson is a "quixotic" and delusional Hercules. In a more serious manner, moreover, Cooper's novel suggests that the threat of multitudinousness inhabits both the mob and the corporate body. This kinship between the two complicates a straightforward reading of Cooper's novel in the anti-corporate, anti-monopoly vein of Jacksonian rhetoric.

[24] David McNally shows how Paine was responding to Edmund Burke's condemnation of the French Revolution (77–81).

[25] For Anne Mellor, the myth of Hercules and the hydra also informs the giant and Promethean creation of Dr. Frankenstein, conveying a sense of the multitude as formless agent of protean power as well as a monstrous terror.

3

Satanic Corporate Agents in the Marketplace: Hawthorne, Melville, De Forest, and the Uses of Allegory

By the beginning of the 1840s, the US economy had temporarily recovered from the financial panic that followed the end of the Second Bank and its financial politics, and it offered a new vista for entrepreneurial individuals. New technologies (steam power in particular) and the expansion of the market from regional to national meant new opportunities, and with rising immigration rates, more people than ever sought out these opportunities in America. Against this backdrop, and because of the need for better transportation infrastructures, critics of corporate monopoly finally got their wish: general incorporation statutes became more and more common and helped to turn corporations from a special privilege of the few into a common business tool for the many—or so it seemed. What this trend also meant was that corporate enterprises became part of a new financial landscape that was not always easily understandable or readable for the enterprising common man. In fact, we could say that the democratization of the corporate form (through general incorporation statutes) also meant a privatization and individualization of the risks involved in corporate finance. Accordingly, in a changing economic landscape—in which more business opportunities than ever were becoming available to the common man, but financial panics and depression also meant the very real possibility of a swift downward turn of fortune— corporations and the strangers that represented them also became associated with the hoaxes, frauds, and confidence games that unsettled middle-class America in the antebellum period. Most of the time, this meant that they encountered corporate agents: the representatives of corporations that acted in their names and interests, at least in theory. Rather than an embodiment of the corporation, the corporate agent became an emblem of the anonymity and obscurity of corporate enterprise—essentially, a problem of knowledge in the market.

Covering the period from the 1840s to the 1870s, this chapter provides a brief overview of the epistemic challenge that the corporation presented in a transforming market and a transforming nation. The first section introduces the economic, social, and cultural changes that characterized the antebellum period and provided the setting for the legal case under consideration in this chapter: *Louisville, Cincinnati and Charleston Rail-road Company v. Thomas W. Letson* (1844). It stands for a US Supreme Court decision which held that corporations were citizens under the Judiciary Act of the Constitution. The final section of the chapter discusses three literary fictions that, taken together, cover tumultuous years in US history, both economically and politically: Nathaniel Hawthorne's "The Celestial Railroad" (1844), Herman Melville's *The Confidence-Man; His Masquerade* (1857), and John William De Forest's *Honest John Vane* (1875). Each is allegorical and satirical, though to varying degrees, and each presents a national narrative modeled after John Bunyan's *Pilgrim's Progress* (1678), in which spiritual growth has been replaced by material growth. In all three of these texts, corporations generally figure as confidence games: they are portrayed as empty of substance and feature a satanic corporate agent whose rhetorical skills are centrally characterized by how he succeeds in emptying language of its substance as well. Taken together, they also outline the transformation of the market from a regional and subsistence-oriented affair to a national, commercial, and financial arena, as well as the transformation of the nation. Through a close reading of the legal arguments in *Louisville Rail-road* v. *Letson*, this chapter will bring these transformations into conversation with parallel concerns over the general nature of corporations, and with the notion of legal personhood in particular. Even before the political debates had reached their peak, *Louisville Rail-road* v. *Letson* would ask questions about the relationship between the whole and its parts (that is, between shareholders, officers, and the corporate entity) that Americans would soon discuss with regard to their country. In fact, at the same time that writers like Hawthorne, Melville, and De Forest turned to allegory to represent corporate agency, the Court began to address the question of the essential nature of the corporate person: was it merely an aggregate of individuals, or was it more than the sum of its parts?

I. From Political to Economic Actor: General Incorporation Statutes and the Market Revolution

The years in which Washington Irving and William Austin published their works and in which the US Supreme Court decided the *Charles River* case proved, in hindsight, to be some of the most prosperous years the US economy had seen since the financial panic of 1819. During these years, "the tools of the market revolution—productive machinery, transportation improvements, easy credit, and marketing facilities—delivered fortunes to thousands of entrepreneurs and promised the same to tens of thousands more who lined up to emulate the successful" (Larsen 92). Then, in the spring and early summer of 1837, a financial panic brought the boom to a sudden close. While contemporaries found more immediate actors and events to blame—such as Nicolas Biddle or Andrew Jackson's pet banks—twentieth-century economic historians have concluded that "large imports of capital from England and the sudden Chinese preference for opium over silver in the Far East trade caused a very real increase in bank reserves in the United States" (Larsen 96). On a larger scale, moreover, Americans were only just beginning to recognize the cyclical nature of their economy. The 1840s saw the economy recover and grow again (another boom following the bust), but by the time Herman Melville published *The Confidence-Man; His Masquerade* in 1857, the US was in the grip of yet another financial panic.

When the economy did recover in the 1840s, corporations, in particular railroad corporations, stood out as important players in the marketplace. "Internal trade, multiplying thirteenfold over the Erie Canal between the 1820s and 1850s and twelvefold down the Mississippi to New Orleans, registered a spectacular advance of territorial specialization in production for market," writes historian Charles Sellers (391). In tandem with more specialized production, however, it was improved transportation that allowed the marketplace to expand so significantly during this period. "Completing a process begun by canals and steamboats, railroads extended market production where water transport could not reach" (Sellers 392). By 1840, Sellers writes, "Americans built nearly twice the trackage of all Europe" (391). Soon, moreover, these enterprises would assume national significance: initial proposals for a transcontinental railroad were debated in Congress in the 1850s, and in 1861, after the outbreak of the Civil War, Congress chartered the first transcontinental railroad, which was also the first federally chartered corporation since the Second Bank of the United States. The Union initially considered the value of such a railroad from a primarily military perspective, but after the Civil War the railroad came to represent what one of John William De Forest's characters (albeit mockingly) calls the closing of "the bloody chasm" (*Honest* 127): a symbol of the nation overcoming distances both physically and symbolically.

In the popular imaginary, the incorporation of canals, railroads, and steamship lines came to signify both individual enterprise and national progress. In the process, corporations' association with monopoly was often outshone by their increasing association with internal improvements and thereby with technological progress and efficiency. In 1830, for example, the Baltimore and Ohio Railroad opened its first section and thereby began to operate as the first common carrier in the United States. Even more importantly, incorporation had become available to the common man through general incorporation statutes. From a public tool and special privilege, the corporation had begun its transformation into a private business instrument available to everyone. As Theodore Sedgwick had put it in 1835, "[w]e must not [. . .] lose sight of the important fact, that the advantages resulting from acts of incorporation are such as, if fairly got, may be fairly enjoyed" (13).

The increasing availability of general incorporation statutes (rather than by special legislation) defined the development of the corporation between the end of Andrew Jackson's presidency and the Civil War. "Some states," William J. Novak writes, "pioneered general incorporation very early," such as "New York in 1811 [and] Connecticut in 1837" (294 n. 111).[1] "As state legislatures made it easier for firms to obtain these now more standard charters," Naomi R. Lamoreaux observes, "the number of corporations increased dramatically" ("Partnerships" 34). She adds that, "between 1826 and 1835 New Jersey authorized on average eleven corporations per year using a special charter system; between 1846 and 1855 it granted on average forty-five per year through a combination of special and general incorporation [. . .]" ("Partnerships" 34). The standardized corporate form that gradually emerged during those years included "perpetual life," "limited liability," and "centralized management based on majority rule and one vote per share" ("Partnerships" 34). Moreover, general incorporation contributed to the larger changes in how Americans conducted business which had been under way since the 1830s: "The personal connections that had defined the commercial world were vanishing, injecting people into a world where it did not matter that they were conducting business with faraway strangers" (Murphy 99).

The expansion of the national marketplace as well as the emergence of novel financial instruments meant new opportunities for the average citizen

---

[1]   Because corporation law is state law, some parts of the US introduce general incorporation earlier than others. Tara Helfman explains that "[th]e 1811 law [passed by New York] made incorporation a matter of right for those who met New York's statutory requirements. Connecticut followed in 1837, enacting the first general incorporation statute allowing entities to incorporate for any lawful purpose" (393). Naomi R. Lamoreaux recounts how general incorporation laws were available in most states by the middle of the nineteenth century and explains the administrative procedure for incorporation as follows: "These laws enabled any group of businesspeople that paid a fee and met specific requirements (such as minimum capitalization) to take out a corporate charter. Initially, they applied only to designated industries and were quite restrictive in their provisions. Over time, however, the range of businesses that could be incorporated widened and the terms on which charters were granted became more attractive" ("Partnerships" 33). It is important to add, as Lamoreaux does, that special charters were not abolished. They continued to exist until the end of the nineteenth century.

to succeed, but also to fail. Nowhere was this more apparent than in the years preceding and following the panic of 1837.

> [T]he antebellum decades witnessed an acceleration in the growth of market relations that made bankruptcy a social, cultural, and political problem of particularly great intensity. During these years, American entrepreneurs forged an increasingly national "credit system" and ever more integrated and competitive markets for goods and services, all of which helped to usher in the modern business cycle. Together, these processes democratized the specter of insolvency, bringing its anxieties and perplexities to a greatly expanded population of market-oriented proprietors. (Balleisen 5)

As Americans became increasingly involved in ever more complex economic networks, it was the confidence in this system, its institutions and agents, that became the economy's real currency. "Confidence was the engine of economic growth, the mysterious sentiment that permitted a country poor in specie but rich in promises to create something from nothing" (Mihm, *Counterfeiters* 10). But with economic expansion and urbanization, the community-based frameworks of conducting business with which Americans were familiar no longer applied. "In the cities of early America, preindustrial methods of ordering the world of strangers were becoming very unreliable" (Halttunen 37). Americans had to learn how to do business with strangers.[2]

The figure of the con artist epitomizes the challenges that this rapid socioeconomic transformation posed for antebellum Americans. Karen Halttunen has shown how the middle class responded to increased social mobility (opportunities to succeed and to fail) by investing in what she calls a sentimental "cult of sincerity." With roots in Puritan and republican ideology, the "cult of sincerity" sought to cultivate transparency and truthfulness in a world of deceit and hypocrisy. In this world, the confidence man came to represent, once more, the republican fear of corruption, specifically the fear of the corruption of the republican youth. Hence, in a world in which con artists donned a variety of masks to deceive their victims—the "masquerade" in Melville's title refers to that—the middle class insisted on the utmost

---

[2] The institutional corollary to this development were intelligence offices and credit reporting agencies. The most successful example of the latter at the time was Lewis Tappan's Mercantile Agency, which opened in 1841. By 1857, the Mercantile Agency "had fifteen branches throughout the United States, as well as offices in Montreal and London" (Balleisen 147). It provided information on individuals and companies, such as "whether a business was reliable for any conceivable engagement, reasonably strong, only good for a limited amount of credit, doubtful, or so suspect that one should only transact business in cash" (Balleisen 149–51).

transparency of character as reflected in appearances and manners. The irony of this insistence on utmost sincerity rests in the fact that, by the 1870s, it had become part of the social performance that was key to one's success in the world of corporate capitalism. In other words, the confidence man had transformed into the self-made man, performing the success and confidence to which he aspired.

Moreover, the figure of the confidence man was not just a general embodiment of the hypocrisy abhorred by sentimental culture and dreaded by republican ideology. He was also explicitly associated with the (financial) market and Wall Street. In his 1969 article "The Original Confidence Man," Johannes D. Bergmann presents the newspaper account which, according to most critics, established the name "confidence man." While swindlers and frauds abounded, Bergmann argues that it was in July 1849 that a man later identified as Mr. Thompson introduced himself to an unsuspecting victim and based his swindle on an explicit appeal to confidence. The *New York Herald* printed a detailed account of the crime on July 8 and three days later, after Thompson had been arrested, followed up with a somewhat angry commentary maintaining that, while one confidence man has been put in jail, a much more successful class of confidence men are still at large: the financiers. "How is it done?" the *Herald* asks rhetorically. "What is the secret? What is the machinery? How does it happen that the 'Confidence Man,' with his genius, address, tact, and skill, sleeps at 'the Tombs,' instead of reposing on softest down in the fashionable faubourgs of the metropolis of the union? Listen. He struck too low! Miserable wretch! He should have gone to Albany and obtained a charter for a new railroad company" (qtd. in Bergmann 564). In his analysis of the newspaper article, Bergmann argues that it specifically condemns those who assume "that wealth is to be admired and respected" (565). The *Herald* thereby draws attention to the fact that American society is willing to accept "the Wall street manipulator's swindle" (Bergmann 565) because it has been ennobled by financial success.

What role did corporations play in this development? How did they figure in the popular imaginary at this point? While the success of infrastructure projects—railroads, canals, etc.—as well as the privatization and democratization of the corporate form through general incorporation statutes meant that corporations' association with monopoly faded somewhat in favor of their association with technological progress and private enterprise, corporations also figured as a problem of seeing and perceiving. As Peter Knight has put it, "Reading the market had to be learned," and corporations presented a particularly challenging cipher (8), which becomes evident when we take a closer look at its legal form. As my discussion of *Louisville, Cincinnati and Charleston Rail-road Company* v. *Thomas W. Letson* (1844) shows, as early as the antebellum period courts and market actors began to recognize the benefits as well as the disadvantages of the so-called corporate veil: the persona that the corporate name presents and behind which individual shareholders could (at least in theory) become unaccountable.

II. Lifting the Veil: *Louisville Rail-road Co. v. Letson*

The story of *Louisville, Cincinnati and Charleston Rail-road Company* v. *Thomas W. Letson* (1844) is both one of the internal improvements that were characteristic of the period and one of its financial failures, because the railroad corporation was one of the many casualties of the panic of 1837. It had been chartered in South Carolina in 1835/6 with the intention of "link[ing] Charleston with Louisville and Cincinnati and promot[ing] a stream of commerce between the South and the West in competition with Northern trade" (Swisher 461). Its president was Robert Y. Haynes, "[an] ardent Southerner and advocate of states' rights" (Swisher 461). The venture folded under the stress of the panic and Haynes's death. The case came to the Supreme Court after it had been decided in favor of Thomas Letson in a federal circuit court. "Letson's suit against the company, where he won damages of some eighteen thousand dollars, was merely one of the innumerable steps toward final settlement" (Swisher 461). Letson had sued the corporation for payment of services which he had rendered for the construction of the line. The company brought up the case by writ of error, maintaining that it should never have been brought to court under federal jurisdiction. Therefore, the US Supreme Court now had to decide whether a citizen of one state could sue a foreign corporation (meaning a corporation chartered in another state) in a federal court on the basis of the Judiciary Act. But how to determine the citizenship of a corporation?

Of course, there was precedent that should have easily settled this question. In *Bank of the United States* v. *Deveaux* (1809), the Marshall Court had ruled that a corporation can sue and be sued in a federal court based on the citizenship of its members—who, in the case of *Deveaux*, had all happened to be members of the same state. That was not the case for the Louisville, Cincinnati and Charleston Rail-road corporation, however, which is why the company's attorneys argued that the case should never have been decided in a federal court in the first place. But Thomas Letson's lawyers and their co-counsel pursued a two-pronged line of attack that basically revised the idea of a corporation as an aggregate of individual shareholders and replaced it with a more unified, organic entity. As Tara Helfman has shown, *Louisville Rail-road* v. *Letson* is exceptional in that it shows how early in the nineteenth century continental theory began to influence the Court's conception of the corporate person. But, as she also points out, the Court's holding is essentially hybrid: it continued to understand the corporation as an artificial creation of the law while granting it separate legal standing. In the course of the arguments, *Louisville Rail-road* v. *Letson* therefore revealed a broad tableau of ideas of the legal and social nature of corporations and their place in the cultural imaginary in this period. The case demonstrates a central concern over seeing and perceiving—essentially, where the law should look to determine identity and agency—as well as a concern over organic and inorganic (or artificial and natural) persons in the marketplace that we also find in the literary fictions by Melville, Hawthorne, and De Forest.

In its ruling, the Court decided in favor of Thomas Letson and held that a corporation can be considered a citizen for the purpose of determining jurisdiction. Herbert Hovenkamp has placed the case at the beginning of a line of reasoning in which corporations gain personhood and citizenship. A modern reader, who has perhaps a case like *Citizens United* v. *Federal Election Commission* (2010) in mind, may think that this was a victory for corporations, but at the time the ruling was an attempt to establish more control over corporations. During this period,

> there was growing discontent with respect to the limitations of the jurisdiction of the federal courts in corporation cases. Corporations were growing larger as well as more numerous and stock was more and widely held [. . .].
> The panic of 1837 and the economic turmoil of the ensuing years increased in the volume of litigation. (Swisher 461)

Hugh Swinton Legaré, who was Letson's co-counsel, explains this motive early in his argument. He situates the conflict sociopolitically when he describes the present moment as

> an age when, more than ever, and [. . .] a country where, most of all, from obvious peculiarities of position and of polity, the spirit of association goes hand in hand with that of commerce, and all great enterprises, without exception, throughout the whole extent of this vast confederacy, are carried on by incorporated companies, local in nothing but their name and origin [. . .]. (*Louisville RR* v. *Letson* 515)[3]

Similar to Joseph Story's reasoning in his *Commentaries on the Law of Agency*, Legaré saw the commercial and political landscape of the US

---

[3] Even more expressly at a later point: if the case does not affirm federal jurisdiction over corporations, "there will soon be an end of all federal jurisdiction *in this most important class of cases*" (*Louisville RR* v. *Letson* 523, my emphasis).

changing—but he saw it changing in favor of corporate bodies, against whom private individuals were powerless.

> If this court has not jurisdiction to protect the rights of a citizen of New York, whose whole fortune—the fruit of his labor—is involved in a controversy with a trading company, thus created, thus composed, thus situated, under that article of the Constitution of the United States which gives to the federal courts cognisance of "controversies between citizens of different states," everybody will admit that there is somewhere a great chasm in our laws, and a serious grievance in our practice. (*Louisville RR* v. *Letson* 515)

While legal personhood would eventually serve to ensure greater autonomy for corporations, in *Louisville Rail-road* v. *Letson* it sought to achieve greater public control over them by making them subject to federal jurisdiction.[4]

But the meaning of legal personality as applied to corporations had to be adapted significantly in order to accommodate such a development in 1844. As the previous chapters have shown, corporations were seen as group entities that were traditionally given legal individuality in order to facilitate their operation within a legal property regime that was entirely geared toward individuals. In a succinct summary, Tara Helfman outlines the theoretical

---

[4] It is unfortunately not within the scope of this chapter to explore the ruling on legal personhood and citizenship in *Louisville Rail-road* v. *Letson* in the light of the Court's decision in *Dred Scott* v. *Sanford* (1857). But even a brief glance at the arguments in both cases reveal the stark contradictions in the Court's decisions. Dred Scott had sued his owner for his freedom, arguing that his residence in a free territory (Missouri) made him a free man. The majority opinion, written by Taney, ruled that Scott was a slave, not a citizen, and could therefore not sue in a federal court. Moreover, it stated that no descendant of African slaves had ever been nor could ever be a citizen within the definition of Article III. Don E. Fehrenbacher has compared *Louisville Rail-road* v. *Letson* and *Dred Scott* and has come to the conclusion "that [the decision in *Dred Scott*] was essentially visceral in origin—that law, logic, and history were distorted to serve a passionate purpose" ("Sectional Crisis" 561). He explains, "In at least three respects Taney's *Dred Scott* opinion was incompatible with the *Letson* decision: (1) He insisted that no new meaning not intended by the framers of the Constitution could be given to the word 'citizen.' (2) He declared that a litigant under the diverse-citizenship clause must be not only a state citizen but a citizen of the United States. (3) He refused to consider the possibility that a Negro might be a citizen under the diverse-citizenship clause without necessarily being entitled to full protection under the privileges-and-immunities clause" ("Taney" 562 n. 20). For more on *Dred Scott* see Fehrenbacher, *The Dred Scott Case: Its Significance in American Law and Politics* and Colin Dayan, *The Law is a White Dog*. Also note Peter Jaros's discussion of black disenfranchisement and corporate legal personhood during the Jacksonian era in his article on *Sheppard Lee*.

development of the legal understanding of corporations in the nineteenth century as follows:

> Looking back through nearly two hundred years of precedent, scholars have identified three distinct theories underlying the federal judiciary's approach to the nature of corporate legal personality: the aggregate entity theory, the artificial entity theory, and the real entity theory. Under the aggregate entity theory, the corporation is merely the sum of its parts, an assemblage of the rights of its individual shareholders. Under the artificial entity theory, the corporation is more than the sum of its parts: the corporation, as a creature of the law, possesses a distinct personality separate from that of its members. Finally, under the real entity theory, the corporation is a creation of the market with a capacity to act that is different in kind from that of its members. (384–5)

In order to achieve even the kind of moderate understanding of individual personhood that the Taney Court would adopt in *Louisville Rail-road v. Letson*, it had to address the relationship between the sum and its parts: between the shareholders and the corporate entity. In a very explicit fashion, this process of redefining emerges as a restructuring of a visual regime, because Letson's attorneys had to show the Court a new way of seeing, perceiving, and thereby formally recognizing the corporation. Legaré in particular argued that the corporation is not identical with all the natural persons which it consists of; it is not, in Roman law terms, a *societas*, like a partnership, but a *universitas*. Its agents, directors, or trustees represent a corporate citizen who cannot otherwise appear in court but through the instrumentality of agents. But, Legaré insisted, the corporation was yet more than the sum of its parts.

By contrast, for the railroad's lawyers, the case was much simpler. The precedent in *Deveaux* provided federal jurisdiction only on the basis of the shareholders' citizenship and it merely suggested (though it did not explicitly make this argument) that, in order to determine the citizenship of the corporate entity, all its members had to be citizens of the same state. This requirement narrowed the scope of federal jurisdiction, but it was consistent with precedent.[5] Because this was not the case in the Louisville, Cincinnati and Charleston Rail-road Company, whose members came from several different states and even included the state of South Carolina itself, *Louisville Rail-road v. Letson* gave the Court the opportunity to reconsider the issue of diversity.

---

[5]   *Strawbridge* v. *Curtiss* (1806), whose "limiting effect" was partly removed by a statute passed in 1839. Swisher notes that *Deveaux* was decided "during the period of Jeffersonian democracy, which was hostile to the federal courts and to large-scale business enterprise" (459).

In the following passage, the corporation's attorney sums up their position, which was in line with the decision in *Deveaux*:

> [T]he corporation being only the modes [*sic*] in which they are associated, affecting very materially the nature and extent of their rights and obligations, the forms of proceeding, and the nature and extent of the remedies for or against them, but not at all affecting their liability to the jurisdiction of the federal courts. For if they did, then all men might be withdrawn from the jurisdiction of the federal courts by charters of incorporation. (*Louisville RR* v. *Letson* 507)

In other words, while it is a special legal faculty that allows them to organize their property, the corporation has no impact on the individuals' standing in court as citizens; and since their diversity does not conclusively allow the court to establish a single citizenship for the corporation based on the shareholders, the case should not have been decided in a circuit court.

Letson's lawyers, James Louis Pettigru and Henry Lesesne, introduced a novel argument that was based on making a distinction between the members of the corporation, between the shareholders and the corporate officers. Not all members are equally relevant, they argued. "The *interest* of the corporation is, in fact, represented by the official members of the company" (*Louisville RR* v. *Letson* 508, my emphasis). As such, only these official members are important when it comes to determining the citizenship of a corporation. To make this argument, moreover, Pettigru and Lesesne introduced a new metaphor to conceive of a corporation: they called it "a state in miniature" (*Louisville RR* v. *Letson* 510).[6] Like a state, they added, a corporation has a "head" which consists of its presidents and directors. They are the corporation's "official members," whereas "[t]he private persons are represented by the corporate name, not as persons, but as a faculty. The only persons who have any individuality in the corporate name, or can be called persons suing, are the official members" (*Louisville RR* v. *Letson* 511). In the case of the Louisville Rail-road all "official members" were citizens of South Carolina, so that, they concluded, the precedent in *Deveaux* applied to the case. What is important here is that, by introducing the metaphor of the head of state, Letson's attorneys already

---

[6] "A corporation is but a state in miniature, but in political societies, the persons in whom the powers of government are vested, are everywhere considered trustees for the rest of the community" (*Louisville RR* v. *Letson* 510). The president and the director of the company "have the government of the company" (*Louisville RR* v. *Letson* 511).

take a first rhetorical step away from the more mechanical metaphor of the corporation as aggregate.[7]

But their co-counsel, Hugh Swinton Legaré, went even further by prioritizing organic metaphors and arguing for real corporate personhood. Legaré was attorney general and a friend of Joseph Story,[8] who had spent time in Germany and introduced "continental" jurisprudence into the case about forty to fifty years before it became fashionable to do so (*Louisville RR* v. *Letson* 520). Legaré maintained that the agents by which the corporation acts and appears in court represent the corporate entity as an ideal body that is more than the aggregate of shareholders, because the latter's identity is lost in the whole to which they submit like "a chemical compound" (*Louisville RR* v. *Letson* 520). In this regard, Legaré's metaphors strikingly anticipate the arguments of treatise writers that portray corporations in organic terms and combinations (trusts) in mechanical terms in the 1880s and 1890s. In her analysis of *Letson*, Tara Helfman explains that in the 1830s, during his time in Europe, Legaré had studied the work of Carl Friedrich von Savigny. In the Roman legal tradition in which Savigny and the continental jurists were writing, all persons were creations of the law; in other words, all rights were dependent on the state. That was particularly the case for corporations, whose legal personhood originated in the distinction between *societas* and *universitas*: while the former described contract-based associations of a more private nature, such as partnerships, the latter were seen as public and in this capacity extensions of the state. Only *universitas* were recognized as legal persons in Roman law. Invoking "the more accurate and scientific language of the continental jurists," Legaré went beyond what was established legal doctrine in the US at this point (*Louisville RR* v. *Letson* 520). In a corporation, he explained, "the whole is essentially and unchangeably different from all the parts, which are as completely merged and lost in it as the ingredients are in a chemical compound" (*Louisville RR* v. *Letson* 520). The shareholders give up their identity and rights to the greater whole; they no longer figure in their individual character. Instead, organic metaphors present a step toward providing the corporation with a body and a legal standing of its own.

---

[7] Böckenförde, in his discussion of the metaphors of organism, organizations, and political bodies, notes, for example, that the *dead mechanism* or mere *aggregate* is the opposite of the state as living *organism* (590). See my discussion of combinations in Chapter 5.

[8] Legaré died not long after *Louisville Rail-road* v. *Letson*, and Story commemorated him in a lecture that, as his son explains, was subsequently published in the *Law Reporter* for August 1844. "I pronounce him a great loss, as one of the most valuable lights of jurisprudence that it has been my happiness to know,—my misfortune to lose" (Story, *Life & Letters* 456).

Deciding who has standing in court—a group of shareholders, corporate agents, or a corporate entity—turns into an argument over the "substance" or "essence" of a corporation. Letson's lawyers argue that the railroad company is suing in its corporate name, instead of shareholders suing in their individual names; hence, they insist, they sue in their corporate capacity, i.e. as a corporation represented by their official members. Their co-counsel Legaré, however, argues that the *name* itself, not the shareholders, must be considered as the corporation's "essence": "a 'juridical person,' is, as I have said, a creature of the law, known to it under a given name, whose essence is in that name, and the social identity it implies [. . .]" (*Louisville RR v. Letson* 520). While Legaré thereby invests the corporate name with substance, the plaintiff's counsel insists on its insubstantiality. The railroad's attorney maintains that the natural persons of the shareholders "are the substance, the real parties [of the corporation]," while "the corporate character and style are only the form and name under which they are presented" (*Louisville RR v. Letson* 500). He holds that precedent has established the custom of lifting the veil of the name to establish citizenship in such cases. "That being ascertained, the veil of the corporation is again thrown over the individuals, and in all other respects [. . .] the Circuit Court [. . .] loses sight of the individuals, and sees nothing but the legal entity" (*Louisville RR v. Letson* 529–30). The metaphor of the veil is not only highly reminiscent of the market masquerades that are the subject of the literary fictions by Hawthorne, Melville, and De Forest; it also introduces an entire field of metaphors that concern seeing and perceiving.

The metaphor of the corporate veil came to *Letson* by way of precedent. In *Bank of the United States* v. *Deveaux* (1809), the US Supreme Court had to decide on federal jurisdiction over corporations on the basis of the Judiciary Act for the first time. Until *Deveaux*, legal doctrine had generally followed the logic outlined above and had recognized corporations only in their corporate capacity so long as they sued in their corporate name. But in *Deveaux*, the First Bank of the United States argued that it could sue in a federal court because its members did not give up their individual identity and thus individual rights through incorporation but remained in possession and full standing behind "the veil which the name interposes" (*Bank of the US v. Deveaux* 75). The court had merely to "raise the veil" to see and recognize the individuals, whose rights it was bound to protect (*Bank of the US v. Deveaux* 75). In his *Commentaries*, James Kent explains that, "The court can look beyond the corporate name and notice the character of the members, who are not considered, to every intent, as placed out of view, and merged into the corporation" (qtd. in Swisher 459). In hindsight and with Marshall's decision in *Dartmouth* in mind, it is conclusive that the Court would decide that it would recognize the right-bearing individuals that constitute the corporation.[9] Even though Marshall's ruling in *Dartmouth* has traditionally been cited as expressing the grant or concession theory, according to which the corporation is a creature of the state and wholly dependent on its charter, Tara Helfman has pointed out that Marshall followed the common-law tradition, which recognized the rights of the individuals who composed the corporation. As Helfman also explains, this view was not in contradiction with the idea that the corporation was also a person in law created by the state charter, since (as *Deveaux* amply illustrates) Marshall's decisions set the corporate entity only in those cases aside in which doing otherwise would violate the shareholders' constitutional rights. In fact, *Deveaux* probably presents the first case in which an American court decided to, what today is called, pierce the corporate veil.[10]

While there is next to no research available on the origin of the metaphor of the corporate veil, the rhetoric in *Louisville Rail-road* v. *Letson* suggests that it can be seen as part of a larger set of garment metaphors in the law as well as of a long tradition of specular metaphors originating in Judeo-Christian, Egyptian, Roman, and Greek thought. By itself, *Deveaux*'s use of the metaphor emphasizes the specific quality of the veil as a garment that covers the face, but not so as to fully disguise or blind its wearer. A veil has to be at least semi-transparent so as to make it possible for its wearer to move about. Moreover, a veil can be and is sometimes even meant to be lifted, such as in the case of the bridal veil. Its insubstantiality is what distinguishes a veil from a scarf or a mask. In *Deveaux*, this insubstantiality and the suggestion of the lifting of the veil as a customary ritual makes sense because *Deveaux*'s innovation consists of suggesting that the corporate persona, the name, is not impermeable; that it can be seen through, lifted, and/or pierced. The difference and the similarity between a veil and a mask, moreover, is noteworthy. The mask of the actors in Roman and Greek theater, the *persona*, is at the root of the word *person* and has come to signify not just the role that the actor portrays, but his or her identity. In Cooper's *The Bravo*, the mask symbolized the difference between public and private selves, the need to protect the

[9] Though it must be noted that Marshall does consider both options in the ruling and also finds precedent for both. The precedent for the Court's ruling in *Deveaux* is *The Mayor and Commonality* v. *Wood*, in which, as Justice Marshall explains, "[t]he judges unanimously declared that they could look beyond the corporate name, and notice the character of the individual" (*Deveaux* 90). For a discussion of *Wood* as well as of *Sutton's Hospital* (the Charterhouse case) see Helfman, "Transatlantic Influences on American Corporate Jurisprudence: Theorizing the Corporation in the United States."

[10] According to Carol Goforth, I. Maurice Wormser established the expression of *piercing* the veil, and Wormser's 1912 article "Piercing the Veil of the Corporate Entity" identifies *Deveaux* as the first case in which the corporate veil is lifted.

latter through a performance of the former. By comparison, a veil is much less material or protective. The law can lift the veil at all times. That the law should do the lifting also makes sense when seen alongside other uses of garment metaphors, such as, at the most basic level, the phrase *clothing in rights*. The law *clothes* the body of persons and other entities in rights and special properties, such as immortality and individuality. And if the law can clothe, it can also unveil.

The sovereign power of the law that the metaphor of the veil thus implies receives further corroboration when we look at the historical tradition of legal visual metaphors to which the veil belongs. In *Louisville Rail-road* v. *Letson*, the metaphor of the veil means that settling the question of jurisdiction becomes a matter of where the law chooses to look: whether it assumes that the name is a veil that is only thinly disguising a group of individuals, or whether it is the face of the corporate citizen that gives it standing in court.[11] Both the counsel of the plaintiff and of the defendant ask the court to consider, "how far [is] it necessary or proper to look?" (*Louisville RR* v. *Letson* 524). The court is urged "to look beyond," "to look to," "to regard," and "to notice." Inherent in the law's visual capacity is the power to create, as is evident in Marshall's ruling in *Dartmouth*: the corporation "exist[s] only in contemplation of the law." The ultimate symbol of the law's visual power is "the eye of the law" (*Louisville RR* v. *Letson* 515), which, as Michael Stolleis has shown, can be traced back to the metaphor of the eye of God.[12]

The all-seeing eye, Stolleis writes, is the most common symbol of God's omnipotence in the metaphorical language of monotheistic religions. Earlier precursors can be found in Roman and Greek antiquity, such as the eye of justice (*Justitiae oculus*), a metaphor which probably symbolized both the value of justice and, similar to the all-seeing power of God, law's ability to penetrate all conflicts and establish justice (Stolleis 24). Moreover, today's blindfolded female allegory is a variant of earlier female figures that were precisely not blind: the all-seeing figure represented law's attention to detail, its recognition of all facts evenly; blindfolded, it represents law's equal justice irrespective of the identity of the persons in front of it. In a sad twist, the blindfold will come to represent law's literal blindness, its unpredictability. Later, in seventeenth- and eighteenth-century iconography, for example, the metaphor of the eye is also used to convey sovereign power, control, and fairness. This metaphor of the "all-knowing, all-caring, and all-controlling" sovereign transfers unto the

---

[11] In *Louisville Rail-road* v. *Letson*, the veil is not only a symbol for the name but also occasionally for the charter; for example, *Louisville RR* v. *Letson* 523.

[12] As in *Dartmouth*, seeing implies more than just perceiving, since it is through the "contemplation of law" that the corporation exists.

state as legitimate power becomes secularized and depersonalized (Stolleis 34; my translation); a process that is expressed in John Adams's phrase "a government of laws and not of men" (see Stolleis 46). As sovereign, the people themselves are the origin of the law, and henceforth, the law (their guardian) never sleeps, as Stolleis puts it (see 48).

Even though the Court finally decided in favor of Thomas Letson and held that a corporation can be deemed a citizen for the purpose of determining jurisdiction, the ruling is ultimately not based exclusively on Legaré's Continental reasoning. Tara Helfman points out that the court's reference to the corporation as "artificial" in its recognition of the corporate person suggests that it does not fully adopt the organic rhetoric of chemical compounds and all that is implied by it.

> A corporation created by a state to perform its functions under the authority of that state and only suable there, though it may have members out of the state, seems to us to be a person, though an artificial one, inhabiting and belonging to that state, and therefore entitled, for the purpose of suing and being sued, to be deemed a citizen of that state. (*Louisville RR* v. *Letson* 555)

Quoting English jurist Sir Frederick Pollock, Helfman explains that "artificial" qualified the corporation as the work or creation of jurists. "[B]y 'artificial person,' the common law tradition conceived of the corporation as an artifact, a legal person created 'in accordance with the rules of art'— the lawyer's art" (Helfman 407). While the counsel encouraged the Court to adopt a new vision of the corporation, the Court did not go so far as to liberate it from the state. Qualifying the corporate person as "artificial," the Court emphasized that it was still the creation of the lawyer and the law, and therefore a being whose existence depended on the state legislature that had chartered it. As Helfman also points out, and as is particularly important for the larger argument of this book, the Court did not go beyond settling the question of jurisdiction in its consideration of corporate citizenship rights in *Louisville Rail-road* v. *Letson*. This would change after the Civil War, specifically in the *California Tax Cases* of the 1880s that are the subject of Chapter 4. What is important, however, is that even as the Court began to consider a broader array of constitutional rights and protections for the corporate person, it did not cease to define it as essentially a collective entity and a representation of the aggregate rights of its natural members.

III. Satanic Agents and Diabolical Corporations in Three Literary Fictions

If the law in *Louisville Rail-road* v. *Letson* showed an unusually high preoccupation with questions of seeing and perceiving truth, the same can be said of the three literary fictions that form the basis of this section. Published between the antebellum period and the end of Reconstruction, they provide glimpses into the transformation that the market, the nation, and the role of corporations in both underwent in the popular imaginary. All three depict corporations as tools of con artists, and all three cast corporate agents in satanical guise. In Hawthorne's "The Celestial Railroad," Mr. Smooth-it-away travels alongside the homodiegetic narrator and represents a newly chartered railroad, whereas Melville's *The Confidence-Man* features several episodes of con-artistry that include a transfer-agent for the Black Rapids Coal Mine; and in De Forest's *Honest John Vane*, Darius Dorman represents the Great Subfluvial, a diabolical version of the transcontinental railroads. In each of these texts, the intertextual clues signal the corporate agents' diabolical nature to the readers, as in fact, each text can be said to have been modeled (to a greater or lesser degree) after John Bunyan's Christian allegory *The Pilgrim's Progress* (1678). Bunyan's *Progress*, which was particularly popular during the antebellum period, tells the story of the soul's long and dangerous journey to heaven and spiritual salvation. In the texts of Hawthorne, Melville, and De Forest, however, the meaning of "progress" is changed: now it refers to the economic and technological advancements of the Industrial Revolution, and to the fact that citizens appear to strive less for spiritual salvation than material gain. As a result, all three texts present national allegories of progress that are highly critical of incorporation's expeditious and rationalizing logic.

The popularity of Bunyan's *Pilgrim's Progress* during the antebellum period, David S. Reynolds explains, was part of a larger trend in which religious and literary discourses began to intersect on account of the "shift in the style of popular religious discourse from the doctrinal to the imaginative" (15). Reynolds refers to Louisa May Alcott's *Little Women* as an example and points out that "each of the four heroines is described as carrying her little bundle of sin through her personal Vanity Fair toward a Celestial City that promises to be a merely idealized version of her earthly home" (38). Allegory, Reynolds maintains, had become "a most flexible and adaptable" genre by the early 1830s, used not only by Hawthorne and Melville but also by Alcott (38). Yet Cindy Weinstein also notes a difference in the way that allegory's referentiality was employed by Nathaniel Hawthorne as opposed to, for instance, Susan Warner's use of *Pilgrim's Progress* in *The Wide, Wide World* (1850). When the heroine receives a copy of Bunyan's work, the narrative emphasizes that the work's accessibility is a consequence of the correspondence between surface and content, between inside and outside, which "transparently mirror one another" (Weinstein 224). Weinstein suggests that, in Hawthorne's story, this correspondence does not obtain, or is at least depicted as precarious due to the influence of market forces.

Hawthorne's "The Celestial Railroad" is the most explicit of the three in its intertextual reference to *The Pilgrim's Progress*, and it tells what we could call the contemporary sequel to Bunyan's Christian allegory. More satire than sentimental tale, the story riffs on the double meaning of progress by having its protagonist take the train to heaven. Along the route, money and the harmonizing, incorporating effects of common interests have smoothed the way for the travelers in the shape of tunnels, bridges, and new, customer-friendly personnel. On this trip, the homodiegetic narrator is accompanied by a corporate agent, Mr. Smooth-it-away, who is revealed as one of Satan's minions at the end of the story. Like Austin's "Martha Gardner; or, Moral Re-Action," "The Celestial Railroad" was first published in a Democratic magazine, the *United States Magazine and Democratic Review*. Nina Baym explains that, "Hawthorne clearly expect[ed] his audience to consist of literate Bostonians and New Yorkers attached to the Democratic Party" (*Hawthorne's Career* 100). Karen Halttunen adds that, to some extent, too, Hawthorne was addressing the newly mobile middle classes and the "aspiring young men and women who hoped to fulfil the promise of the allegedly open society of Jacksonian America, either by entering the ranks of the middle class from below or by rising within those ranks to higher and higher levels of gentility" (xv).

Uncritical belief in progress and easy solutions to complex, even existential problems (such as the soul's salvation) is the target of satire in "The Celestial Railroad." The story's controlling metaphor is progress: it alludes to Bunyan, but also to technological, spiritual, and economic advancement. On the level of the basic narrative, progress is also the primary joke, because the narrator assumes the perspective of the writer of a travel narrative and treats Bunyan's Christian in the same manner. The word's reference to the physical journey from the City of Destruction to the Celestial City is still present insofar as the anonymous homodiegetic narrator repeatedly comments on "Bunyan's road-book" and how the landmarks described therein—the Wicket-Gate, the Interpreter's House, the Hill of Difficulty, and so on—have changed since Christian's last visit (Hawthorne, "Celestial Railroad" 517). Referring to Bunyan's work as a "road-book," the story activates and draws on the conventions of travel narratives, which were also published in the *Democratic Review*. Such narratives also included pilgrimages: "Pilgrimage narratives [. . .] accurately relate travels in Europe and the Orient in a light, often humorous tone" (Post-Lauria 21). The conventions of the genre also set the tone and the discursive framework of the narrator's relationship to the reader of "The Celestial Railroad," whom he repeatedly addresses via references to Christian: "The reader of Bunyan will be glad to know that Christian's old friend Evangelist [. . .] now presides at the ticket-office" (Hawthorne, "Celestial Railroad" 515). The anonymous narrator praises "the new method of going on pilgrimage" because of the ease and convenience with which it can now be conducted, and he explains how technological as well as economic advancements have made this ease possible (Hawthorne, "Celestial Railroad" 516).

The railroad is therefore a symbol of technological advancement as well as, by virtue of being a corporation, of economic progress. But the "Celestial Railroad" is also a fraud. At the beginning of the story, the reader learns that the railroad was "[established] by the public spirit of some of the inhabitants [of the City of Destruction]" (Hawthorne, "Celestial Railroad" 515). Later, however, the traveler is warned that the Lord of the Celestial City "has refused and will ever refuse, to grant an act of incorporation for this railroad," which is why no pilgrims will ever arrive in the Celestial City as long as they take the train (Hawthorne, "Celestial Railroad" 522). In legal terms, this means that the railroad was operating as a quasi corporation. Such enterprises were often based on private contract or organized as "unincorporated stock associations," such as we have seen in *Astoria* (Hurst 14). The Celestial Railroad, in other words, is not a celestial creation at all.

To some extent, Hawthorne's portrait of incorporation is reminiscent of Cooper's critique of expediency as the primary principle ruling corporations—a principle that subordinates everything to the imperatives of efficiency and rationality. Incorporation, as Hawthorne's narrator explains, has produced "harmony between the townspeople and pilgrims": "[A]s the new railroad brings with it great trade and a constant influx of strangers, the lord of Vanity Fair is its chief patron, and the capitalists of the city are among the largest stockholders" (Hawthorne, "Celestial Railroad" 520). By achieving harmony,[13] the town's community as well as its visitors can maximize the

---

[13] As a term that signifies a specific model of economic and social organization, harmony's significance will increase steadily in the course of the nineteenth century. In antebellum America, it is associated with Henry C. Carey, who is often called the architect of Henry Clay's American System. This plan, as Brook Thomas explains, "hoped to overcome sectional differences by harmonizing the interests of manufacturing, commerce, and agriculture through an activist government that stimulated the economy with internal improvements and tariff protection" (*Reconstruction* 234–5). What is even more interesting with respect to how harmony is employed here is Carey's emphasis on associations. "The agrarian vision of a single-class society of self-employed, independent proprietors appeared in Carey's revisionist political economy as the end result of, instead of the point of departure for, the market revolution. The true origin and basis of market relations themselves, he came to believe, lay not in class interests but in psychosocial 'association'; of which a cash and credit economy and corporate business enterprise represented the highest expressions" (Sklansky 80). On Carey and harmony's role in economic discourses on monopoly and corporate management see Chapter 5.

pleasurable effects of their stay at Vanity Fair. This is also the purpose of several "ingenious methods [that] constitute a sort of machinery" at the fair (Hawthorne, "Celestial Railroad" 520). Through these effortless methods, "thought and study are done to every person's hand" and literacy is made obsolete (Hawthorne, "Celestial Railroad" 520). "[M]achinery" refers to the efficiency of the methods, as well as to the harmonious interaction between its parts, whether ministers and lecturers in the case of the knowledge-machinery, or an entire society, as in the case of the second ingenious invention of Vanity Fair.

> There is another species of machine for the wholesale manufacture of individual morality. This excellent result is effected by societies for all manner of virtuous purposes; with which a man has merely to connect himself, throwing, as it were, his quota of virtue into the common stock; and the president and directors will take care that the aggregate amount be well applied. (Hawthorne, "Celestial Railroad" 520)

This "species of machine" is less an actual factory than a corporation in which "virtue" is the capital stock. The passage mocks the association of corporations with the common good, the idea that corporations serve a public purpose, by suggesting incorporation merely serves to increase personal profits. The suggestion of speculation and gambling that is only implied here becomes explicit in another corporate dimension of the Fair: the stock market.

> There was a sort of stock or scrip, called Conscience, which seemed to be in great demand, and would purchase almost anything. Indeed, few rich commodities were to be obtained without paying a heavy sum in this particular stock, and a man's business was seldom very lucrative, unless he knew precisely when and how to throw his hoard of Conscience into the market. Yet as this stock was the only thing of permanent value, whoever parted with it was sure to find himself a loser, in the long run. (Hawthorne, "Celestial Railroad" 521)

Like the railroad itself, incorporation increases safety, efficiency, and ease. Cindy Weinstein argues that incorporation ultimately erases all difference by erasing all conflict under the imperative of "compromise [and] improvement" (66), such as when the narrator recounts that the feud between Beelzebub and the keeper of the Wicket-Gate has been resolved in a manner reminiscent of disputes over railway routes and private land.

In a manner further comparable to Austin and Cooper, Hawthorne's use of incorporation associates expediency with non-human entities. Whether technological, financial, or managerial, corporations are associated with the idea of rationalization, which the story's moral rejects as the lazy man's solution. It satirizes the confusion of progress with efficiency, and it suggests that in the process, expediency has replaced morality—the very danger of which Cooper's dark tale of republican decline in *The Bravo* (1831) had tried to warn its readers. But while the corporation in *The Bravo* was still figured as a governmental conspiracy and thus as a political actor, in Hawthorne's "Celestial Railroad" corruption is figured much more mundanely as material affluence and ease. As the encounter between natural citizen and corporate citizen is brought to the level of everyday private lives, however, the figure of the corporate agent becomes more significant.

As mentioned earlier, Hawthorne's use of a satanic corporate agent anticipates strikingly similar figures in the work of Melville and De Forest. The preeminent quality that characterizes Mr. Smooth-it-away is his eloquence.[14] Throughout the story, the corporate agent not only glosses over unpleasant incidents, but reinterprets events for the narrator in such a way that they end up meaning the opposite. Cindy Weinstein points out that Mr. Smooth-it-away consistently "drive[s] a wedge between names and what they stand for" (61). When he wants "to visit the Palace Beautiful, and be introduced to the charming young ladies—Miss Prudence, Miss Piety, Miss Charity, and the rest—who have the kindness to entertain pilgrims there," Mr. Smooth-it-away convinces him that far from being young and charming, these ladies are unfashionable "old maids" (Hawthorne, "Celestial Railroad" 518). While he himself is accurately named, Weinstein suggests that Mr. Smooth-it-away's purpose is to destroy this accuracy, or rather identity, in all other names. For Weinstein, the corporate agent's linguistic skills are part of a larger theme in the story, originating in an economic logic that she describes as a "principle" of unequal exchange that impacts language itself (62). While the names seem to reveal the truth about characters in the manner in which proper names do in Bunyan's text, they also highlight those occasions in the story in which meaning is just not stable or fixed, but contradictory. As a result, language is all but emptied of any substance in "The Celestial Railroad."

Despite such strong social criticism, Hawthorne's story is ultimately humorous and ends not with the narrator going to hell, but waking up and realizing that it was all a dream—a relief that neither Melville nor De Forest grants their readers. But the humor of the story also relies precisely on the role of the (implied) reader and, more specifically, on the reader's implied

---

[14] Larry J. Reynolds has suggested that Mr. Smooth-it-away is "a sly caricature of Emerson" (17). As evidence he refers to the scene in which the train crosses a bridge that had been built over a swamp, the "Slough of Despond." Mr. Smooth-it-away explains that the foundations have been rendered solid by throwing philosophical books of various kinds into the swamp, which Reynolds reads as "a fair jab at Transcendental eclecticism" (L. J. Reynolds 17).

prior knowledge of *Pilgrim's Progress*. Five times the narrator addresses the "Christian reader" or "benevolent reader," and each time he does, he underscores the relationship between the reader and himself as one of peers who have both read and know Bunyan's work well. It is this knowledge of Bunyan that provides readers with the framework necessary to (morally) orient themselves in the landscape of the story and hence to recognize the corporation as con game. "The reader of John Bunyan will be glad to know," the narrator informs us, for example, "that Christian's old friend Evangelist, who was accustomed to supply each pilgrim with a mystic roll, now presides at the ticket-office" (Hawthorne, "Celestial Railroad" 515). The story's set-up puts the reader in the position of a superior interpreter, a reader of allegory (and thus of the marketplace). As Levy in his discussion of allegory in *Honest John Vane* remarks, "Allegory fixes a point of moral reference in a world devoid of morality [. . .]" (96). Because the "Christian reader" knows that the topic of Bunyan's *Progress* is a serious one—the soul's salvation—and because he knows that there are no shortcuts to salvation, he can recognize the traveler's folly.

Hence, unlike Cooper, who uses an all-seeing and all-knowing narrator to educate his readers about corporate power, Hawthorne uses allegory to provide the reader with epistemic certainty. Romantic writers often considered allegory conventional and even mechanical. It stood in contrast to the symbol, which was understood to establish meaning through an organic and spontaneous connection between sign and idea. In her extensive study of the distinction between symbol and allegory as one between what was deemed natural as opposed to artificial, Cindy Weinstein has connected Poe's, Hawthorne's, and Melville's use of allegory to their refusal to erase the labor of the author,[15] and argues that they chose artificiality to emphasize that literature is the product of the artist's labor. Yet Weinstein pays no special attention to the fact that both Hawthorne and Melville occasionally pair allegory and satire, as is the case in "The Celestial Railroad" and *The Confidence-Man*. Of course, through its emergence from the medieval tradition of morality plays, satire was already an element of Bunyan's *The Pilgrim's Progress*. Yet in "The Celestial Railroad," Hawthorne amps up the satirical elements, and not simply because it makes his story entertaining. Distinguishing satire from irony, one critic explains that "[c]lassical satire demands conformity to a standard of behavior and a conviction that life will be improved if people do what

---

[15] For a classical study of symbolism in the American Renaissance see Feidelson, *Symbolism and American Literature*. For Hawthorne's work specifically see Berlant, *The Anatomy of National Fantasy: Hawthorne, Utopia, and Everyday Life*.

is right—and there is no doubt that right and wrong can, and should be, clearly defined" (Pavlovskis-Petit 512). Hence satire, like allegory, can provide the kind of epistemic certainty that allows Hawthorne's readers to recognize that the moral of "The Celestial Railroad" is precisely directed against the kind of rhetorical free-for-all Mr. Smooth-it-away practices in the service of the corporation. By contrast, Herman Melville's *The Confidence-Man; His Masquerade* (1857) poses a much more fundamental critique of the loss of substance of both language and persons in the marketplace by refusing such epistemic certainty at the end.

Corporations and corporate agents are not *The Confidence-Man*'s main concern, but they are prominent among the confidence games that the text presents, and they can be said to inform the story's basic setting. Scholars of Melville's work have often pointed out that the steamboat *Fidèle* travels south, from St. Louis to New Orleans, and thus along the infamous slave-trading route as well as through frontier territory. But despite following a journey down the river, the story can be said to never leave the singular site that it explores: the market. The setting of the steamer is presented as a marketplace from the beginning—and, as many scholars have pointed out, the polyphony of voices in the initial chapters ties economic practice to pioneer spirit and, ultimately, to national character.

> Merchants on 'change seem the passengers that buzz on her decks, while, from quarters unseen, comes a murmur as of bees in the comb. Fine promenades, doomed saloons, long galleries, sunny balconies, confidential passages, bridal chambers, state-rooms plenty as pigeonholes, and out-of-the-way retreats like secret drawers in an escritoire, present like facilities for publicity or privacy. Auctioneer or coiner, with equal ease, might somewhere here drive his trade. (Melville 15)

Representative of a heterogeneous society, the ship's passengers are nonetheless all similar in that they resemble merchants on the exchange: they want to do business. The boat is portrayed as a corporate commonwealth: all the passengers (all Americans) are like merchants on the exchange here—they are out to pursue their self-interest.

There is reason to read the *Fidèle* as a corporate body. For example, Jennifer Greiman has argued that the text begins in fact with a presentation of collective agency, when the narrator describes the crowd on board the *Fidèle*. The strangeness of the mute initially serves as an other against which the heterogeneous mass can define its sameness. Yet after he has fallen asleep, maintaining collective agency becomes a problem, both for the crowd and the author writing their story. "The problem, of course, is how to narrate this multiple that is no longer acting as a mass, no longer generating itself around a center.

To do this, the narrator marshals a long chain of figures, beginning with the thing that temporarily contains them—the riverboat itself" (Greiman 188–9). A container "defined by an extraordinary leakiness," the *Fidèle's* structure may remain the same but what defines it, the "flow" of strangers, is continuously changing (Greiman 189). Not just changing, but producing an "excess" of strangeness, as Greiman notes, the steamer "as a traveling theater," a mobile site of performance, also symbolizes what Greiman considers to be the meaning of theatricality in the novel: "[t]heatricality reveals that faith in the authenticity of the self may be the ultimate confidence game" (187).

Similar to Hawthorne's "Celestial Railroad," the *Fidèle* represents America's faith in progress and a society confident in its belief in the democratic promise. But in the course of the story, one novel scheme of progress after another is employed to bedazzle rather than empower the many, and in no area more so than the financial. In this regard, the book obviously draws on the spirit of its historical moment. "Historians have long noted," observes Lara Langer Cohen,

> the ubiquity of hoaxes, confidence games, and other forms of "humbug" during these years. From Richard Adams Locke's moon hoax to P. T. Barnum's Feejee Mermaid, from table-rappers to perpetual motion machines, deception, it seems, established itself as the national pastime in the nineteenth-century United States. (1–2)

The book ultimately raises the question of who benefits from progress—and what the social costs of such progress are.

While critics have disagreed over whether or not *The Confidence-Man* should be read or was intended as allegory, its similarities with Hawthorne's story (both in subject matter and style) are striking. While parallels to Bunyan's *The Pilgrim's Progress* can be drawn, scholars often also point out that the *Fidèle* is a version of the "ship of fools" trope, the most well-known of which is Stephan Brant's 1414 allegory of the same name.[16] The text itself compares the passengers not just to "Merchants on 'change," but also to "Chaucer's Canterbury pilgrims, or those oriental ones crossing the Red Sea toward Mecca in the festival month" (Melville 16). Hence it ultimately casts the *Fidèle's* passengers in the role of commercial pilgrims. Leaving not through the "Gate of Dreams" like Hawthorne's narrator, but through the famous gate of the West, St. Louis, the passengers are not after spiritual salvation but after material gain. In this regard, the journey itself is also more

---

[16] See for example John Bryant's *Melville and Repose* (1993). Post-Lauria argues that Melville could have been inspired by a review of Goethe's *Faust*.

important than the destination, since it is aboard the ship that the passengers meet strangers and the opportunities that come with them. Moreover, like Hawthorne's tale, the novel also updates the motif of the journey by placing the pilgrims on a steamboat. This mode of transportation also allows Melville to toy with satanic allusions to coal, fire, and steam. Finally, the setting on a river—a metaphor of change at least since Heraclitus—also reinforces the themes of mutability, metamorphosis, and the fluidity of identities in the marketplace.

Much less debate has been spent on the question of the text's satirical qualities. Most often, these are read in the context of the picaresque novel, a genre that traditionally features a roguish protagonist, little character development, and a string of episodes rather than a fully developed plot. But we can also read the text's satirical qualities in conjunction with its allegorical and ironical ones. Surprisingly, the effect is different from that produced by Hawthorne's use of allegory and satire, because Melville's text is much more ambivalent about its message. Rather than supporting epistemic certainties, Melville's use of satire in conjunction with irony renders them doubtful.[17] Going so far as to call the novel an "anti-allegorical representation of the confidence game," Frank Palmeri also makes this connection between irony and uncertainty in allegorical narratives: "Institutions that ground belief and behavior characteristically employ allegory to assert their authority; the use of irony by narrative satire registers and encourages the undermining of such institutions" (92).

The ambiguity of Melville's use of satire, irony, and allegory also informs his use of the (satanic) corporate agent, who makes his appearance in the shape of John Truman, the president and transfer-agent of the Black Rapids

[17] One of the greatest ambiguities still revolves around two possible, yet entirely contradictory readings of the confidence man as either Satan or Christ (see Fiedler, *Love and Death in the American Novel*). For example, Wadlington notes "the Confidence-Man's unmistakable traditional associations with Satan," but then adds: "An excellent case can also be made for considering the Confidence-Man as Christ [. . .]" (168). This theme also connects the novel to a non-picaresque tradition of satire beginning with Erasmus's *The Praise of Folly* (1511). Featuring "the medieval allegorical figure of Folly" as its speaker, the text presents her in "a sequence of personae ranging from a carnivalesque entertainer, who abuses many of the time-honored commonplaces of medieval satire (besotted lovers, drunks, and so on), to a proponent of true Christianity as the highest form of folly, namely, an abandonment of a common-sense kind of reason such as is favored, or at least paid lip service to, by such fools as we all are" (Pavlovskis-Petit 516, 515). As Zoja Pavlovskis-Petit explains, Erasmus's work takes its cue from "the ironic Pauline passage on faith in Christ as 'folly'"—which also captures the central irony of *The Confidence-Man*'s discourse on charity (520). Erasmus's *Folly* shares this descent with later satirical works, such as Nikolai Gogol's *The Overcoat* (1843).

Coal Mining Company. The company's name is an obvious allusion to hell, and the company is making a profit from a deep and dark underground operation. In chapter 9, Truman is introduced by way of looking for his prior alter ego, John Ringman, the confidence man's former disguise. This basic pattern of reference and sequence reigns throughout the novel, at least until the appearance of the Cosmopolitan, the final disguise in the "masquerade." In the case of Mr. Truman, what is remarkable is his intention to help Mr. Ringman financially, because, as he explains it to the collegian, "we have been so very prosperous lately in our affairs—by we, I mean the Black Rapids Coal Company—that, really, out of my abundance, associative and individual, it is but fair that a charitable investment or two should be made, don't you think so?" (Melville 54–5). Truman's reference to his "abundance, associative and individual" identifies him as a corporate agent and a shareholder, but also as a representative of the wealthy middle class to which his victim, the "collegian," evidently aspires. "I like prosperous fellows, comfortable fellows; fellows that talk comfortably and prosperously, like you. Such fellows are generally honest" (Melville 57). It is the poetic reflection of a comfortable and prosperous life that the collegian finds in Truman and hopes to achieve by buying stock in the company.

This similarity is not insignificant when we consider the possible connection between Truman and Thurlow Weed, a New York lobbyist. A Whig politician, editor of the *Albany Evening Journal*, and cofounder of the Republican Party, Weed's rhetorical abilities as lobbyist are captured, Helen Trimpi notes, in the description in a later chapter of the novel that presents him as "'Orpheus in his gay descent to Tartarus,' while he 'lightly hums to himself an opera snatch'" (qtd. in Trimpi 109–10). Poetical, rhetorical, and satanical qualities combined, Truman is therefore also the corporate agent as lobbyist that the figure of Mr. Smooth-it-away had already implied. Called "[t]he Lucifer of the Lobby" by a contemporary observer, Weed was for "much of his life [. . .] the chief political boss—the wooer of funds and support and the dispenser of patronage and legislative favors—for (successively) the Anti-Masonic Party, the Whig Party, and the Republican Party in New York State and at national conventions" (Trimpi 115; 114). Business corporations and political machines, this comparison suggests, employ agents that share the ability to persuade and "smooth-it-away." What Hawthorne's and Melville's characters suggest, moreover, will find its full expression in De Forest's rendition of Darius Dorman, the satanic agent who establishes the rapport between the corporation and the politicians responsible for its subsidies.

Among the confidence man's victims in Melville's novel, the collegian is also a good example of the duplicitousness of everyday appearances and common morality. In fact, he dupes the reader. In chapter 5 he is approached by the Man with the Weed, Mr. Ringman, whose eloquence he is unable to resist, except by sheer flight: "From the outset, the sophomore [. . .] had struggled with an ever-increasing embarrassment, arising, perhaps, from such strange remarks coming from a stranger—such persistent and prolonged remarks, too. In vain had he more than once sought to break the spell by venturing a deprecatory or leave-taking word" (Melville 36). But when responding to Mr. Truman's wish to help Ringman financially, the collegian explains that he had "humored" the latter: "By the way, strange how that man with the weed, you were inquiring for, seemed to take me for some soft sentimentalist, only because I kept quiet, and thought, because I had a copy of Tacitus with me, that I was reading him for his gloom, instead of his gossip" (Melville 57). While the transfer-agent wants to give Ringman money, the collegian replies that if he sees Ringman again, "I will send for the steward and have him and his misfortunes consigned overboard" (Melville 59). Not at all the "soft sentimentalist" the latter mistook him for, the collegian reveals himself a hardened capitalist (Melville 57). Melville thus exposes the dark side of the middle-class ethos at which Hawthorne only hints, when he has the narrator approvingly report that conversation among the pilgrims on the train has "thrown [religion] tastefully into the back-ground" ("Celestial Railroad" 431).[18] If humanity were a corporation, the confidence man replies to the collegian, "the stock of human nature" per his example would be pronounced "of a hardening heart and a softening brain" (Melville 58).

The collegian is therefore one of the most extreme examples in Melville's work of the novel's revision of the pilgrim-narrative, in which it replaces the quest for spiritual salvation with one for material gain.[19] But while this theme can be seen as a continuation of Hawthorne's critique of a naive and even dangerous faith in progress, Melville's novel ultimately challenges all certainties by refusing to expose the confidence man. What some critics have considered a serious flaw may, however, be the novel's greatest asset. Unlike "The Celestial Railroad," which allows its reader a position of epistemic certainty by alluding to Bunyan's allegory as a shared inter-text and leaving it intact,

[18] As one critic notes, "[Melville] takes great pains to show the elective affinities between the con men and their victims" (Malkmus 610).

[19] Consider his investment choices: he buys stock in the Black Rapids Coal Company, but refuses opportunities to invest in "the New Jerusalem" (the millennial city upon the hill) and in a fellow human being (the Man with the Weed). By making him a collegian, Melville may also have been satirizing what the character summarily calls "the popular notion touching the nature of the modern scholar" (58). At the beginning of his lecture, "The American Scholar," Emerson mentions the scholar's "speculative" pursuits. This reference to philosophical inquiry into moral truths may thus have been turned into a ruthless quest for material profit by Melville.

The Confidence-Man has sent generations of readers on what Matthew Seybold has recently called "a wild goose chase" (81). In "Quite an Original Failure: Melville's Imagined Reader in *The Confidence-Man*," Seybold maintains that allegorical readings of the novel have failed, citing interpretations of the confidence man as Satan, Jesus, Dionysus, and Vishnu (80). In his own article, Seybold persuasively argues that the text's allegorical properties are part of a larger strategy that foregrounds readerly practice itself, and which is connected to the desire to identify or expose the confidence man. For Seybold, the text's symbolic density thus prepares the reader for the metafictional interludes in which Melville, Seybold contends, suggests that a work's originality depends not only on writerly craft, but also on readerly experience and taste.

In a similar vein, Peter Knight maintains that "[*The Confidence-Man*] offers a self-reflexive meditation on the problem of reading in a market society," which Knight connects to the transitional nature of the antebellum period as poised between a modern and a sentimental economy (147). In this sense, Knight argues, the novel reveals that the con trick relied essentially on "mimicking the rhetoric and reassurance of a contract infused with the 'Wall Street spirit,' while, at the same time, appealing to an older tradition of personal connections" (145). This observation is perhaps particularly relevant to the encounters with corporate agents. As Chapter 1 of this book has explained, legal agencies were modeled after the laws and customs that defined master-servant relationships and were as such still understood in quite personal terms. That this was no longer appropriate to the realities of a rapidly expanding national marketplace, one in which business was conducted not only outside one's community but across state lines, has been pointed out by modern critics. For example, Morton Horwitz notes that "[a]lmost from the moment Story's treatise was published, judges and jurists struggled to free themselves from its categories" (*1870–1960* 42).

From a cultural perspective, however, it is more significant that the social and performative characteristics of the con artist not only remain a feature of the corporate agent in US culture, but become even more central in the course of the nineteenth century. In the concluding chapter of her study, Karen Halttunen shows how the con man's art of appearances is reinterpreted as a positive skill through its absorption into the figure of the self-made man. In Horatio Alger's *Ragged Dick* stories, she finds that the protagonist's rise "depends on three qualities new to American success ideology: aggressiveness, charm, and the arts of the confidence man" (202). The latter is now encoded in terms such as "personal magnetism." Echoing Warren Susman's diagnosis of personality being "an effort to solve the problem of the self in a changed social structure that imposes its own special demands on the self," Halttunen explicitly relates this merger of confidence man and self-made man to corporate organization: "After 1870, a new success literature was emerging that effectively instructed its readers to cultivate the arts of the confidence man in order to succeed in the corporate business world" (198).[20] As private replaced public associations, corporate agents, we may say, became a social norm.

While it does not at all approve of this development, De Forest's *Honest John Vane* (1875) offers a glimpse into it. Published after the Civil War, the novel is yet another American retelling of Bunyan's *Pilgrim's Progress* and one that assumes yet a darker, even grotesque tone as it challenges the nation's notions of its progress.[21] This progress is still industrial and economic, but it is also quite explicitly connected to what the book mockingly refers to as "the bloody chasm": the political, economic, and social rift between the North and the South (127). In this regard, *Honest John Vane* is generally less well known than *Miss Ravenel's Conversion from Secession to Loyalty*, which De Forest had published in 1867. *Honest John Vane* tells the story of an everyman character who becomes a politician through the support of a dubious lobbyist, Darius Dorman, and who is quickly caught up in the corruption spawned by what the novel calls "the great Subfluvial Tunnel Road" or simply "the Great Subfluvial" (De Forest, *Honest* 125). In effect, *Honest John Vane* completes the transformation I have outlined above: its protagonist starts out as a mark, a victim of a satanic agent, and successfully, though awkwardly, transforms into a confidence man himself—one who is widely acknowledged to be an honest, self-made man. (In one of the many grotesque twists of the novel, John Vane sells iceboxes before he begins his descent into hell: his career in Washington.) Yet De Forest does not design John Vane as an evil character, just a mediocre one: "[John Vane] was one of those heroes of industry and conquerors of circumstances known as self-made men, whose successes are so full of encouragement to the millions born into mediocrity [. . .]" (De Forest, *Honest* 69). In this regard, the novel joins in the contemporary chorus of voices that loudly questioned the success of the great American experiment, universal suffrage; others included Henry Adams's *Democracy* (1880) and María Amparo Ruiz de Burton's *The Squatter and the Don* (1885). In fact, the novel explores a theme that will become painfully commonplace after the Civil War and, in particular, during the Grant administration: political corruption through

---

[20] While Halttunen analyzes Andrew Carnegie, my study takes a closer look at John D. Rockefeller in Chapter 5.

[21] About the confession that one of the characters gives during a hearing at the end of the novel, the narrator remarks, "It was a new and perversely reversed and altogether bedeviled rendering of the *Pilgrim's Progress* into American politics [. . .]" (De Forest, *Honest* 224). This is also a quite accurate characterization of De Forest's novel.

corporations. One of the most dramatic installments of this theme was the Crédit Mobilier scandal, which involved what was otherwise seen as a noble national enterprise: the transcontinental railroads.

The idea of constructing a transcontinental railroad was initially pursued during the early 1850s, when Secretary of War Jefferson Davis "was authorized to send his Army Topographical Corps to survey five possible transcontinental routes" (Bain 48). As I will discuss in more detail in the next chapter, Davis favored the southern route along the 32nd parallel,[22] but the plan "[fell] victim to the stalemate between the North and the South and the unwillingness of private capital to build the road" (White, *Railroaded* 17). With the beginning of the Civil War, however, a new incentive emerged for building a railroad through what was considered empty land: military supply and control over western territories. In 1862, Congress passed the first of four Pacific Railroad Acts and thereby issued the first federal charter since the First and Second National Banks. Congress chartered the Union Pacific Railroad as a "trunk line" and five more corporations as "branches that would connect it to various points on the Missouri" (White, *Railroaded* 19). The Central Pacific Railroad, a California corporation, existed prior to the Act and was backed by the capitalists that were commonly known as the Big Four: Collis P. Huntington, Leland Stanford, Mark Hopkins, and Charles Crocker.[23] Extensive land grants to the corporation, dispossessing Native Americans, as well as $50 million in government bonds subsidized the enterprise.[24]

Both California and federal law provided several obstacles, among which a personal liability clause proved most pertinent to the promoters. These personal liability clauses meant that "[i]f the railroad failed to pay the debts that its construction created, the debtors could sue the stockholders" (White, *Railroaded* 28). To evade the provision, the presidents of the Union Pacific "purchased an investment company [. . .] originally designed to build a southern transcontinental. Its only real asset was its very broad and flexible charter" (White, *Railroaded* 28). After renaming it, the Crédit Mobilier

---

[22] See Bain 51–2.

[23] At the beginning the group included Edwin Crocker, a lawyer and Charles's brother.

[24] That the land granted to the railroad did not actually belong to the US, but to Native Americans, seemed an advantage. "Instead of land grants from the public domain complicated by competing claims from settlers, land might pass directly from Indians to railroads" (White, *Railroaded* 25). This was first put into practice by Senator Samuel Pomeroy of Kansas, otherwise known as Senator Dilworthy in Twain's *The Gilded Age*. He included a provision for the sale of land to a railroad in a treaty with the Kickapoo tribe, against which the latter protested but to no avail. "The treaty stood as a model of how treaties could deliver land directly to corporations, which could then sell the land at a markup to finance railroads" (White, *Railroaded* 25).

served as a shield between stockholders and debtors: it was "a limited liability venture," and

> [b]y the terms of its charter, neither the Crédit Mobilier nor its stockholders were responsible for the failure of any firms whose stocks it acquired. Second, the Crédit Mobilier not only was a finance company but it could also be a construction company that was to build the railroads. (White, *Railroaded* 28)

In its latter role, it meant the Union Pacific was negotiating with itself, and the Crédit Mobilier would charge more for construction than the actual cost. In 1872, four years after the line's completion and during the presidential campaign, Charles Dana's *New York Sun* broke the story, "proclaim[ing]," as Richard White records, "the Crédit Mobilier 'The King of Frauds'" (*Railroaded* 63).

What is significant about De Forest's treatment of the scandal is how the novel correlates its protagonist's utter moral emptiness with the emptiness of the corporate enterprise. While it is a reputation "easily [acquired]," by the standards of his community John Vane starts out as an honest man (De Forest, *Honest* 94). But once he leaves this community, he adapts to the corrupt standards of Washington. In the words of Darius Dorman: "I have looked into the very bottom of John Vane's thimbleful of soul. I know every sort and fashion of man that he will make up into, under the scissoring of diverse circumstances. John has no character of his own. [. . .] If his constituents ever find him out, they won't call him Honest John Vane, but Weathercock Vane" (De Forest, *Honest* 133). At the end of the novel, "his cockle-shell of a character" emptied out, only his reputation remains, and yet John Vane succeeds in "getting up a new and revised edition of his character as Honest John Vane" that ultimately allows him not only to stay in office but to actually prosper in Washington (De Forest, *Honest* 198, 225). The metaphor of the "shell" correlates with De Forest's depiction of the Union Pacific Railroad as "the great Subfluvial Tunnel Road": not only subterranean (like the Black Rapids Coal Mine), a tunnel is also a decidedly empty structure. It is an appropriate symbol for a fake holding company with no capital of its own and as such a mere front. As subsequent chapters will show, such empty tunnels or shells would become more prevalent in law as well as in literature; in 1890, novelist Charles W. Chesnutt calls such a fictional enterprise "the Universal Subterranean Development Company" (*Business Career* 194).[25]

---

[25] Chesnutt may have been referring to the Union Pacific, given that one of the characters also refers to the Crédit Mobilier scandal (*Business Career* 193).

The hollowness of John Vane and other characters in the novel also signifies upon the novel's position between political allegory and naturalism. Leo B. Levy sees *Honest John Vane* as a proto-naturalist novel and has argued that "the categorizing which allegory promotes [. . .] also lends itself to the reductive view of character found in naturalistic fiction" (96). Yet as this brief overview of corporate agents in literary fictions has also shown, there is a close association between corporations and language's loss of substance. In "The Celestial Railroad," Mr. Smooth-it-away persistently manipulates words and names to convey the progress that the corporation supposedly represents, while the con artist's use of language in Melville's *The Confidence-Man* fully destabilizes meaning without the relief of allegorical knowledge. Darius Dorman's and ultimately John Vane's dealings with a shell corporation therefore can be said to epitomize this tendency toward emptiness or lack of substance, which this chapter has related to the mid-nineteenth-century changes in how Americans made use of the corporate form and the ways in which courts and lawyers interpreted it.

The next chapter focuses on a single literary text and on the legal and political debates over corporations in California during the 1880s. María Amparo Ruiz de Burton's *The Squatter and the Don* (1885) shares similarities with De Forest's work, in particular in how it dramatizes corporate monopoly and corruption as a problem of national (dis)unity. It is also connected to *Louisville Rail-road* v. *Letson* in that it criticizes the transportation monopoly of the Southern Pacific Railroad, which is the corporation in the *California Tax Cases*, in which the Court would indirectly comment on whether corporations should be considered persons under the Fourteenth Amendment. And it is connected, through its subject as much as through its treatment thereof, to better-known literary treatments of the so-called Mussel Slough shooting, such as Frank Norris's *The Octopus* (1901). Emerging from this legal, political, and literary network, *The Squatter and the Don* presents a unique take on the late nineteenth-century formation of corporate monopoly through its interrogation of the latter's private and public properties—or, as the period would call it, its "quasi public" nature.

4

Incorporating the Nation:
Ruiz de Burton and
"Quasi Public" Corporations

When President Abraham Lincoln signed the Pacific Railway Act in 1862, the document created the Union Pacific Railroad, the first federally chartered corporation since the Second Bank of the United States. The purpose of this corporation was to build the eastern part of the first transcontinental railroad. The western part, building from Sacramento, was given to the Central Pacific Railroad, a company that had been incorporated in California the previous year. To finance the undertaking, the Act also authorized the issuance of government bonds and federal grants of land to the railroads. Before the outbreak of war, the project had taken up years of debates in Congress. Among the proposed routes, a line along the 32nd parallel had been favored by the southern states, whereas the northern states had preferred a central route. In 1862, the building of the transcontinental railroad was a matter of the preservation of the West for the Union North. "The railroad to the Pacific," C. Vann Woodward explains, "was part of the struggle for control over the Western territories, and part of the contest for sectional balance of power; it was behind the Kansas-Nebraska Act and the repeal of the Missouri Compromise" (92).

After the war and during Reconstruction, it became a matter of national unity: of bringing North and South closer together by facilitating travel and commerce across the continent. Published in 1886, Henry Field's collection of travel sketches, *Blood Is Thicker Than Water*, illustrates this point. When his train arrives at Danville, Virginia, the cars have to be lifted onto the southern tracks on account of the difference in width of northern and southern gauges. Field marvels at the process, and then adds:

> In a few weeks the gauge of the whole railway system of the South is to be changed to conform to that of the North. It will cost millions, but the object is thought to be worth it all. May we not interpret this as a happy symbol of

other changes by which the course of things North and South is hereafter to be run on the same track to the end of common prosperity? (16)

And even though the sentiment is declared by the satanic railroad agent, even De Forest's *Honest John Vane* expresses this idea repeatedly: "Close up the bloody chasm. Bind together the national unity in chains of cast-iron" (De Forest, *Honest* 126–7). As De Forest's work stresses throughout, in all of this lay a certain irony: whether it was the fact that the Union Pacific was part of the largest case of corporate fraud the country had seen so far (the Crédit Mobilier scandal), or the fact that Henry Field was the brother of Stephen Field, who would be instrumental in laying the foundations for corporations' Fourteenth Amendment protections. But for other writers, the turn of (national) events in which corporations had begun to figure so prominently was less ironic than desperate and outrageous. This is particularly apparent from a cluster of texts that depict California's Central Pacific and Southern Pacific Railroads and the infamous railroad monopoly that controlled traffic in California at the end of the nineteenth century. Among these texts are María Amparo Ruiz de Burton's *The Squatter and the Don* (1885), Josiah Royce's *The Feud of Oakfield Creek* (1887), and Frank Norris's *The Octopus* (1901).

With these works, specifically the novels by Ruiz de Burton and Norris, and the events that inspired and influenced them, the following two chapters refocus on corporations as monopolies and as collective entities rivaling the power of the people. The Central Pacific had been incorporated in California in 1861 by a group of merchants and hardware dealers who would become known as the Big Four: Leland Stanford, Collis P. Huntington, Mark Hopkins, and Charles Crocker. Stanford and Huntington acted as president and vice president of the Central Pacific respectively. In 1868, the group also bought the Southern Pacific Railroad, which had originally been incorporated for the purpose of building a connection between San Francisco and San Diego. In 1885, the Southern Pacific bought and merged lines with the Central Pacific. In 1886, the Southern Pacific became party to one of the popularly best-known corporate law cases in the nineteenth century, the *Santa Clara* case. In the popular imaginary, moreover, the Southern Pacific became strongly associated with what continues to be one of the best-known corporate tropes: the octopus.

The present chapter takes as its point of departure the debates over railroad monopoly and the relationship between state and private corporations during California's Second Constitutional Convention (1878–9). I argue that the scholarly focus on the assumed triumph of corporate personhood during this period has eclipsed the significance that so-called quasi-public corporations held in the popular imaginary as well as the (racial) anxiety raised by the corporation's inherent multitudinousness. While the previous chapter stressed the effect of the corporation's development into a tool of private business rather than an instrument of public utility, the present chapter shows that this was by no means a complete transformation, whether legally or culturally. After discussing the anti-monopoly rhetoric of the Convention and how the latter's debate would lead to *Santa Clara*, Section III turns to María Amparo Ruiz de Burton's *The Squatter and the Don* (1885). Ruiz de Burton's unique vision of what California delegates called "monster monopolies" draws on and goes beyond established anti-monopoly rhetoric, and it ultimately aligns different corporate bodies in an effort to sketch a republican future for California and the nation (*Debates I* 402). Unlike De Forest's satire or Norris's romantic naturalism, the sentimental style of Ruiz de Burton's novel allows her to explore the theme of national unity and republican grandeur through the metaphors of family and marriage and thereby emphasizes issues of contract, obligation, and accountability vis-à-vis the corporation. In the final section of this chapter, I take a closer look at the aspect of race in the discourse on corporations during this period. In particular, I show how anti-monopoly and anti-Chinese discourses intersected precisely because they violated the ideology of liberal individualism that defined much of Reconstruction.

I. California's Constitutional Convention

While not primarily about corporations or railroad monopolies, California's Second Constitutional Convention (1878–9) set in motion a chain of events that would lead to one of today's most well-known corporate rights cases, *Santa Clara County* v. *Southern Pacific Railroad Company* (1886). The case is known for its headnote: a brief commentary that was added by J. C. Bancroft Davis, the court reporter on the day, in which Chief Justice Morrison Waite is reported to have noted that "[t]he court does not wish to hear argument on the question whether the provision in the Fourteenth Amendment to the Constitution [. . .] applies to these corporations. We are all of opinion that it does" (*Santa Clara* v. *Southern Pacific* 396). Twentieth-century scholarship has tended to identify *Santa Clara* and its headnote as the beginning of modern corporate personhood, and late twentieth-century court rulings have certainly contributed to such retrospective interpretation. But there is ample evidence that in 1886, the US Supreme Court did not yet regard corporations as individual legal persons worthy of constitutional protection, but continued to understand them as group entities whose individuals were the subjects of constitutional rights. The focus on corporate personhood has also tended to eclipse the fact that, during this period, Americans understood some private corporations to be "quasi public." In *Munn* v. *Illinois* (1876), the US Supreme Court ruled that some private enterprises, such as railroads or grain elevators, exercised "a sort of public office," because the public had an interest in their use (*Munn* v. *Illinois* 130). Accordingly, the state would step in to regulate those enterprises for the common good if the need arose. To some extent, this conviction also fueled the debates over the role of corporations in California during the Constitutional Convention in Sacramento, and no group was more outspokenly anti-corporate than the Workingmen's Party.

The delegates that were sent to the Convention in 1878 consisted of Republicans, Democrats, and representatives from two recent populist movements: the Workingmen's Party of California (WPC) and the Grange, both of whose politics were decidedly anti-railroad. The Grange was a farmers' movement that had begun as an anti-monopoly group in the West in the 1860s and that led to the passage of new regulatory laws in Illinois, Iowa, Wisconsin, and Minnesota, among others. After the Civil War, the Grange—or the National Grange of the Order of Patrons of Husbandry—had spread quickly through the northern states. "By the early 1870s, the Upper Mississippi Valley was the centre of the railroad regulatory movement. By then, the Grangers (an agrarian self-help group) were established throughout the region" (Ritter 51).

The Workingmen's Party in California was a more recent phenomenon. It was a movement that was both anti-corporate and anti-Chinese, and it consolidated the high number of unemployed men who wandered the streets of San Francisco. At its center stood Dennis Kearney, a thirty-one-year-old Irishman who had stepped up one night in September of 1877 and addressed the crowd. Within weeks, such meetings became regular, and by early 1878, the movement had organized into a party that carried elections. The anti-monopoly rhetoric that the Workingmen employed was not new, of course, and was reminiscent of the Jacksonian era. For example, in their principles of organization they opposed the concentration of capital for which corporations had figured in the 1830s: "We propose to destroy the great money power of the rich by a system of taxation that will make great wealth impossible in the future" (Davis 366). They also evoked the destruction of the republic by an oligarchy:

> The rich have ruled us until they have ruined us. We will now take our own affairs into our own hands. The republic must and shall be preserved, and only workingmen will do it. Our shoddy aristocrats want an emperor and a standing army to shoot down the people. (Davis 367)

Yet the WPC were not alone in their critique of corporate monopoly.

Historians identify three main areas in which the delegates to the Constitutional Convention had to address the role and influence of the railroad corporations in California: land ownership, transportation, and taxation. The distribution of land ownership was a problem because after the Civil War too much land was in private hands in California. By 1869, historian R. Jeffrey Lustig notes, "almost a third of the state's 100 million acres [. . .] had been claimed" (49). The Central Pacific, which later became part of the Southern Pacific, held "12 percent of the state's land area" based on federal grants (49). "In addition to almost 9 million acres tied up in former Mexican land grants," Lustig explains, "another 8 million acres of federal lands intended for schools, swampland reclamation, and public services had been disposed of by speculators" (49). Secondly, the Central Pacific Railroad held a transportation and freight monopoly that meant farmers had no choice but to pay the railroad's rates if they wanted to sell their wheat. Controlling transportation in California also meant that the corporation held the power to decide "which businesses and towns would boom and which would bust" (Lustig 50). Thirdly, California's 1849 Constitution provided for uniform and equal taxation but did not define what constituted taxable property. As a result, California's tax system favored corporations and wealthy businessmen because "bank credits in 1878 were not classified as taxable property, large landholdings held for speculation were taxed only lightly, and portions of railroad property were totally untaxed" (Lustig 50).

The delegates formed committees for these issues that would regularly report back to the delegates at large. The "Committee on Corporations Other Than Municipal" was chaired by Morris M. Estee, a Republican lawyer. Highly critical of corporate monopoly in California, Estee was nonetheless a pragmatist. In a speech to the delegates, he explained that combinations were inevitable and described the present moment of corporate power as "a new era":

> [N]early all the great business enterprises of the country are in the hands of corporations. The insurance business is conducted by corporations, the banking business is conducted by corporations, the mining business is in the hands of corporations, the entire carrying trade of the country, not only of the Pacific Coast but of the whole nation, is in the hands of corporations. Natural persons no longer control these great interests. (*Debates I* 377)

The railroads, moreover, presented an unprecedented influence in people's lives, whether with regard to their transportation of resources and commodities or with regard to how they had become indispensable to individual mobility. Nobody, Estee observed, plans a visit "to his old home in the East" without thinking of taking the railroad (*Debates I* 377). But precisely because railroad monopoly had become "so immense—[. . .] [so] grand in all its proportions," it had also become a threat to the republic. "The political and financial power of railroads in the United States are immense, and have become a grand *imperium in imperio*—a government within a government, a power within a power" (*Debates I* 377). Yet, despite such immense power, the people could decide to regulate these corporations—and the US Supreme Court had handed them the legal tools to do so.

The Supreme Court case to which Morris Estee and others referred in this respect was *Munn v. The State of Illinois* (1876). This was one of the so-called Granger cases, a set of six lawsuits that challenged the constitutionality of states' regulation of private companies. Except for Munn & Scott, all the companies were incorporated railroads, and in all cases, regulation was based on statutory reservation clauses; that is, the states had reserved the right to amend corporate charters either in their constitutions or as part of the original charters. *Munn v. Illinois* received the most detailed opinion of the Court, though it may seem an odd choice for a representative case: instead of a railroad, it concerned a grain elevator business in Chicago that was not even incorporated. Nonetheless, even in these unusual circumstances the Court ruled that regulation was not dependent upon a charter detailing privileges and duties, but followed from the nature of the market in which a business was engaged. In other words, the right to regulate the business did not depend on whether the property had been *chartered* for public use, but whether it was *put* to public use. In Chief Justice Morrison Waite's words: "Common carriers exercise a sort of public office" (*Munn v. Illinois* 130). Though it was not employed in *Munn v. Illinois*, the term that was most commonly used to designate corporations of such a nature was "quasi public."

The first remedy for corporate monopoly proposed by Estee's Committee was the creation of a railroad commission that would assess and set transportation rates in California and that would receive the power to enforce those rates. In practice, however, the commission was a paper tiger because "[it] never effectively fixed freight rates and passenger fares below what the Southern Pacific or other lines were prepared to accept. In some instances, railroad commissioners were simply paid off" (Rolston 548). The second remedy proposed by the Committee was taxation. The Constitution of 1849 called for "equal and uniform" taxation and therefore allowed individuals and corporations equally to deduct mortgages and other forms of debt prior to the tax assessment. But as one delegate put it, it was precisely for that reason that taxation of real estate had long ceased to be "equal and uniform" in California. Section 4 of Article XIII ("Revenue and Taxation") of California's new Constitution would therefore except "railroads and other quasi public corporations" from this provision.

II. The *California Tax Cases*

There is a direct connection between the new Constitution's exception for "railroads and other quasi public corporations" in California and one of the most famous corporate rights cases, *Santa Clara County* v. *Southern Pacific Railroad Company*. Scholars often refer to *Dartmouth College* (1819) and *Santa Clara* (1886) in the same breath and imply that separate corporate personhood had become a universally accepted fact by the late nineteenth century, such as in the following example:

> In the *Dartmouth College* v. *Woodward* case of 1819, Chief Justice John Marshall incisively shifted the matrix by defining the corporation as an artificial person, created only in law. By 1886, when the Supreme Court applied several aspects of the Fourteenth Amendment to corporations, constitutional law was fine-tuning the similarities and differences between these artificial persons and human persons. (Leverenz 26)

However, as should be evident by now, such statements about the nineteenth-century ascendancy of corporate personhood oversimplify a complex development. Moreover, they ignore the debate over what constituted "quasi public" corporations, over the conditions under which the sovereign could legitimately regulate private property, and, ultimately, over the role of collectives in a democracy.

To explore these questions we must first take a closer look at the *California Tax Cases*, a set of lawsuits in which the counties sued the Southern Pacific for outstanding tax payments and of which *Santa Clara* would emerge as the most prominent. As I will explain in more detail presently, the US Supreme Court did not actually rule on the question of whether corporations were protected by the Fourteenth Amendment. In order to understand the extent to which it was possible at the time to conceive of corporations' rights in those terms at all, we have to turn to a prior case, in which Henry Field's brother Stephen played a pivotal role. But even in the case of the most pro-corporate rulings, it is evident that courts did not understand corporations as individual legal persons and subjects of constitutional protections in the way that much later scholarship (and some jurisprudence) have suggested. Rather, the courts understood the question as one of the protections of individual shareholders' and members' rights, because they still thought of corporations as aggregates of individuals. As group entities, moreover, corporations were part of a much larger debate over the place and power of collectives in the republic.

The conflict over the taxation of railroad property in California reached the US Supreme Court because the railroads simply refused to pay the newly calculated taxes. The counties which were responsible for the collection of those taxes, among them Santa Clara and San Mateo counties, sued the Southern Pacific and Central Pacific railroads for payment. While the California Supreme Court found in favor of the counties, the Ninth Circuit Court found in favor of the railroads. By December 1885, the tax cases reached the US Supreme Court under Chief Justice Morrison Waite, which issued an opinion in *Santa Clara* that consolidated the cases.

The key to *Santa Clara*'s fame is the defense's challenge of Section 4 of Article XIII of California's new Constitution on the basis of the Fourteenth Amendment's Equal Protection Clause. The railroads' lawyers argued that the Section "denied [corporations] the equal protection of the laws guaranteed by the Fourteenth Amendment of the Federal Constitution" (*San Mateo County v. Southern Pacific* 246). The counties' lawyers, on the other hand, insisted that "the power of taxation possessed by the State is unlimited, except by the Constitution of the United States" and averred "[t]hat corporations are not persons within the meaning of that amendment" (*San Mateo County v. Southern Pacific* 247). The Supreme Court ultimately ruled in favor of the railroads, but it did so on much narrower grounds than the defense had proposed. Writing for the majority, Justice John Harlan explained that in calculating the railroads' taxable property, the State Board had included "the value of the fences" that ran along the railroad tracks and separated them from adjacent properties, but "that the fences did not constitute a part of such roadway" (*Santa Clara v. Southern Pacific* 411). The case could therefore be decided without the Court having to "consider the grave questions of constitutional law upon which the case was determined below" (*Santa Clara v. Southern Pacific* 411).

Despite the fact that the US Supreme Court decided the *California Tax Cases* in favor of the railroad corporations by pointing out that the State Board had made a mistake when it calculated the companies' taxable property, scholars have often interpreted *Santa Clara* as a case that affirmed corporate rights and sometimes even as the beginning of the natural entity theory. Such interpretations usually focus on the case's famous headnote, which precedes the opinion of the Court. Headnotes (as well as syllabi) are composed by court reporters and make the court rulings more accessible, but they are not part of the actual ruling. In the case of *Santa Clara*, the court reporter was J. C. Bancroft Davis, who had a reputation for writing syllabi and headnotes that expressed his personal interpretation of cases more than the official record.[1] Even though *Santa Clara* was explicitly not decided on constitutional grounds, Davis's headnote observes,

> One of the points made and discussed at length in the brief of counsel for defendants in error was that "Corporations are persons within the meaning

[1]   See Adam Winkler's discussion of Davis, 149–50.

of the Fourteenth Amendment to the Constitution of the United States."
Before argument MR. CHIEF JUSTICE WAITE said: The court does
not wish to hear argument on the question whether the provision in the
Fourteenth Amendment to the Constitution, which forbids a State to deny
to any person within its jurisdiction the equal protection of the laws, applies
to these corporations. We are all of opinion that it does. (*Santa Clara* v.
Southern Pacific 396)

The headnote clearly misrepresents the case, and yet it has enjoyed a long
afterlife. For one thing, it may have received the attention that it has because
of the "conspiracy theory" of the Fourteenth Amendment, which emerged
from Charles and Mary Beard's *The Rise of American Civilization* (1927).
Having studied the *California Tax Cases* as well as the debates over the passage
of the Fourteenth Amendment during Reconstruction, the Beards argued
that the wording of the Fourteenth Amendment (in particular the choice of
"person" rather than "citizen") was carefully chosen so as to allow the future
protection of economic interests rather than African Americans' civil rights.[2]
Whereas this theory has long been debunked, a more lasting reason why the
headnote has retained its influence over corporate law may have been the fact
that it was quickly written into actual rulings. As Adam Winkler has pointed
out, in the years following *Santa Clara*, Supreme Court Justice Stephen Field
slipped the headnote's misrepresentation of *Santa Clara* into at least two cases
and thereby gave it life.[3]

But it is important to stress that even as Justice Field promoted the
idea that corporations are persons within the meaning of the Fourteenth
Amendment's Equal Protection Clause, he was not advocating corporations'
separate legal personhood in the way that those in favor of the natural entity
would have (or as Legaré had suggested in *Louisville Rail-road* v. *Letson*). For
Field, corporations had a right to equal protection of the laws because they
consisted of people: "Private corporations are, it is true, artificial persons,
but [. . .] they consist of aggregations of individuals united for some legitimate business" (*San Mateo County* v. *Southern Pacific* 264). Field had laid

---

[2] For a detailed discussion of the "conspiracy theory" see Graham, *Everyman's Constitution:
Historical Essays on the Fourteenth Amendment, the "Conspiracy Theory," and American
Constitutionalism*; Adam Winkler presents a highly accessible summary of the contro-
versy in *We the Corporations*. Also see *Corporations and American Democracy* by Novak and
Lamoreaux.

[3] The cases were *Pembina Consolidated Silver Mining Company* v. *Pennsylvania* (1888) and
Minneapolis & St. Louis Railway Company v. *Beckwith* (1889). Winkler notes, "Field embed-
ded in his majority opinion language that would go far to serve the interests of railroads and
other corporations for generations to come" (156).

out his interpretation in his ruling in *San Mateo County* v. *Southern Pacific Railroad* (1882), when he served as a judge in the Ninth District Court. The *San Mateo* decision preceded the Supreme Court's in *Santa Clara*, but it is nonetheless instructive because it reveals how corporations were understood as aggregate entities and would still receive rights that are commonly understood to apply to individuals.

In effect, Field explored a line of reasoning going back to at least the Marshall Court's decision in *Deveaux* (1809): that incorporation did not deprive the individual members of their rights.[4] In his ruling in *San Mateo* (1882), Field emphasized the existence of "private individual[s]" behind the corporation of whose rights the corporate persona was only a representation.

> [W]e think that it is well established by numerous adjudications of the Supreme Court of the United States, and of the several States, that whenever a provision of the Constitution, or of a law, guarantees to persons the enjoyment of property, or affords to them means for its protection, or prohibits legislation injuriously affecting it, the benefits of the provision extend to corporations, and that the Courts will always look beyond the name of the artificial being to the individuals whom it represents. (*San Mateo County* v. *Southern Pacific* 265)

At a time when piercing the corporate veil became associated more with questions of corporate liability, Field was reminding his audience that piercing the veil should work both ways: to hold shareholders, managers, etc. accountable and liable, but also to protect their rights. While the delegates at the California Convention had rhetorically asked, "Why should a corporation be more favored than a private individual?" (*Debates I* 401), Field essentially asked, why should it be favored less?

III. Ruiz de Burton's *The Squatter and the Don*

For the delegates at the Convention in Sacramento, as much as for the majority of California's citizens, the question of corporations' equal treatment was not a merely academic one. As the speeches of and exchanges among delegates across the political spectrum show, the railroad corporations had reached a scale of control and power within the state that evoked fears of *imperium in imperio*. The Central Pacific Railroad and the Southern Pacific were not some "peanut stand" corporations, but "monster monopolies" (*Debates I* 169, 402). Reminiscent of Jacksonian fears of a secret takeover of the republic

---

[4] For a detailed discussion, see Helfman, "Transatlantic Influences on American Corporate Jurisprudence: Theorizing the Corporation in the United States."

by oligarchical powers, delegates such as Clitus Barbour, a prominent San Francisco lawyer and delegate of the Workingmen's Party, described the corporations as an organized threat to the sovereignty of the people.

> What are the attributes of sovereignty? Eminent domain—the right to take private property for public use, on compensation? The Central Pacific Railroad Company goes around over the State and bullies the citizen with this assumption of power. Nay, sir, bullies the State itself, and even assumes the right to take public property for their own private use. Is it the power of taxation? The railroad company knows no limit to the boundless claim to exercise this right beyond the capacity of the people to bear. [. . .] Three or four men sit down in a room and with one scratch of a pen extract a million from the industries of the country. And yet you tell me that there is no necessity for controlling a power like this. They run their car wheels over the liberties of the people, crushing in their devastating career a hecatomb of human hopes, and rear upon their ruins an empire of arbitrary power. [. . .] The question is, who shall exercise the sovereign power of the State? These railroad corporations never injured me. I fear not their threats and I care not for their favors. But my philosophy teaches me that [. . .] if we expect to maintain in California anything like a republican form of government, these corporations must be controlled, and the means must be devised to do so effectually. (*Debates I* 534)

For Clitus Barbour, as for others, the Central Pacific had begun to replace the government of the people by exercising powers reserved for the people and for the benefit of the common good. Eminent domain as well as police powers were reserved for the state, to be exercised only in the interest of the general welfare—and not for private interests. In California's "quasi public" corporations, this distinction had become blurred.

María Amparo Ruiz de Burton's novel *The Squatter and the Don* (1885) draws recognizably on the debates over California's "monster monopolies." The novel's title, for example, is a reference to the Mussel Slough shooting, which occurred in the San Joaquin Valley in 1880.[5] The shooting took place when representatives of the Southern Pacific Railroad, accompanied by a US Marshal, tried to forcibly evict a community of farmers from land that was legally the railroad's. In the aftermath of the violence that ensured, "Mussel Slough came to be venerated by farm, labor, and anti-monopoly civic groups as a site of anti-railroad martyrdom" (Henderson 130). What's more, *The*

---

[5] On the status of Mussel Slough in California's public discourse at the time see Conlogue, "Farmers' Rhetoric of Defense: California Settlers versus the Southern Pacific Railroad."

Squatter and the Don was first published under the pseudonym "C. Loyal" or "Citizen Loyal," and it concludes with a chapter in which the narrator once more highlights the power of the railroads in California, fittingly titled "Out with the Invader."

Accordingly, much early scholarship on *The Squatter and the Don* has understood the novel in terms of social protest or reform fiction.[6] The references to Mussel Slough, for example, have been taken as a sign that the novel is "siding with the vigilante unrest that grew out of [the Mussel Slough shooting]" (Aranda Jr., "Vigilantism" 11). As the work of a recovered Chicana author whose novels were republished in the early 1990s, *The Squatter and the Don* was also initially celebrated as giving voice to the subaltern. But such readings have since been complicated—by scholars who have explored what José F. Aranda Jr. has described as "contradictory impulses" in Ruiz de Burton's work, in particular the racist depiction of African Americans and *Indios* and the endorsement of a white aristocratic *Californio* elite,[7] and also by scholars such as Brook Thomas, who has pointed out that the novel endorses not an agrarian but a commercial future for California (*Reconstruction* 213). Indeed, Ruiz de Burton's novel offers a view of corporations at that time that is anti-monopoly, yet not anti-corporate.

"Contradictory impulses" are part of Ruiz de Burton's rather unique vision of the role and power of corporations in California, with which she had also had personal experience. For starters, she was the first Mexican American woman to publish literature written in English. Born in Baja California in 1831, she had met her husband, Lieutenant Colonel Henry S. Burton, during the Mexican-American War. In 1852 the couple moved to San Diego, a rural region at the time, where Burton had been "ordered to serve as a commander of the garrison" (*S&D* vi). While in San Diego, the couple invested in railway lines that would eventually be incorporated into the Texas Pacific, the Southern Pacific's rival. During the 1860s the Burtons lived on the East Coast, where Ruiz de Burton "met politicians of all kinds" and even "attended Abraham Lincoln's inauguration" (*S&D* vii). After her husband's death in 1869, Ruiz de Burton struggled financially. She had two children and herself to support, with "no 'real assets'—since titles to what she claimed were nebulous, encumbered, or tied up in litigation" (Ruiz de Burton, *Conflicts* 374).

---

[6] See, for example, Warford, "'An Eloquent and Impassioned Plea': The Rhetoric of Ruiz de Burton's *The Squatter and the Don*."

[7] For a discussion of how class trumps over ethnicity in the novel's construction of an imagined community see Raab, "The Imagined Inter-American Community of María Amparo Ruiz de Burton," as well as Ruiz de Burton's earlier novel, *Who Would Have Thought It?*

In addition to existing debts, Ruiz de Burton needed money to defend her land titles in court: two tracts of land that she and her husband had bought in Baja California, one of which she hoped would prove rich with copper and silver, and another which had been in her family since 1805 (S&D vii, viii). She wrote two novels, a play, and in addition a legal brief, a mining prospectus, and several newspaper articles (S&D viii). In The Squatter and the Don, her knowledge of California politics and her experience in writing (and arguing about) legal and economic questions provide a unique perspective on corporate monopoly.

In particular, the novel criticizes "quasi public" corporate enterprises: corporations that not only exercised "a sort of public office," but had also received public grants and subsidies to do so. In The Squatter and the Don, this mixing of public money and private enterprise destroys the democracy of the market and the law of competition. Moreover, the novel connects these matters of commerce to matters of sovereignty by including the issue of Californio landownership and of the future of the post-Reconstruction South. The metaphor that connects such matters of private enterprise, state sovereignty, and imperialism is the metaphor of the body. By highlighting the structural homology between bodies corporate and bodies politic, The Squatter and the Don succeeds in going beyond established anti-monopoly rhetoric and complicating our understanding of corporate power and agency in this period.

The novel is set in the first half of the 1870s and basically tells the story of two families, as reflected in its title. The novel's focus, however, is on the Alamar family. The Alamares are of old Spanish stock and have lived as land-owners in Alta California since before the Mexican-American War, yet by the beginning of the novel, they have been increasingly marginalized and will ultimately be dispossessed by legislation that favors Anglo farmers over Mexican ranchers. Representative of a virtuous Spanish American past, yet separated from Mexico after the treaty of Guadalupe Hidalgo (1848), the Alamares patiently endure a growing number of so-called squatters on their property in Southern California while they wait for the federal government to officially recognize and thereby also to protect their ownership of the estate. The head of the family is Don Mariano Alamar, a kind father and experienced rancher who tries to protect his real estate and his cattle from the so-called squatters. The latter's views are represented by a second family, the Darrells. Their patriarch is William Darrell, a stubborn Yankee who moves his family to Southern California to start a new life on a farm. The conflict between these two families is about who has a lawful claim to the land, and while it is to some extent modeled after the event popularly known as the Battle of

Mussel Slough, the historical conflicts on which it is ultimately based originate in the United States' imperialist expansionism.[8]

The war between Mexico and the United States ended with the Treaty of Guadelupe Hidalgo in 1848, which "ced[ed] almost half of [Mexico's] territory (which incorporated present-day states of California, New Mexico, Nevada, and parts of Colorado, Arizona, Utah, and even Oklahoma) to the United States, in return for $15 million" (Acuña 56). The original treaty not only promised citizenship to the Mexicans who chose to stay in California (such as the Alamar family in *The Squatter and the Don*), it also promised protection for their land grants. However, the article specifying protection of property was deleted a few months later by the US Senate,[9] and only three years after the treaty Congress passed the "California Land Act of 1851": "Proposed by Senator William Gwin of California, this bill forced all landed *californios* to have their grants and titles reviewed for certification by the Land Commission, in effect placing all titles in abeyance" (Ruiz de Burton, *Conflicts* 87). At the beginning of the novel, the reader learns that the Don's title is still not cleared (it is January 1872), and that therefore his property officially belongs to the United States and hence can be settled by whoever stakes a claim. To add to the conflicts arising from the arrival of strangers, who—from the Don's perspective—are "squatters" illegally occupying his land, Congress has also passed laws for taxes and liability that disadvantage the Mexican grantees: "we (the landowners)," as the Don explains, "have to pay the taxes on the land cultivated by the preemptors, and upon all the improvements they make and enjoy" (*S&D* 27). Moreover, a new "no fence law" requires the ranchers, rather than the farmers, to fence in their (much larger) property to keep cattle from trespassing upon farmland, thereby presenting an example of special interest legislation that puts *Californios* at a disadvantage (*S&D* 47).

While this is the conflict to which the novel's title refers, it gradually drops into the background as a larger one comes into view. This second conflict is between two railroad corporations over who will build a southern line into California. In the novel, the two corporations are the Southern Pacific Railroad, represented by Leland Stanford, and the Texas Pacific Railroad, represented by Tom Scott. The Alamar family is part of this plot as well because Don Mariano (as well as his friend James Mechlin) have invested in San Diego real estate in anticipation of the new railroad line that will connect the town

---

[8]   As I will discuss in more detail in the next chapter, Ruiz de Burton models the conflict after the Mussel Slough event to the extent that she identifies one party with the railroad corporations and the other as small landowners. But in contrast to the real conflict, it is the squatters that are identified with the railroads in her novel.

[9]   See Acuña 56–9.

to the nation's commercial network. The Southern Pacific ultimately succeeds in maintaining its monopoly in California, and beats the Texas Pacific—however, without completing the line for San Diego. As a direct consequence of this decision, Don Mariano goes bankrupt and ultimately dies of grief.

Once more, the novel's plot of corporate competition and corruption is based on historical events, but altered in such a way that they express more powerfully the novel's anti-monopoly message. Originally chartered in 1871, the Texas Pacific Railway was supposed to build a line between Marshall, Texas, and San Diego along the 32nd parallel, which had been considered as an option for a transcontinental railroad before the Civil War. "[The Texas Pacific] was the last road to receive a substantial federal land grant: roughly eighteen million acres," as well as the "federal and state land grants" that its "failed predecessors" had been given (White, *Railroaded* 94). The Texas Pacific Railroad's charter also stipulated that the Central Pacific Railroad (in the novel, the competitor is the Southern Pacific) had rights to build into Southern California and meet the Texas Pacific at the border of California and Arizona. But as Brook Thomas explains, the Central Pacific did not stop at the border but went ahead and built along the route that the Texas Pacific was intending to use, "without the government subsidies demanded by [the Texas Pacific]" (*Reconstruction* 222).

The crucial difference between the historical Texas Pacific and the Texas Pacific as represented in Ruiz de Burton's novel is the significance of subsidies in the building of those railroad lines. At the center of its anti-monopoly critique, the novel sets up a contrast between private enterprise and "quasi public" corporations, in which the former is presented as more beneficial for society than the latter. And even though the Texas Pacific did receive public subsidies, the novel aligns it with private enterprise, since its plans to build a line to San Diego would have greatly benefited the individual, private investors in Southern California. When the Southern Pacific succeeds in cutting off the Texas Pacific and decides to bypass San Diego, the novel reveals the economically devastating consequences for the region through the bankruptcy and death of both Don Mariano and his friend James Mechlin, who commits suicide.

The Alamar family teeters on the brink of poverty for several grueling chapters before the novel's third and romantic plot saves them. All along, Don Mariano's daughter Mercedes and William Darrell's son Clarence—the children of the squatter and the don—have been falling in love. Finally, Clarence marries Mercedes, and because he turns out to be a successful financier, he can pay the Alamar family's debts and move them to San Francisco to open a new business. It is through these three interrelated plots that Ruiz de Burton develops her critique of corporate monopoly: the story of the conflict between the squatter and the don over landownership, the story of the battle between the Southern Pacific and Texas Pacific Railroads over the transportation monopoly in California, and finally, the love story of Mercedes Alamar and Clarence Darrell.

The Body Corporate and the Body Politic

As should be evident by now, *The Squatter and the Don* is anti-monopoly but not anti-corporate. In fact, as recent scholarship has shown, Ruiz de Burton's vision for California's future as well as for the future of the South in general was decidedly commercial (rather than agrarian), and corporations played a significant role in that vision. The faultline that runs between "good" and "bad" railroads in the novel is defined by the nature of their property, whether it is private or "quasi public" property (cp. Thomas, *Reconstruction* 216). As we have seen, this critical view of the "quasi public" was common among the delegates of the Constitutional Convention too, but not only on account of the monopoly power that the "quasi public" corporations had seized. There was also a moral aspect to it, which becomes evident in the following passage from John Sharpstein Hager, a Democrat and judge from San Francisco.

> I have heretofore alluded to the fact that this railroad was built by the munificence of the Government of the United States, and the people of the State of California—one half composed of the Union Pacific and the other of the Central Pacific—constitute our great transcontinental road [*sic*]. If the Central Pacific had remained satisfied with this great transcontinental road, there probably might have been less complaint against them. They have been ungrateful to their benefactors. They are not only controlling their end of this great transcontinental road, but it has been and is their intention and ambition to control all the railroads and all the avenues of commerce in this State. [. . .] They own also the Southern Pacific Railroad, which they are now constructing—not without subsidy, [. . .] for they have valuable land subsidy; not for the purpose of controlling the trade of Arizona, as has been said, but for the purpose of heading off Tom Scott and other parties in building a competing transcontinental road, which might interfere with their monopoly. (*Debates I* 593)

The delegate's moral outrage centered on the corporation's ungratefulness—a language that is appropriate to the corporate charter understood as a "sovereign gift" rather than to the corporate charter as a private contract (Barkan 19). But even though the Central Pacific had been authorized by Congress to build the western line of the transcontinental railroad in 1862 and had received land grants and financial subsidies to do so, it was also a private enterprise that had been originally incorporated in California in 1861 and would become part of the Southern Pacific Railroad in 1885. While it served public interests, the "quasi public" corporation was in effect a "hybrid of private and public firms" (Alexander 262).

Like Hager, Ruiz de Burton's novel expresses outrage at the fact that the railroad uses public resources to private ends and refuses to take responsibility for how its actions impact the public welfare. But if the courts, in Justice Stephen Field's words, "will always look beyond the name of the artificial being to the individuals whom it represents" (*San Mateo County* v. *Southern Pacific* 265) to protect those individuals' rights, literature can do the same to hold those individuals accountable. In *The Squatter and the Don*, Ruiz de Burton "pierces the corporate veil" for her readers after the Southern Pacific has defeated its competitor: Don Mariano and his friends and co-investors travel to San Francisco to talk to Leland Stanford and persuade him to continue the work begun by Tom Scott, that is, to complete the line to San Diego (Ramirez 445).

Not an unpleasant man, Stanford is clearly presented in this scene not only as the corporation's president but also as a representative of California's business elite. However, when the Don and his friends question the fairness of preventing the Texas Pacific Railroad from enjoying the "Congressional aid" from which the Southern Pacific benefited, Stanford loses his temper.

> "The Government gave you a grant of many millions of acres to help build it, as the Central Pacific was constructed with Government subsidies, and the earning of the Central Pacific were used to construct the Southern Pacific, it follows that you were helped by the Government to build both," said Mr. Holman.

> "You are talking of something you know nothing about. The help the Government gave us was to guarantee the interest of our bonds. We accepted that help, because we knew that, as private individuals, we might not command the credit necessary to place our bonds in the market, that's all. As for the land subsidy, we will pay every cent of its price with our services. We do not ask of the Government to give us anything gratis. We will give value received for everything." (*S&D* 310)

What is striking about this exchange is how strongly Ruiz de Burton has the fictional Stanford reject the idea that his company had received what Joshua Barkan has called the "sovereign gift." Not a public grant based on what is best for the public welfare, but a simple business transaction in Stanford's eyes, he rejects the symbolic debts incurred by the grant. To lift the corporate veil for her readers is therefore not the sole purpose of Ruiz de Burton's narrative. This is evident from her second narrative strategy.[10]

---

[10] Pablo A. Ramirez and Brook Thomas have shown how Ruiz de Burton relies on Herbert Spencer's anti-monopoly ideas for her argument against a cutthroat capitalist ethic. While I find their readings quite persuasive, the focus of my analysis here is more on the legal than

To criticize the role of corporate power in the republic, the novel's major narrative strategy is to foreground the structural kinship between the body corporate and the body politic on several levels through its use of the metaphor of the body. This is particularly apparent in the novel's portrait of San Diego, and of the consequences of the Southern Pacific's decision to abandon the plan for a railroad line to the town. The organic metaphors that dominate this aspect of the narrative either present San Diego in terms of a child waiting to grow up, or Southern California in general as a limb of the national body. In each case, death and mutilation ensue when the corporation cuts off the region from the nation's commercial blood flow. The following passage imagines the town's transformation from a rural village to a commercial center, if the Texas Pacific Railroad succeeds in building its line:

> These little one-story wooden cottages were intended for temporary dwellings only. By and by the roomy stone or brick mansions would be erected, when the Texas Pacific Railroad—the highway of traffic across the continent—should bring through San Diego the commerce between Asia and the Atlantic Seaboard, between China and Europe. San Diego lived her short hour of hope and prosperity, and smiled and went to sleep on the brink of her own grave [. . .]. (S&D 318)

The second passage follows a description of the legal battles in San Diego's courts after the railroad plans have been crushed:

> But this order of things (or rather disorder) could not have been possible if the Texas Pacific Railroad had not been strangled, as San Diego would not then be the poor, crippled, and dwarfed little city that she now is. (S&D 337)

This motif of mutilation, or rather strangulation, is repeated in the narrative of the Alamar and Mechlin families. Similar to San Diego, they experience the foreclosure of their economic hopes and an end to their prosperity in terms of physical disability. For example, Don Mariano's son Victoriano suddenly loses control over his legs and can no longer walk.

> "What is the matter, my boy?" asked [Don Mariano].
>
> "Father, I cannot stand up. From my knees down I have lost all feeling, and have no control of my limbs at all."

the economic aspects of the monopoly debate. See also the next chapter and my discussion of Frank Norris's depiction of Shelgrim.

"Have you rubbed them to start circulation? They are benumbed with the cold, I suppose." (*S&D* 292)

In addition to Victoriano's sudden paralysis, Clarence Darrell takes to bed with a severe case of pneumonia, and George Mechlin is shot in the hip: while the "wound was not mortal, [. . .] it would be of a long and painful convalescence, with the danger, almost certainty, of leaving him lame for life" (*S&D* 287). These injuries and sicknesses reinforce the theme of stunted growth and strangulation that originates in the Southern Pacific Corporation's obstruction of the railroad line; or, in the organicist language that undergirds this motif, in the corporation's cutting off of the city from the commercial blood flow of the nation. They also connect the fate of one region (the Southwest) and one group of individuals (the families of the don and the squatter) to that of the nation. With regard to "quasi public" corporations, moreover, foregrounding the homology between body corporate and body politic also serves to evoke the danger of imperialism and dispossession.

Previous scholars have already noted that the novel combines its critique of monopoly with a critique of US imperialism. This is particularly evident in the plot that concerns the Alamares' contested land-ownership. But additionally, as Pablo A. Ramirez has shown, the novel also connects this imperialist threat to the railroads:

> [T]he text clearly casts the railroad monopolists as the generals and the squatters as the foot soldiers of a protracted war of territorial acquisition against the landed Mexican elite. From the perspective of a conquered subject, both have inflicted injuries on the Californio community. (440)

But I want to suggest that the novel's depiction of this imperialist power of the corporations has even farther implications. This is apparent in the following exchange, which takes place during the interview with Leland Stanford. When Don Mariano and his friends point out that they thought they had made a safe investment in San Diego's future because they could not have foreseen the Southern Pacific's intervention, Stanford asks them why not. To which they reply,

> "We never thought, and do not think now, that it is to your interest to prevent it. But even if we had thought so, we would not have supposed that you would attempt it[.]" [. . .]
>
> "Why not?"
>
> "Because it would have seemed to us impossible that you could have succeeded."

"Why impossible?"

"Because we would have thought that the American people would interfere; that Congress would respect the rights of the Southern people."

Mr. Stanford laughed, saying: "The American people mind their business, and know better than to interfere with ours." (*S&D* 310)

Stanford's response is not simply a veiled reference to the corporation's influence in Washington, but to what the novel presents as the corporation's imperialist as well as populist threat. This contradictory quality is figured through recurrent references to Napoleon Bonaparte.

In keeping with the contemporary anti-monopoly discourse, Napoleon represents corporate monopoly in terms of an illegitimate and immoderate claim to power. This is most explicit in the novel's final chapter, the title of which is a call to arms: "Out with the Invader." It begins with quotes about the character and personality of the historical Bonaparte, in which he is described as vain and ambitious, an infamous invader. Then the narrator points out that while intellectuals agree that Napoleon was an immoral leader, present-day Americans have not yet recognized the immorality of corporate leaders.

> Not infamy, but honor and wealth, is the portion of the men who corrupt and ruin and debase in this country. Honor and wealth for the Napoleons of this land, whose power the sons of California can neither check nor thwart, nor escape, nor withstand. (*S&D* 367)

As with her references to the Southern Pacific as a "hydra-headed monster" (*S&D* 288), Ruiz de Burton is drawing on well-known anti-monopoly rhetoric here. The self-proclaimed emperor figured in magazine caricatures—such as the "King of Combinations" (1901), which depicted John D. Rockefeller in the guise of an emperor (Fig. 4.1)—as well as in the anti-monopoly rhetoric employed by the Workingmen's Party: "Our shoddy aristocrats want an emperor and a standing army to shoot down the people" (Davis 367).

Yet what is different about Ruiz de Burton's use of Napoleon is her association of this figure with the masses rather than with the aristocracy. Her use of this trope takes a republican perspective that underscores Napoleon's association with self-interest, a figure of "vanity and ambition" that can sway and beguile the masses, as the squatters are swayed and beguiled by the monopolists (*S&D* 366). As critics such as Pablo Ramirez have pointed out, the squatters are presented as the railroads' foot soldiers and as such are rendered in unflattering, often grotesque terms. But it is also characters who are presented in overall more sympathetic terms, like William Darrell, who are beguiled by the railroads. This is the painful lesson that Don Mariano and

Figure 4.1 John S. Pughe, "The King of Combinations," *Puck* 49, no. 1251 (February 27, 1901). Library of Congress Prints and Photographs Division, Washington, DC.

his friends must learn when Leland Stanford disabuses them of their belief in "the American people" (*S&D* 310).

Family Inc.

The Squatter and the Don foregrounds the homology between the body corporate and the body politic to evoke the threat of imperialism and dispossession in the "quasi public" corporation, whereas in the private corporation it serves to evoke the promise of liberty and a prosperous Spanish American future. The latter is the case, for example, in the portrayal of the Texas Pacific Railroad. Even though it is tainted by having accepted "Congressional aid" (*S&D* 148), the Texas Pacific is portrayed as a private enterprise in many ways, and in particular because the plan to build a railroad to San Diego energizes the local economy and encourages many individual investors like Don Mariano and Mr. Mechlin. Not only is the plan presented as economically beneficial, but it is also presented as politically beneficial in a way that is markedly different from the Southern Pacific's. While the Southern Pacific is presented as a foreign invader into California, the novel suggests that the Texas Pacific would have consolidated the Southwest and would have supported regional independence and state sovereignty.

This argument of a felicitous Southwestern integration is based on what scholars have described as Ruiz de Burton's alignment of the West with the South. Vincent Pérez, for example, reads the novel as expressing nostalgia for the "true community" of the prewar Mexican hacienda through its sympathy for the South. Accordingly, for Pérez, "[t]he railroad project serves in the novel primarily to establish a sociohistorical kinship between Mexican California and the American South, a solidarity based on a shared condition of military defeat and subjugation by the Yankee 'North'" (33). But Brook Thomas has shown that such an interpretation assumes that the plans for the future of the South were agrarian, which they were not. Contemporary visions for the New South were commercial. Henry W. Grady, journalist, author, and promoter of the New South, declared in a speech in 1886, "The old South rested everything on slavery and agriculture, unconscious that these could neither give nor maintain healthy growth. The new South presents [. . .] a diversified industry that meets the complex needs of this complex age" (19). In this vein, Ruiz de Burton has one of her characters explain to Congress how the future of California and of "the impoverished South" could be saved through the Texas Pacific by impressing on them "the importance, the policy, the humanity, of helping the South, and of giving to the Pacific Coast a competing railway, to get California out of the clutches of a grasping monopoly" (*S&D* 190). In this way, the Texas Pacific would realize the promise of the transcontinental railroads: to tie the nation closer together—only that Ruiz de Burton's vision was rooted in a strong and sovereign Southwest.

This brings us to the second example of a "good" corporation in the novel, though it is not as obvious as the first: the marriage of Mercedes Alamar and Clarence Darrell. They are representatives of a new economic elite that will lead the republic into a better future: *Californio* and Yankee, virtuous and ambitious, communal and individualist. For the couple to represent the future, however, they must first sever ties with their respective paternal regimes. After a fight with his son, Clarence's father drops out of sight for much of the novel, and when he briefly returns toward the end, it is to express his deeply felt regret for how he has treated Don Mariano. Physically as well as symbolically diminished, the squatter is presented as irrelevant to the couple's future and steps aside to let the younger generation take over. Nor is Don Mariano still relevant, though he may live on in their memory as an example of a noble past and its values. The novel suggests that his business and lifestyle represent a virtuous yet obsolete past. One of Don Mariano's daughters, for instance, observes about Clarence's fortune, "I have no faith in stocks" (S&D 85). And Clarence admits, "I think it's a pity that such men as Don Mariano and his sons do not have some other better-paying business than cattle-raising" (S&D 130). The Don's death is therefore part of a necessary passing of the parent generation, the end of his economics and his lifestyle, with the future open for the *Californios* and Californians of Mercedes's and Clarence's generation.

Marriage as a metaphor for national unification was a common device in romances of the Reconstruction, such as, for example, John William De Forest's *Miss Ravenel's Conversion from Secession to Loyalty* (1867) and Lydia Maria Child's *Romance of the Republic* (1867). Ruiz de Burton's first novel, *Who Would Have Thought It?*, also ends in a marriage, one "between the Mexican South and the Anglo North" (Rivera 106). According to John-Michael Rivera, Ruiz de Burton "subverts this popular trope into a binational configuration between the Mexican south and the United States north, thus describing [a] transnational understanding of American culture" (107). José Aranda Jr. goes even further, calling the marriage in *Who Would Have Thought It?* "a union between two colonial enterprises" ("Contradictory" 569). By contrast, Pablo Ramirez maintains that the marriage between Mercedes and Clarence "is a symbol of the [*Californio*] community's decline, for it only serves to highlight the Alamars' marginalization. [. . .] With the loss of the railroad, [the Alamars] must rely on Clarence to fulfil his financial obligations as a good son-in-law in order to avoid complete dispossession" (440). But the novel's conclusion, in particular the marriage, can also be read as Ruiz de Burton's idea of how to create a new body politic in which representation is *not* based exclusively "on the representation of a white masculine demos, a Hobbesian body politic where only 'the artificial [white] man' who is 'naturally' capable of reason is able to enter and represent the people of a given republic" (Rivera 83, brackets in the original). Instead, as Elisa Warford has pointed out, Ruiz de Burton seemed to believe in the "possibility of the mixture benefiting both, producing a better race," which she expressed in a private letter: "[T]he mixture of them can do no less than produce a third, more beautiful, more energetic, stronger, sweeter in character, more temperate and,

I believe, stronger" (Ruiz de Burton qtd. in Warford 11). While race is a complicated issue in Ruiz de Burton's work as well as in the contemporary discourse on corporations, Ruiz de Burton's reimagining of the incorporation of *Californios* into the American body politic provides only benefits to both parties.

Imagined as part of a domestic narrative, incorporation is both a business affair and an affair of the heart, and therefore it is Mercedes's virtue and Clarence's business acumen that the novel presents as the couple's assets. Unlike Don Mariano or Leland Stanford, Clarence makes his fortune (by the end of the novel, he is worth "twelve million dollars," *S&D* 364) through financial speculation: "Clarence had been a lucky investor. With the sum of $2000 bequeathed to him by Mrs. Darrell's Aunt Newton, [. . .] Clarence speculated, and now [at the beginning of the novel] he was worth close on to a million dollars" (*S&D* 65). Throughout the novel, Clarence's ability to take risks at the right moment, even as part of his courtship of Mercedes,[11] is conveyed admiringly. Mercedes represents the virtues of Spanish womanhood: similar to the feminine ideal of self-denial that the heroines of the Reconstruction romances possess, family and tradition are central to her character. Most importantly, these virtues also provide the basis for the novel's revision of liberal individualism and economic agency as represented by Darrell, the "money-making Yankee" (*S&D* 360).[12]

Because on closer inspection, the marriage between Clarence and Mercedes is not simply a union of two, but a union of many; nor is it only a marriage. At the end of the novel, Clarence has married Mercedes and has relocated the Alamar family to San Francisco's Nob Hill, where they live among other millionaires and at the center of California's economic power. Having bought the rancho from his mother-in-law and with his future prospects looking bright, Clarence incorporates. Plans for a private bank in San Diego are mentioned early on in the novel, but for most of the story they are contingent upon the construction of the railroad. Since the Mechlins already

---

[11] Hesitating out of propriety, Clarence does not publicly begin his courtship until Don Mariano tells him, "*Faint heart never won fair lady*" (*S&D* 88, emphasis in the original).

[12] While her description of the squatters/settlers arriving in San Diego with "carpet-bags" (*S&D* 21) establishes the association between the fate of the South and the West and suggests a decidedly negative attitude towards Northerners, Clarence's self-identification as Yankee is evidently positive. Leonard Pitt notes a similarly positive attitude toward "certain Yankee ideals" in the Mexicans of Ruiz de Burton's generation, when he describes California in the 1840s. "The Californians admired certain Yankee ideals, at least in the abstract, and generally thought more highly of the Yankee government than they did of Yankee citizens. [. . .] For the creative economic energy of the Yankees, Californians had both admiration and criticism" (Pitt 23).

own a bank in New York City—and one that remains miraculously unscathed by the Panic of 1873—Clarence turns to George Mechlin with his plan first.[13]

> I have had an idea in my head, a sort of project, I want to talk to you about. [. . .] The two banks in San Diego, I don't think, have a paid-up capital of more than a hundred thousand dollars. I think we could establish a bank of two or three hundred thousand dollars that would be a paying institution. I heard you say that you thought you would like to come to California, so as to be near your family. That gave me the idea of starting a bank. You could be the president and manager, and I would furnish as much of the capital as suited you. (*S&D* 129)

Just as Clarence connects his initial idea for a bank to George's wish to stay close to his family in California (instead of returning to the East Coast), so the project rapidly implicates Clarence's entire extended family: "If you put in twenty-five thousand, I will put in that much for each of the others, Don Gabriel, Tano and Retty, and one hundred thousand for myself, or will put in thirty thousand for Don Gabriel and ninety-five thousand for myself" (*S&D* 129). In this way, Clarence not only marries into the Alamar family—which is connected to the Mechlins by marriage as well—but literally incorporates them: they become shareholders of his bank. Keeping business in the family in such a way is the epitome of private enterprise in *The Squatter and the Don*. Yet, as this chapter's final section will show, unlike in Ruiz de Burton's reimagining of the incorporation of *Californios* into the American body politic, race figured much more prominently and problematically in the contemporary discourse on corporations and corporate monopoly in the US.

IV. Race and the Corporation in California

One of the more puzzling aspects of the anti-corporate rhetoric of the populists in general, but of the Constitutional Convention of 1878 in particular (at least to a modern reader), is how it intersected with the Convention's anti-Chinese agenda. While not all delegates were as critical of corporations as the Workingmen's Party, it is safe to say that the majority of delegates believed that the Chinese population in California needed to be controlled and regulated by the state. Throughout the debates, a deep-seated anti-Chinese racism is apparent, such as in the following assertion: "[The Chinaman] is cruel, treacherous, and revengeful. He has lived under a dominion entirely foreign to our institutions, and subject to a law antagonistic to our own. He holds

---

[13] Brook Thomas notes, "[f]ew authors give as positive an account of bankers as Ruiz de Burton" (*Reconstruction* 236).

in our midst an *imperium in imperio*" (*Debates II* 679). The content of these racist sentiments, specifically the association of the Chinese with feudalism, monopoly, and collectivity, intersected with the contemporary populist rhetoric against corporations.

To some extent, this intersection of anti-Chinese and anti-corporate discourses can be related to the economic and political realities of the time: the fact that "quasi public" corporations employed Chinese laborers on a large scale at the same time that Anglo-Saxon and in particular Irish workers were unemployed, for example. In the 1850s, during the California gold rush, many Chinese laborers had taken up work in the mining camps, with a second community of Chinese immigrants developing in San Francisco. Free-soilers saw the arrival of Chinese laborers, as well as "[p]oorer Sonorans and Chilean contract workers, sometimes known as *peones*," critically (Smith, *Frontier* 10). During this period Chinese labor began to be associated with what was called "coolie" labor, which would become a central theme in later Democratic and Republican anti-Chinese discourse. In the early 1860s, construction began on the Central Pacific Railroad and the railroad received government subsidies that were "issued per mile of track constructed" (Saxton 61). With the high-elevation terrain of the Sierra Nevada ahead of them and the Union Pacific Railroad competing for subsidies, the corporation was desperate to find construction workers, yet white men preferred to seek their fortunes in gold mining.

In 1865 the railroad hired a team of fifty Chinese workers, a decision that proved an instant success for the company. "[Leland] Stanford described the Chinese as 'quiet, peaceable, industrious, economical—ready and apt to learn all the different kinds of work required in railroad building.' They were in fact a construction foreman's dream" (Saxton 62). Historian Alexander Saxton estimates that "the company in three years saved approximately five and a half million dollars by hiring Chinese instead of white unskilled laborers" (63). The number of Chinese workers who died in the harsh Sierra winters is harder to estimate: "By Crocker's own reckoning, the Central kept ten or eleven thousand on the line from 1866 to 1869, but what the rate of replacement may have been he did not specify" (Saxton 65). The incredibly difficult working conditions also account for white men's reluctance to work for the railroad, as well as for their general acquiescence to the entrance of the Chinese into this particular labor market. But by the late 1860s, California and San Francisco in particular saw the rise of so-called anti-coolie clubs, such as "the Pacific Coast Anti-Coolie Association, [which] pledged to protect free white labor from coolie competition, to press for the legal restriction of Chinese immigration, and to expel Chinese immigrants from the state" (Smith, *Frontier* 208). The clubs did not shy from the use of violence: "Chinese were stoned, beaten, run down on the streets" (Saxton 73). Anti-coolie clubs also organized boycotts of Chinese-made goods to promote their own products (Saxton 74).

However, recent scholarship suggests that it was not just material conditions—rising unemployment and thus competition for labor—that fueled anti-Chinese sentiment. It also emerged as a counter-narrative to the prominent anti-Catholic sentiment in San Francisco. By identifying Chinese laborers as racial others, Catholics, specifically Irish immigrants, succeeded in establishing their own membership among the white American citizenry. When the Democratic Party was looking for new alliances to win the election of 1867, anti-coolie clubs as well as trade unions, which were seeking to protect recent gains (such as "the eight-hour day [. . .] [and] closed shop conditions," Saxton 68), offered the Party a new electorate. Its alliance with these two groups contributed to the rehabilitation of the Democratic Party in California,[14] and in 1867 Henry H. Haight carried the election. His platform merged anti-Chinese and anti-monopoly sentiments by arguing that "[c]orporate interests would use their control over Chinese slaves' votes to manipulate state politics and virtually enslave free white men" (Smith, *Frontier* 210). The Republican Party quickly followed suit and, under the pretense of an anti-slavery agenda, became instrumental in the passage of federal anti-Chinese legislation.[15]

Chinese immigration had heretofore been regulated under the Burlingame Treaty of 1868, which had established the right of the Chinese to free immigration to, and travel within, the United States, as well as access to education. But the first two sections of Article XIX that was passed during the Constitutional Convention in California ten years later established the framework for a systematic discrimination against Chinese immigrants. Section 1 does so by targeting Chinese people indirectly, both as an expression of a common racist stereotype according to which the Chinese were a physically

---

[14] "It [. . .] involved commitments to the eight-hour day, to a rising standard of living for workingmen, to effective action against monopoly, against corruption of government by private interest, and against Chinese immigration" (Saxton 111). Once back in power, however, the party would only realize its promise to pass anti-Chinese legislation.

[15] "The Page Law [. . .] purported to enforce existing treaty stipulations by ensuring that all immigration from China and other Asian countries was 'free and voluntary.' Modelled closely on California's 1870 anti-prostitution act, it prohibited the importation of Asian prostitutes and women who "entered into a contract or agreement for a term of service within the United States, for lewd and immoral purposes" (Smith, *Frontier* 221). It was passed in 1875. As Stacy Smith points out, "it set the stage for the Chinese Exclusion Act of 1882" (207).

inferior race and a contagious element within the body politic, and, quite practically, through a loophole in the Treaty.

> The Legislature shall prescribe all necessary regulations for the protection of the State, and the counties, cities, and towns thereof, from the burdens and evils arising from the presence of aliens who are or may become vagrants, paupers, mendicants, criminals, or invalids afflicted with contagious or infectious diseases, and from aliens otherwise dangerous or detrimental to the well-being or peace of the State, and to impose conditions upon which persons may reside in the State, and to provide the means and mode of their removal from the State, upon failure or refusal to comply with such conditions; provided, that nothing contained in this section shall be construed to impair or limit the power of the Legislature to pass such police laws or other regulations as it may deem necessary.

Because the Burlingame Treaty did not include provisions for Chinese citizens "who are or may become vagrants, paupers, mendicants, criminals, or invalids afflicted with contagious or infectious diseases,"[16] this Section was not interfering with the treaty. Section 2 was intended to prevent those who could not be forcibly removed from California from working and thus was intended to cut them off from earning a livelihood.

> No corporation now existing or hereafter formed under the laws of this State, shall, after the adoption of this Constitution, employ directly or indirectly, in any capacity, any Chinese or Mongolian. The Legislature shall pass such laws as may be necessary to enforce this provision.

The absence of the prefix "quasi" in this section makes clear that it was aimed at all private corporations, though the railroads were the largest employers of Chinese laborers. In this piece of legislation, therefore, the intersection between anti-corporate and anti-Chinese interests becomes apparent, and even more so in the Fourteenth Amendment lawsuits that followed it.

Of those lawsuits, *In re Tiburcio Parrott* (1880) presented the most direct challenge to Section 2 of Article XIX. Tiburcio Parrott was the director of a mining corporation in California who had employed Chinese laborers and who was subsequently arrested for violating the newly amended California Penal Code, which (on the basis of Section 2) made it a criminal offense to employ Chinese citizens. Parrott filed a writ of habeas corpus and the case came before the Ninth Circuit Court, which was then presided over by Judges Lorenzo Sawyer and Ogden Hoffman. Parrott's lawyer argued that

---

[16] See *Debates II* 689.

Section 2 violated the Fourteenth Amendment, the Civil Rights Act, and the Burlingame Treaty, whereas California's attorney general maintained that, while that may be true, the State did have a reserved power to alter corporate charters which remained untouched by either the federal Constitution or the treaty. The court ruled against the law, but not based on its discriminatory measure, though the court was well aware of its unconstitutionality. Significantly, the court's opinion focused on the anti-corporate implications of Section 2, specifically its impact on the corporation understood as private property and as an aggregate of private property holders. In fact, the opinion in *In re Parrott* pitches a group of white, property-holding individuals against anonymous Chinese laborers in a way that suggests that Judge Hoffman would not want one group confused with the other.

For Hoffman, the constitutional article prohibiting corporations from employing Chinese laborers is foremost an attack on private property:

> [T]he claim thus put forth [in the Constitution] is well fitted to startle and alarm. It amounts in effect to a declaration that the corporations formed under the laws of this State and their stockholders, hold their property, so far as its beneficial use and enjoyment are concerned, at the mercy of the Legislature, and that rights which in the case of private individuals would be inviolable, have for them no existence. (*Re Parrott* 6)

Nor does Hoffman accept the argument that the State commands a reserved power regarding corporate charters, let alone that the law could constitute an exercise of police power. Contrary to what Herbert Hovenkamp has described as a continuous tendency of the courts to reject arguments based on the Contract Clause since the Taney Court, Justice Hoffman insists on its relevance. In his discussion of what constitutes the States' reserved power regarding corporations, his interpretation is narrow and essentially based on *Dartmouth*. As such it also stands in striking contrast to the Supreme Court's decision in *Munn* v. *Illinois*: "It would be a 'mockery, a delusion, and a snare' to say to a corporation: 'The title to the property you have lawfully acquired we may not disturb, but we may prescribe such conditions as to its use, as will utterly destroy its beneficial value'" (*In re Parrott* 10). While difficult to define, the power authorized by statutes of reservation is not "unrestrained" (*In re Parrott* 6), but guided by reasonableness. It is the criterion of reasonableness—which Hoffman does not define, but which he quotes from earlier rulings—that the law does not fulfill. Instead, it only uses the statutes of reservations as a front to target Chinese immigrants: "Can it be said to be in good faith—that is, in the fair and just exercise of the reserved power to regulate corporations for the protection of the stockholders, their creditors, and the general public?" (*In re Parrott* 12).

Underlying Hoffman's opinion is the recognition of an opposition between two groups, one white and owning property, the other Chinese and owning only their labor. While these groups sometimes disappear behind corporate legal personhood and treaty rights, the opinion still contains this basic juxtaposition. Hoffman emphasizes that there are natural persons "[b]ehind the artificial or ideal being created by the Statute and called a corporation" who do not lose their rights when they incorporate. As we have seen, his piercing the veil in such a way is important for his argument. But even more striking is the figurative shuffle that unfolds as he explains why he points to the white, property-owning natural persons rather than building his case on a violation of the Burlingame Treaty. While it is only an "ideal being," it turns out that in its position as "trustee, agent, and representative of the shareholders," it possesses substantial and individualistic legal reality (*In re Parrott* 11).

> I am therefore of the opinion [. . .] [t]hat the corporations [. . .] are not compelled to shelter themselves behind the treaty right of the Chinese, to reside here, to labor for their living, and accept employment when offered; but they may stand firmly on their own right to employ laborers of their choosing, and on such terms as may be agreed upon, subject only to such police laws as the State may enact with respect to them, in common with private individuals. (*In re Parrott* 12)

The image of corporations seeking "shelter [. . .] *behind* the treaty right of the Chinese" is a curious one, in particular as it is followed by Hoffman's assertion of the corporations' firm stand on their own right, as if shielding the shareholders from illegitimate access to their property. This shuffling and reshuffling of bodies into, out of, and from behind artificial creations, whether corporations or treaty rights, is evidence of what Brook Thomas has described as Hoffman's operation within a contractualist and individualist framework of law: "Hoffman's decision helped to illustrate the extent to which corporate capitalism in the United States operated—as it still does—within a legal system devoted to the notion of individual rights" (*Realism* 238).

Race also plays a role in Justice Field's opinion in *San Mateo County* v. *Southern Pacific Railroad* (1882), the case in which Field laid out why he believed that corporations are persons within the meaning of the Fourteenth Amendment's Equal Protection Clause. As explained earlier in this chapter, the case revolved around the Convention's decision to assess the property of "quasi public" corporations differently for purposes of taxation. The defense challenged the Section on the grounds that it "denied the equal protection of the laws guaranteed by the Fourteenth Amendment of the Federal Constitution" (*San Mateo County* v. *Southern Pacific* 246). The plaintiff, on the other hand, insisted that "the power of taxation possessed by the State is unlimited, except by the Constitution of the United States" (*San Mateo County* v. *Southern Pacific* 247). Moreover, they referred to the narrow construction of the Fourteenth Amendment delivered in the *Slaughter-House Cases* and, in addition, averred "[t]hat corporations are not persons within the meaning of that amendment" (*San Mateo County* v. *Southern Pacific* 247). But as he had in his dissent in the *Slaughter-House Cases*, Justice Field maintained that "the Fourteenth Amendment had radically altered the constitutional relationship between the states and the federal government" (Horwitz, *1870–1960* 69). It had provided Congress with a tool to protect citizens from unjust state legislation and "the generality of the language used extends the protection of its provisions to persons of every race and condition" (*San Mateo County* v. *Southern Pacific* 259).

In the back of both Justice Field's and Justice Sawyer's minds was the plaintiff's argument in *Parrott* that the Constitution violated the Chinese laborers' Fourteenth Amendment rights. Justice Sawyer wrote in his concurring opinion that Chinese laborers "were among the first to invoke this very provision of the Fourteenth Amendment to protect them, under the word 'person,' in the right to earn an honest living by honest labor"—referring to three cases that involved Chinese immigrants, among them *In re Ah Chong* (1880), in which Justice Field had overruled a California law that had restricted the immigration of Chinese women (*San Mateo County* v. *Southern Pacific* 286).[17] It was evidently a noteworthy move in his eyes. In Justice Field's words, the Amendment "stands in the Constitution as a perpetual shield against all unequal and partial legislation by the States, and the injustice which follows from it, whether directed against the most humble, or the most powerful; against the despised laborer from China, or the envied master of millions" (*San Mateo County* v. *Southern Pacific* 261–2).

But while all these factors—from the railroads' large-scale employment of underpaid Chinese immigrants to the legal consequences of the Constitutional Convention's new legislation—explain the material realities of the association between Chinese persons and corporations, its ideological foundations are of longer making. What I mean by that is well illustrated by a caricature that was published in the San Francisco–based magazine *The Wasp* in March 1882, during what we have seen was a period of intense anti-Chinese labor

---

[17] For a discussion see Smith, *Freedom's Frontier* 207–30. In *Chy Lung* v. *Freeman* (1875), Field also ruled in favor of a group of female Chinese immigrants who had been prevented from entering San Francisco because the commissioner of immigration thought that they were prostitutes. Anne Anlin Cheng provides a fascinating reading of the case in which she explores the role of ornament and artifice in the creation of legal personhood; see "Ornament and Law" in Anker and Meyler, ed., *New Directions in Law and Literature*.

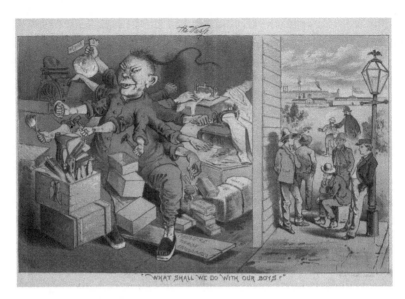

Figure 4.2 G. Frederick Keller, "What Shall We Do With Our Boys?" *The Wasp* 8, no. 292 (January–June 1882). Bancroft Library, University of California, Berkeley.

activity (Fig. 4.2). Its diptych structure contrasts a group of idle young white men, who seem to be waiting outside a warehouse on the right, with a single barely human character amid stacks of crates and boxes on the left. The character's clothes, hairstyle, and exaggerated facial features identify him as a "coolie," the racial stereotype of a Chinese laborer. From his body, ten arms protrude and engage in sewing, hammering, packing, and so on. A human octopus capable of replacing the labor of five men, the cartoon's headline suggests that this figure is monopolizing labor: "What Shall We Do With Our Boys?" the headline asks, while the Chinese octopus character has one foot resting on a sign which reads "Chinese Trade Monopoly." As Saxton argues, writers like Henry George maintained that cheap, inexhaustible Chinese labor was benefiting the capitalists rather than the common man and was therefore contributing to corporate monopolies.

The association of the Chinese more generally with anti-monopoly rhetoric was reinforced by the common stereotype of China as a feudalistic society. Historian Harry Scheiber explains that in the course of the California Constitutional Convention, "[n]ot only the Workingmen, but also many elements of the two major parties expressed [the] concern to recapture the republic, somehow, for the people—to get rid of an 'imported feudalism' that had validated monopoly landholdings and encouraged the appearance of great disparities in wealth" ("Race" 42). As Colleen Lye has pointed out, this "popular use of inherited notions of Oriental despotism" had its roots in "[a] tradition of European political economy, beginning in the eighteenth century with Montesquieu and culminating with Marx and Engels' theory of an 'Asiatic mode of production,' [which] thought to identify the traits that distinguished non-European from European forms of precapitalism" (*Asia* 68). But while anti-monopoly rhetoric could therefore encompass both corporations and the Chinese, it was also the stereotype of the "coolie," of the Chinese as a collectivized rather than individualized society, that afforded the association between Chinese persons and corporate persons in the popular imaginary.

In the caricature, the figure's collective nature is not only evident from its many arms, but is also conveyed through the diptych structure. The "coolie" figure, the caricature suggests, incorporates the many in the figure of a single, though many-handed, body. Its monstrous, non-human qualities evoke earlier associations of crowds with many-headed beasts. The plebeian crowd of the revolutionary and early republican period thus returns in the racialized, collectivist other. "The coolie is a figural variant of modernity's economic masses; by definition the coolie lacks individuality" (Lye, *Asia* 54). Moreover, the figure's body and the way it executes tasks also add to its non-human, now clearly mechanistic properties. Focusing on the transformation of labor under industrialization, Lye adds, "The coolie signifies [. . .] the prospect of [the body's] mechanical abstraction" (*Asia* 56).

The association of corporate multitudinousness (the fact that corporations were groups of people and as such received constitutional protections) with racial otherness required an extraordinary ideological policing. The corporation, in other words, needed to be harnessed into the framework of liberal individualism, and most urgently so where it intersected with matters of race and economic agency. African American lawyer and novelist Charles W. Chesnutt captures this tension and the contradictions that surface in attempts to negotiate it in "The Partners," a short story published in 1901. Set in the post-bellum South, the story tells of two black freedmen, William Cain and Rufus Green, and their attempts to make a living by their own labor. After a while, a Northern philanthropist arrives and, after buying a former plantation, offers each of them a plot of land for a fair price and with the intention to "[encourage] industry and thrift among the Negroes" (Chesnutt, "Partners" 254). The crux of the matter is, however, that the philanthropist insists that they own and work the land individually. Yet William and Rufus are not only friends, they are actual partners. At the beginning of the story, we learn that Rufus is much less skilled than William because he did not have any opportunity to learn a trade during slavery. But William suggests that they establish a partnership, and for this purpose the two have an "agreement" drawn up for them which formally declares that "William Cain and Rufus Green is gone in partners this day to work at whatever their hands find to do" (Chesnutt, "Partners" 254).

The story suggests that it is not just formal training, but also—and as a consequence thereof—"the prospect of facing the world alone" that is daunting for Rufus, because "slavery had not been a good school for training in self-reliance" (Chesnutt, "Partners" 253). It is this very "self-reliance," however, that the Northern philanthropist wants purportedly to instill in the freedmen when he insists on their *individual* ownership of the former plantation land. Yet in the course of the story, it is his isolated situation that brings ruin onto Rufus and his family. The story points to the glaring contradiction that underlies his proposition: "The good philanthropist, waiving for the moment his theory of self-reliance—of which indeed his whole generous scheme was a contradiction—gave his beneficiaries advice and oversight for several years [. . .]" (Chesnutt, "Partners" 254–5). For Brook Thomas, Chesnutt's story thereby reveals the tension between the ideology of free labor and of paternalism during Reconstruction. But it is also, as he points out, revealing a contradiction to a larger shift in which "[f]reedmen [. . .] were held to a standard of self-reliance that did not apply to the white business community" (*Reconstruction* 206). In the words of Chesnutt's narrator, "A thoughtful student of history might have suggested to the philanthropist that the power of highly developed races lies mainly in their ability to *combine* for the better accomplishment of a common purpose" ("Partners" 254, my emphasis). Yet, to the extent that the contemporary discourse on racialized collectivity—such as in the examples of the caricature or Chesnutt's short story—allowed to distinguish between legitimate and illegitimate forms of collectivity, it allowed white entrepreneurs to exploit ever more assertively the opportunities that corporate collectivity offered. As the next chapter shows, by the end of the nineteenth century, white American businessmen like J. P. Morgan and John D. Rockefeller had indeed mastered the art of combination.

5

The End of Individualism:
Tarbell, Norris, and the Power
of Combinations

The final decade of the century had begun with yet another financial panic, but it would close with "the most significant merger movement in American history," as Alfred D. Chandler Jr. writes. "In industry after industry the giant enterprise appeared" ("Industrial Corporation" 74). It was the era of trusts, of industrial concentration and consolidation; in short, of combination. Under the influence of the natural sciences, and in particular of Darwin's theory of evolution, the emerging profession of American economists declared this trend "inevitable": like any organism, they maintained, the industrial sector would grow ever larger and more complex. In the words of John D. Rockefeller: "The day of combination is here to stay. Individualism has gone, never to return" (qtd. in Nevins 622).[1]

Legislation tried to stem the tide of what was a new age of monopoly, such as in the form of the creation of the Interstate Commerce Commission (1887) and the Sherman Anti-Trust Act (1890). The Act, which refers to "contract[s], combination[s] [. . .] or conspirac[ies], in restraint of trade or commerce," popularized the term *combination*, which became closely associated with trusts but also more generally with the phenomenon of large-scale industrial organization. Over time, *combination*'s more neutral meaning was almost replaced by its criminal meaning. Both dimensions yet informed Cooper's use of the word in *The Bravo*, for example, and the entry on "conspiracy" in the 1839 edition of *Bouvier's Law Dictionary* still reads, "CONSPIRACY, crim. Law, torts. An agreement between two or more persons to do an unlawful act, or any of those acts which become by the combination injurious to others." By 1892, however, *Bouvier's* has a separate entry on "combination" and the

---

[1] Statement made in a conversation with W. O. Inglis, who was assembling material for a biography in 1915. The material was incorporated into Allan Nevins's biography *John D. Rockefeller: The Heroic Age of American Enterprise* (1940).

emphasis has shifted: "COMBINATION. A union of men for the purpose of violating the law. A union of different elements."

When John D. Rockefeller signed the first trust agreement in January of 1882, it was to circumvent state law on foreign corporations that limited the Standard Oil Company's ability to own out-of-state ("foreign") corporations. Devised with the help of the company's attorney, S. T. Dodd, this new form of trust was an agreement by which the shareholders of several companies abdicated control over their property to a separate body of trustees. This structure was based on the common-law trust, a legal device used to provide for widows and orphans, which gave control over property to an appointed guardian who would manage the estate in their interests. Moreover, by signing the agreement, Rockefeller achieved the vertical integration of nearly forty companies, including companies from out of state. The resulting trust was not a corporation, and until the passage of the Sherman Act, the agreement presented an extra-legal but not an illegal document. In fact, for a short period the trust epitomized the most elusive, intangible, and ominous qualities of the corporate form itself. As Ida Tarbell put it in her *History of the Standard Oil Company* (1904), "You could argue [the trust's] existence from its effects, but you could not prove it" (*History II* 141).

Faced with such an elusive power, visual artists, journalists, and literary writers took recourse to an established anti-monopoly rhetoric and adapted it to the era's changing views on group action or collective agency. Among the tropes that would become most closely associated with the trusts in the popular imaginary of the late nineteenth and early twentieth centuries was the octopus. As the previous chapter has argued, the Chinese octopus cartoon that was published in *The Wasp* in 1882 was both a stab at monopoly and at Chinese immigration: both special privilege and Chinese culture were popularly associated with feudalism.[2] Moreover, corporate monopoly evoked a form of collective agency that was deemed alien to white Anglo-Saxon culture in California in the late nineteenth century and one that, as I noted in the previous chapter, found its racialized expression in the figure of the "coolie." We can expand this reading by considering the fact that Frederick G. Keller, the artist who had drawn the image, was also responsible for two cartoons depicting the Mussel Slough incident. Only a week after the cartoon depicting a Chinese laborer as an octopus, Keller took on the Southern Pacific Railroad in a cartoon titled "The Ogre of Mussel Slough" (March 12, 1882). This cartoon presents a two-headed giant—the railroad's presidents, Leland Stanford and Charles Crocker—grabbing for naught in a desolate landscape.

---

[2] See Chapter 1 of this study for corporate monopoly's association with feudalism.

Figure 5.1 G. Frederick Keller, "The Curse of California," *The Wasp* 9, no. 316 (August 19, 1882). Bancroft Library, University of California, Berkeley.

In August of the same year Keller published the famous "Curse of California" cartoon, in which he has moved Stanford and Leland inside the (single) head of a full-fledged octopus, now labeled "Railroad Monopoly" (Fig. 5.1). Not only does the octopus's trace lead through the popular imaginary on trusts and combinations at the end of the nineteenth century, however; it also connects California's struggle with the Southern Pacific to the rise of foreign monopolies such as the Standard Oil Company. Additionally, it hints at the more significant struggles in legal, literary, and economic discourses of the time to reconcile the success of combinations, and thus of collective economic agency, with the master narrative of liberal individualism.

To understand how writers, artists, and lawyers made sense of the rise of corporate capitalism at the end of the nineteenth century, and specifically to learn more about the representation of collectives and collective agency in law, literature, and art, this chapter looks at a variety of materials. It begins by taking a closer look at combinations in the legal imaginary: The discussion of two legal treatises and the opinions in *Northern Securities Company* v. *United States* (1904) shows that the emergence of powerful combinations in the market prompted foundational debates over the place of collectives and the nature of associational agency in US society. In essence, these debates revolved around the question of whether collective agency in the market was conspiratorial or cooperative in nature. Accordingly, legal writers would draw on either organic or inorganic metaphors to represent combinations and corporate agency. In a similar effort to represent to their readers the intangible and invisible agency of corporations, magazine writers and artists relied on metonymy and personification, thereby rhetorically restoring to the corporation the substance of which the trust form and the holding company had emptied it.

The main part of this chapter focuses on Ida Tarbell's *History of the Standard Oil Company* (1904) and Frank Norris's *The Octopus* (1901). I argue that both Tarbell and Norris present stories of conflicts that are not between the individual and the group but between different types of organizations. Both tell stories of corporate agency as trans-individual, and both highlight the qualities that characterize the new and more successful type of business— qualities that we associate with the managerial revolution today. Rather than the rugged, self-reliant individual, their stories—broadly speaking—present the success of agents, or at least of men capable of organizing others and thinking beyond their individual self-interest. This is not surprising if we consider the corporation's development at the end of the nineteenth and beginning of the twentieth century. This development culminated in the merger movement, which allowed for ever larger industrial organizations and the rise of the managerial class that followed the triumph of majority rule and the internal reorganization of corporations during this period. Contrary to common opinion, the late nineteenth century was the age of collectives rather than of the ruthless individual.

Concluding this study's investigation into the narrativization of corporations in the nineteenth century, the chapter interprets Tarbell's and Norris's narrativization of collective (economic) agency in the context of the debates over combinations. It shows that both drew on the visual rhetoric established by popular discourse as well as the legal and economic rhetoric of the period. While the latter developed a set of organic and inorganic metaphors to present legal and illegal combinations, that is, combinations as cooperation or conspiracy, the former's dominant rhetorical devices consisted in metonymy and personification. Tarbell and Norris built on this legal and popular imaginary to present the triumph of large industrial organizations as an epochal shift in US (business) culture. While Tarbell overall remains critical, Norris's novel ultimately celebrates the rise of corporate capitalism.

I. From Trust to Merger: Late Nineteenth-Century Corporate Forms

Scholars often characterize the last two decades of the nineteenth century by efforts to devise more efficient and more coherent forms of organization in fields of science, politics, and industry:[3] what historian Robert Wiebe has called "a search for order," resulting in a deep structural transformation that Alan Trachtenberg famously described as "the incorporation of America." The search for new forms of organization resulted in the brief but influential era of trusts, which would dominate public debate over industrial organization. This was partly due to a series of spectacular legal cases between 1888 and 1892, in which state courts persecuted monopolies in almost every area of commercial life: the Diamond Match Trust, the Standard Oil Trust, the Sugar Trust, and the Whiskey Trust.[4] While at first the courts drew on the common law regarding restraints of trade to deal with the trusts, it soon became clear that more efficient legislation would be needed. In 1890 the passage of federal legislation, the Sherman Act, made restraints of trade and commerce illegal, empowering the courts to persecute what the Act called "combinations." In its first section, it stated,

> Every contract, combination in the form of trust or otherwise, or conspiracy, in restraint of trade or commerce among the several States, or with foreign nations, is hereby declared to be illegal. Every person who shall make any such contract or engage in any such combination or conspiracy, shall be deemed guilty of a misdemeanor [. . .]

The Act did not become relevant for another five years, however, since the depression at the beginning of the decade temporarily slowed down industrial development in the US. But by 1895, "the trust movement accelerated sharply and turned into the greatest merger mania America has ever experienced, lasting almost a decade" (Hovenkamp, *Enterprise & Law* 242). At this point, however, the trust (as informal agreement) had practically been replaced by the holding company and the merger, new forms of business organization made possible by changes in state incorporation laws. In other words, the extra-legal trust form had been returned to the corporate form proper, yet under very different conditions.

By the middle of the nineteenth century, lawyers had begun to argue that, rather than through a grant from the state, the corporation came into being as free individuals entered into contractual relations with one another. As an aggregate of contracting individuals, it was quite as normal and natural a mode of doing business as a partnership and as such, it was private.

---

[3] See also Alfred D. Chandler, *Strategy and Structure* (1962) and *The Visible Hand* (1977), and Samuel P. Hays, *The Response to Industrialism, 1885–1914* (1957).

[4] *Richardson* v. *Buhl et al.* (Michigan, 1889); *State* v. *Standard Oil Co.* (Ohio, 1892); *The People* v. *The North Sugar Refining Co.* (State of New York, 1890); *State* v. *Nebraska Distilling Co.* (Nebraska, 1890).

Accordingly, agency and rights rested in the individual members. As the previous chapter has shown, this contractualist reasoning still provided the basis of the *California Tax Cases*, including *Santa Clara County* v. *Southern Pacific Railroad Company* (1886). The court had not based its ruling on the so-called natural entity theory,[5] according to which the corporate person was a separate entity from its shareholders; rather, it had agreed with the corporation's lawyer, John N. Pomeroy, that the natural persons who compose the corporation had a legitimate claim to protection under the Amendment that was not lost through incorporation. In effect, the court had treated the corporation as an aggregate of shareholders and as private, like a partnership.

In 1889, the New Jersey state legislature decided to pass new incorporation statutes, legalized holding companies and thereby allowed corporations to own one another. The state benefited almost immediately from an influx of new businesses that relocated to New Jersey, among them the Standard Oil Company in 1899: "After the passage of the New Jersey Act, the entire expenses of the state of New Jersey were paid out of corporation fees" (Horwitz, *1870–1960* 84). In practice, the holding company was a firm incorporated with comparatively little capital stock of its own and with the sole purpose of holding the stock of other companies.

> Under the 1891 and 1893 amendments, a New Jersey corporation could be formed with only nominal capital paid in, agree to acquire a controlling interest in the shares of another corporation, and then issue shares with a stated value sufficient to pay for the transaction. The shares of the acquired firms were the paid-in capital necessary to support issuance of the holding company's shares. (Hovenkamp, *Enterprise & Law* 258)

The most important quality of the holding company was the fact that it seemed to supersede the combination by incorporating a single company. Lawyers believed that the holding company was therefore not a combination within the meaning of the Sherman Act. Holding companies did, however, continue to incur charges of *ultra vires*,[6] and the Supreme Court decision in

---

[5] For other accounts of the development of the corporate form during this period, and corporate personhood in particular, see, for example, Hovenkamp's *Enterprise and American Law 1836–1937* (42–8); and Gregory A. Mark's "The Personification of the Business Corporation in American Law." For a classical though somewhat dated account, see James Willard Hurst's *The Legitimacy of the Business Corporation in the Law of the United States 1780–1970*.

[6] Cp. Horwitz, *1870–1960* 86. For a discussion of how these charges were related to the problem of dealing with foreign corporations and inter-state commerce see Hovenkamp, *Enterprise & Law* 260–2. "By 1899 the states had chartered 121 corporations with a capitalization of $10 million or more each. Of these, 61 were chartered in New Jersey. By 1899

Northern Securities Company v. *United States* (1904) held that the holding company presented a combination within the meaning of the Sherman Act. In the light of these decisions, enterprises increasingly took to mergers by direct sales of assets. Mergers were rarely charged with *ultra vires*, because, as Horwitz explains, "by the time the transactions were challenged in court they had already become executed contracts" (*1870–1960* 86). But the merger movement was only possible because of the transformation that the corporate form's internal hierarchy was undergoing during this period. It was a transformation in which shareholders were rapidly becoming unimportant for the definition of corporations, and it was tied to the idea of the corporation's organic existence.

An important step in the transformation of the corporation was the redefinition of its internal hierarchies. As the natural entity theory gained support, lawyers and legal scholars argued that the corporation was not only a natural mode of doing business, as the contractualists had argued, but that corporations existed prior to law. Like all associations, they argued, corporations were a fundamental social fact that occurred independently of the state and required legal sanction only *after* they had come into existence. "Contrary to the contractualists, they insisted that groups were just as real as individuals and that, in addition, the corporation was separate and distinct from its shareholders" (Horwitz, *1870–1960* 101). The claim that groups were "real" drew on the ideas of German legal historian Otto von Gierke, whose work on voluntary associations and corporations influenced Chicago law professor Ernst Freund and was partly translated by British legal historian Frederic William Maitland in 1900.[7] American lawyers and legal scholars used Gierke's work because it argued in favor of the autonomy of groups: they were not dependent on the sovereign's power of creation but existed independently of the Prince or State, and thereby provided the cornerstones of an autonomous civil sphere. In this respect, Gierke's ideas would have pleased María Amparo Ruiz de Burton. In his introduction to another selection of Gierke's work, Anthony Black explains that "the *early* Gierke [. . .] believed that fellowships would resolve the problems of individual and society, and of autonomy and authority, by generating truly willed and therefore truly free forms of association" (Gierke, *Community* xviii). Sadly, in the American

---

every combination that had been dissolved in state quo warranto proceedings during the 1890s had reorganized as a New Jersey corporation" (Hovenkamp, *Enterprise & Law* 258).

[7] Maitland was one of "the English pluralists," which also included Harold Laski. See Turner 21–3.

context, Gierke's ideas did not support civil society but ultimately contributed to ever greater concentrations of wealth.[8]

The difference between "real" (or natural) and "artificial" that lawyers began to pursue during this period also had implications for the status of corporations as legal persons. The Romanist tradition distinguished between *universitas* and *societas*, corporations and partnerships, with only the former having the status of a *persona ficta*. This status was entirely dependent on the grant of the sovereign, which meant that it could never become a rival body to the corporate body of the sovereign. Against this conception, Gierke argued from a Germanist tradition which had recognized the autonomy of *Genossenschaften*, or fellowships. Summarizing Gierke's view, Maitland explains that "our German Fellowship is no fiction, no symbol, no piece of the State's machinery, no collective name for individuals, but a living organism and a real person, with body and members and a will of its own. [. . .] [I]t is a *Gesammtperson* [. . .]" (Gierke, *Political Theories* xxvi).[9] The "group-will" (*Political Theories* xxvi) which Gierke likewise believed to rest in this person posed conceptual problems of its own, however. They were related to the internal hierarchy and management structure of corporations.

As long as corporations were conceived as aggregates of separate, property-owning individuals, courts required *unanimous* shareholder consent: "Any fundamental corporate change was regarded as a breach of the individual shareholder's contract, as well as, in effect an unconsented taking of his property" (Horwitz, *1870–1960* 87). But in the course of the 1890s, state legislatures began to pass incorporation statutes that allowed for *majority* rule, which was soon tied to the idea of the corporate person as a separate entity. In 1897, Ernst Freund considered the problem of how to conceive of

---

[8] It is important to note that the emergence of the natural entity theory at this point did not mean that this conception of the corporation replaced the artificial entity theory or the aggregate model. In her reading of *Hale v. Henkel* (1906), Lamoreaux argues that the turn of the century even saw "the resurgence of the artificial entity theory" ("Partnerships" 50). It is therefore probably more accurate to speak of a "general drift" from artificial to natural entity at the turn of the century (Lipartito, "Utopian" 117 n. 56). See Harold Laski's "The Personality of Associations" (1916), published in the *Harvard Law Review*, for a contemporary account of the natural or real entity theory.

[9] Maitland's introduction to *Political Theories of the Middle Ages* is in itself a fascinating, even poetic text. Take, for instance, the following passage, in which Maitland describes the foundational assumption of the concession or grant theory: "The corporation is, and must be, the creature of the State. Into its nostrils the State must breathe the breath of a fictitious life, for otherwise it would be no animated body but individualistic dust" (Gierke, *Political Theories* xxx). For a recent discussion of metaphor in Maitland's work see Gearey, "'We Want to Live': Metaphor and Ethical Life in F. W. Maitland's Jurisprudence of the Trust."

the "corporate will," if it no longer rested in a unanimous decision (52). By accepting the majority's decision for that of the entire body of shareholders, law was compromising out of expediency, he explained.

> The justification of this legal expedient lies in the fact that the will of the majority may be presumed to express correctly what would be the result of forced unanimity; a presumption not always agreeable to fact [. . .]. In so far as the presumption fails to be correct, it cannot be denied that *a will* which is not identical with the corporate will *is imputed to the corporation*, just as we impute the will of the agent to the principal without insisting that it should in all cases accord with the principal's will. (qtd. in Horwitz, *1870–1960* 89, my emphasis)

From a mere contract, the corporation had progressed to the status of a subject, to which the law imputed "a will which is not identical with the corporate will." Freed from the shareholders and thus from the natural bodies of which it had been a representation, the corporate person could begin to take on a life of its own.[10] As Horwitz notes, this internal reorganization also had an influence on how Americans imagined the corporation. "After 1900, [. . .] directors were more frequently treated as equivalent to the corporation itself. This realignment of legal powers within the corporation thus made the entity theory more plausible" (*1870–1960* 74). In other words, as directors and professional managers took over operational control, their individuality replaced the collective in the public's perception of the corporate body.

II. Combinations in the Legal Imaginary

With the proliferation of corporate forms in the final two decades of the nineteenth century, and most urgently, with the passage of the Sherman Act in 1890, courts and lawyers were faced with the task of defining the legal boundaries of collective agency in the market. Understanding the market increasingly in evolutionary terms and as ruled by "inevitable growth," they

---

[10] During the following decade, the natural entity theory and corporate personality were gradually accepted by the Court, though artificial and aggregate theories continued to be in use, too. *Hale* v. *Henkel* (1906), for example, extended Fourth but not Fifth Amendment protection to corporations, arguing that "[t]he right of a person under the Fifth Amendment to refuse to incriminate himself is purely a personal privilege of the witness. [. . .] The question whether a corporation is a "person" within the meaning of this Amendment really does not arise [. . .] since it can only be heard by oral evidence in the person of some one of its agents or employees" (*Hale* v. *Henkel* 69–70). But only a few years later, in *Southern Railway Co.* v. *Greene*, "the Court came out clearly for the position that the corporation as such was entitled to constitutional protection under the equal protection clause, *without any reference to its shareholders*" (Avi-Yonah and Sivan 164, my emphasis).

drew on organic as well as inorganic metaphors to convey the differences between the organizational forms of trust, combination, consolidation, and corporation. A closer look at two treatises as well as at the court's decision on holding companies in the *Northern Securities* case (1904) provides a brief overview of this corporate taxonomy in the popular imaginary at the time.

Cooperation or Conspiracy?

Two legal treatises from this period illustrate the rhetorical means by which lawyers were trying to convey the difference between legal and illegal combinations. The first is William W. Cook's treatise on corporations, *The Corporation Problem* (1891), published a year after the Sherman Act. It works with a mostly consistent dichotomy in which corporations are associated with consolidation and trusts with combination. Cook was a prominent corporate law scholar who published several influential treatises on the law of corporations, trusts, and in particular on stockholder law. He was also a member of the New York state senate judiciary committee in 1887 (Letwin 81 n. 1). In Cook's treatise, consolidation is part of a field of organic metaphors, such as "absorptions, and amalgamations," that originate in the natural sciences (167). Combination, by contrast, is a mechanical metaphor that highlights an arrangement of discrete individual parts. As noted earlier, even *Bouvier's Law Dictionary* (1892) still provided combination's technical alongside its legal definition: "A union of men for the purpose of violating the law. A union of different elements." As Cook compares and evaluates corporations and trusts, his emphasis respectively on the organic or inorganic quality of either metaphor shapes his narrative of the emergence of business organizations.

Cook's description of the history of railroad corporations in the United States, the problems that they have created, and the various possible solutions draws almost exclusively on consolidation, with combination reserved for his discussion of the trusts.[11]

> [V]ery probably the most striking feature of the railroad situation to-day is the swift and uncontrollable tendency toward consolidation. Trunk lines are being united, while short and disconnected roads are being absorbed. [. . .] A few great transcontinental systems of railroads are beginning to assume enormous proportions, and when their work has been accomplished it will be found that all other roads have been absorbed. (Cook 167)

---

[11] "Combination" is used twelve times in the first four chapters; it is used 31 times in his chapter on trusts.

Consolidation is a manifestation of "the law of industrial development" and presents a "swift and uncontrollable tendency" among railroads, which can proceed peaceably, "by gradual purchase, absorption, and consolidation," or "fierce[ly]," through "railroad wars and foreclosures" (Cook 173, 178, 179). For Cook, this process is an instance of Herbert Spencer's "law of the survival of the fittest" (216). It is both a *tendency* (an inherent quality) and a *result* of the struggle itself. Moreover, Cook's use of the rhetoric of evolution not only conveys his understanding of the processes of growth and centralization in business as inevitable, but also in more political terms as war: "It may be that the weaker roads must be crushed until they are absorbed by the greater" (177). In this manner, organic metaphors facilitated the exchange not only between law and the natural sciences, but also between law and political economy.

Organic and inorganic metaphors also convey a different sense of unity and hence ultimately also of authorship. Consolidation suggests a loss of individual identity on behalf of the larger entity, while combination suggests that separate parts are arranged in relation to each other without necessarily giving up their individual discreteness. Cook conveys this meaning when he describes the trust as machine: "But the original and simon pure trust is a unique piece of handiwork. It is well fitted to baffle investigation and to work out its schemes secretly, silently, and effectively. [. . .] It is a skilfully constructed intricate machine [. . .]" (Cook 222). The machine qualities that Cook is emphasizing are intricacy, efficiency, and complexity, rather than size or power. The machine's parts work together smoothly, without any friction, and as a result almost obscure their inner workings: "It is well fitted to baffle investigation" (Cook 222). As a consequence of its intricacy and complexity, it distributes responsibility to the point of obscuring the source of its motion. Because it maintains the individual discreteness of its constituent companies, the combination is ideally suited for a "'dark-lantern' affair" (Cook 223), and in Cook's opinion, it promotes "power without responsibility" (220). Combination's association with mechanicalness thereby turns into artificiality and ultimately into artifice. In this way, the man-made device becomes an image for the dispersal and concealment of agency, for "'dark-lantern' affair[s]" (Cook 223), and thus for conspiracy.

The specific use of inorganic metaphors also reflects Cook's ambivalence about trusts. On the one hand, mechanical metaphors, as opposed to organic metaphors, raise the question of authorship, as Laura Muenkler has observed (see 193). Whether the famous metaphor of the clockwork or Cook's "unique piece of handiwork" (Cook 222), when put in opposition to organic metaphors, as in the case of Cook's treatise, they highlight the question of control and creation. But whereas the above examples do underline the conspiratorial dimension of this "machine," Cook also admires the American "ingenuity" (222) of which combinations are the product.

> It is true that the wonderful success of modern business is dependent upon combination; that by combination capital is obtained, enterprises of magnitude conducted, great results accomplished; and that every partnership and every corporation is a combination. But these arguments do not justify the trust mode of combination. [. . .] In short, the trust is not a natural mode of doing business on a large scale. (Cook 227–8)

Cook's observation also alerts us to another implication of the metaphor that follows from its inorganic origins: unlike Cooper's operator-less, noiseless machine, Cook identifies "the restless American" (216), who wants to artificially accelerate the natural process of consolidation as its creator: "he has stopped the workings of the natural laws of trade and has substituted his own makeshift" (216). Because Cook is convinced that "the laws of trade are stronger than the laws of men," he is positive that a natural mode of consolidation will prevail and result in the rise of what he calls "large corporations," otherwise known as holding companies or "New Jersey corporations" (168). Classical republicanism and the anti-monopoly discourse of the Jacksonian era associated (conspiratorial) combinations with self- or special interest and corruption. A similar explanation for the failure of trusts is provided by Cook. He refers to the "competing concerns" that constitute combinations as "various discordant elements" (Cook 218), whose jarring cacophony of voices dooms combinations. "Hence it is that most of the trusts now existing, being merely contract agreements to act together, will be broken up by the acts of the members themselves, who will secretly or openly violate their contract" (Cook 236). Cook's use of a musical metaphor ("discordant") for conveying the relationship among the parts of a combination evokes the liberal notion of a harmony of interests. The trusts, Cook argues, cannot harmonize their individualistic constituents: "being *merely* contract agreements to act together" (Cook 236), they lack something that goes beyond private contract, something that can compel the members to act together for a common purpose. An enduring harmony of elements, Cook suggests, is only possible through incorporation: "Unity and single ownership of all the property" (236, emphasis in the original).

In *The Law of Combinations* (1901), the Chicago lawyer and journalist Arthur J. Eddy strips combinations of some of their mechanistic associations to render them more natural. Joseph Dorfman describes Eddy "as an ardent free-trader" who would cause quite a stir with the publication of his book *The New Competition* (1912), in which he "contended that the 'old competition' which the Sherman Anti-Trust Act sought to restore was cutthroat

competition; that true competition was 'co-operative competition,' the competition embodied in sound trade associations—for a number of which he
was the attorney" (Dorfman, *III* 315). Written ten years after Cook, *The Law
of Combinations* must be read against the backdrop of the emergence of the
natural entity theory as well as the US Supreme Court's inclusive reading of
the Sherman Act as criminalizing every contract, combination, or conspiracy
in restraint of trade. By criminalizing every contract, Eddy suggests, the court
has narrowed the meaning of combination to conspiracy, and Eddy's treatise
can be read as an elaborate attempt at revising this meaning: from conspiracy
to cooperation. For this purpose, Eddy draws on organic images and the
rhetoric of evolution to portray combinations as originating in a human pro-
pensity to associate.

> Evolution of the simple combination.—Most forms of co-operation,
> whether partnerships, associations or corporations, are simple combina-
> tions. [. . .] The simplest combination conceivable is the co-operation of
> two individuals. The bond or agreement which holds them together may
> be of a very intangible character, but so long as they co-operate together to
> attain any object they are in combination. [. . .] The evolution of the simple
> combination can be traced in the economic tendency of men to make use
> of the advantage of co-operation. (Eddy 516)

This is a far cry from Cook's mechanical understanding of the inner
workings of a combination. For Eddy, cooperation is grounded in human
nature and social life, and the law can only recognize and acknowledge this
tendency, which in itself precedes it.

The naturalization of the combination is therefore partly achieved by
rooting it in man's nature, which is portrayed as social rather than individual,
let alone antagonistic (as suggested by Cook's use or social Darwinist rhetoric). In this sense, combination is an organic manifestation of the "intangible"
"bond or agreement" between two individuals. The treatise even contains an
American ur-scene of cooperation:

> It is a dangerous extension of the power of the courts in the administration
> of the criminal law to say that an individual may do certain things and not
> be liable criminally, but if he leans over his fence and talks with his neighbor
> and asks his neighbor's help, both are immediately subject to indictment,
> not for doing or attempting to do anything, but for agreeing to do together
> that which either could do separately—the agreement is criminal, though
> none of the acts contemplated are. (Eddy 229–30)

Eddy's invocation of the right to associate could not be more contrary to
Cook's earlier depiction of "'dark-lantern' affair[s]" (Cook 223), and evokes

the mythical frontier beginnings of American society itself: A man leaning over a fence to talk to his neighbor is a public act, occurring in broad daylight, and as neighborly exchange is emblematic of a democratic society. The fence itself implies a host of associations, beginning with respect for private property as well as separations that are overcome by the friendly gesture of leaning over and talking. Not self-interest but cooperation motivates the combination. The analogy is also meant to suggest that a corporation should be treated as an individual: If the acts of two neighbors are equal to that of a single man, then, Eddy argues, the acts of a corporate body must likewise be equal to that of a single person.

While this association between man's nature and combination is the necessary link that allows Eddy to render combinations more natural, his central argument borrows even more strongly from the natural sciences. Conspiracy itself is declared to be only one of many garden varieties of organization. "Combination is the generic term of which conspiracy is the illegal species" (Eddy 116). The reason that Eddy is so intent on classifying and clarifying is because,

> It is so easy to obscure right notions by the use of sounding phrases, such as "gigantic aggregation," "enormous combinations," "vast aggregations of capital," "huge monopolies," etc.,—many such phrases might be culled from decisions in this connection,—that it would be a wise rule to rigidly exclude all such terms from the discussion of the subject, for they mean nothing and lead to nothing except erroneous conclusions. (Eddy 604)

Eddy suggests that judicial decisions have tended to foreground the size of combinations and even more importantly, have tended to reflexively apply the superlative: *gigantic, enormous, vast, huge,* all of which suggest deviation from an implied norm. By drawing up a classification of combinations, like a family tree, Eddy wants to establish the simultaneous existence of "varieties of simple combinations" (516), which are per se based on the cooperative nature of human interaction, and thus to attune the courts' perception to these varieties.

However, the metaphor of combination remains a problem for Eddy because the separate elements of combination continue to suggest the possibility of a conspiratorial activity in the first place. Hence, Eddy finally returns the combination to the corporate form. The last step in this evolutionary scheme that begins with simple combinations is

> Corporate combinations [. . .]—Combinations formed by the sale or lease of the properties, assets and good will of several parties or corporations *to one large corporation* organized for the purpose of acquiring the several properties. (Eddy 516, my emphasis)

In this way, Eddy returns the combination to its corporate origins, yet now the corporate form is clearly identified as a single unit. At the same time, it presents a hybrid entity, a corporate combination—a body still consisting of separate parts—which only becomes "one large corporation" in the sub-clause and after a transfer of material and spiritual goods: "assets and good will." In this respect, Eddy confirms Cook and goes beyond him: while it was single ownership of all property that unified the corporate body in Cook's view, for Eddy incorporation also requires a moral component.

All Form, No Substance: the US Supreme Court and the Holding Company

The legal significance of *Northern Securities Company* v. *United States* (1904) lies in the fact that it presented the first case of a holding company before the United States Supreme Court. Until then, legal scholars like Arthur J. Eddy were convinced that the holding company, or "New Jersey corpora-tion," as it was commonly called, was not a combination within the meaning of the Sherman Act because "it was a legal structure for a single business firm, created by the sale of one corporation's property to another corporation" (Hovenkamp, *Enterprise & Law* 264). The Supreme Court, led by Justice Harlan, thought otherwise. The decision was not unanimous, however, and in its aftermath lawyers insisted that "corporate asset acquisitions and hold-ing companies legal under state law could not be considered 'combinations' under the Sherman Act. Identifying what constituted the business 'firm' was a prerogative that belonged to the states" (Hovenkamp, *Enterprise & Law* 265).

Writing for the majority, Justice Harlan therefore needs to show what dis-tinguishes holding companies from corporations. Laying out the argument that a holding company (incorporated under New Jersey law) is a combina-tion within the meaning of the Sherman Act, he begins by reconstructing the events that led to the lawsuit.

> Prior to November 13, 1901, defendant Hill and associate stockholders of the Great Northern Railway Company, and defendant Morgan and associ-ate stockholders of the Northern Pacific Railway Company, entered into a combination to form, under the laws of New Jersey, a *holding* corporation, to be called the Northern Securities Company [. . .]. (*Northern Securities* v. *United States* 322–3, emphasis in the original)

Notice how the defendants "entered into a combination to form [. . .] a *holding* corporation." "Entering into" suggests some form of vessel that can contain Morgan, Hill, and the stockholders. At the same time, they "form" this container: the "*holding* company." Thus, what Harlan is saying is that they entered one container to form another container, and this image is later repeated when he describes the process again: "The stockholders of these two competing companies disappeared as such for the moment, but immediately reappeared as stockholders of the holding company [. . .]" (*Northern Securities* v. *United States* 327). This image of containers within containers—an array of nesting dolls—is perceived as threatening because, as the following observation from Justice Brewer's concurring opinion makes evident,

> this process might be extended until a single corporation whose stock was owned by three or four parties would be in practical control of both roads, or, having before us the possibilities of combination, the control of the whole transportation system of the country [. . .]. (*Northern Securities* v. *United States* 364)

Despite its appearance in the shape of a single entity, Harlan and Brewer are saying, the holding company still contains separate elements who are its principals and the source of its agency.

The metaphor of the company as container, moreover, allows both organic and mechanical associations. It is the basis of Harlan's declaration "that it is a mere depositary, custodian, holder or trustee of the stocks of the Great Northern and Northern Pacific Railway companies" (*Northern Securities* v. *United States* 325). Containing and thereby obscuring multiple constituents, the company conceals the source of its agency. This is also why Harlan dwells on the metaphor used by J. P. Morgan in his testimony.[12]

> In his testimony, he was asked, "Why put the stocks of both these [constituent companies; *insertion in the original*] into one holding company?" He frankly answered: "In the first place, this holding company was simply a question of *custodian*, because it had no other alliances." That disclosed the actual nature of the transaction, which was only to organize the Northern Securities Company as a *holding* company, in whose hands, not as a real purchaser or absolute owner, but simply as custodian, were to be placed the stocks of the constituent companies—such custodian to represent the combination formed between the shareholders of the constituent companies [. . .]. (*Northern Securities* v. *United States* 355, emphasis in the original)

In this passage, metaphor and metonymy are virtually stacked into each other. The body whose "hands" Harlan refers to is that of the holding company, and as metaphorical body it is given a role and a name: that of the custodian who acts in the interests of others, thus "represent[ing] the combination" synecdochically as "its head and front" (*Northern Securities* v. *United*

---

[12] The only other judge to employ this term is Justice White (dissenting opinion), who uses it once.

States 347). In fact, Harlan's rhetoric evokes earlier cases, such as *Louisville Rail-road* v. *Letson* (1844), in which the metaphor of the veil expressed a logic of internal and external identity. Why head and hands are not enough to legitimize the holding company as corporate person (and thus to distinguish it from a trust) becomes evident in Harlan's description of the company's purchase: "There was no actual investment, in any substantial sense [. . .]. If it was, in form, such a transaction, it was not, in fact, one of that kind" (*Northern Securities* v. *United States* 354–5). In other words, the container was not properly filled—not invested with substance. Like De Forest's "Great Subfluvial" in *Honest John Vane*, it is an empty shell, whose form is made to disguise its emptiness like a garment or a "veil," but whose "actual nature" is "disclosed" by Morgan's remark. Clearly, the main purpose of the holding company is an immaterial one for Harlan, mere representation.

It is no coincidence that Harlan's and Brewer's descriptions, in particular the figurative register of containers and custodians, is evocative of the debates in *Louisville Rail-road* v. *Letson* (1844) and *Deveaux* (1809) over whether courts can legitimately lift and lower the corporate veil as they try to determine corporate citizenship. Writing in 1912, I. Maurice Wormser identifies *Deveaux* as the first case in which an American court acknowledged this question (and its import for equity) and then proceeds to an overview of the conditions under which courts lift, or rather pierce, the veil that includes Brewer's concurrence in *Northern Securities* (507). Common to those conditions and criteria is the instrumentalization of the corporate form—what Wormser, referring to Brewer's concurrence, calls "the sham and subterfuge of incorporation" (507). He explains that incorporation is a mere "sham and subterfuge" if there is "evidence that the corporation created is only an adjunct of the business of its creator,—a mere agency, or instrumentality, through which it acts,—a mere business department, or bureau, so to speak" (502). Drawing on inorganic metaphors, Wormser explains that a holding company turns a corporation into an agent and thereby instrumentalizes the form.[13]

In Brewer's vision of the nesting dolls, a republican fear of factions and *imperium in imperio* is also manifest. In fact, Harlan twice uses the phrase *at the mercy of* to describe the position of the American people if corporations remained unchecked.

> If such combination be not destroyed, [. . .] the entire commerce of the
> immense territory in the northern part of the United States between the

---

[13] See Thomas K. Cheng for a comparison of English and American courts on piercing the veil. According to Cheng, "[i]n the United States, the instrumentality doctrine was first formulated in 1931 by Frederick J. Powell" (348).

Great Lakes and the Pacific at Puget Sound will be at the mercy of a single holding corporation, organized in a State distant from the people of that territory. (*Northern Securities v. United States* 328–9)

"Destroy," "at the mercy of," "territory," "State"—Harlan is clearly drawing on a set of metaphors that is equating business with war and in this particular case, nothing less than foreign invasion. Reminiscent of Ruiz de Burton's call to oust "the Invader" at the end of *The Squatter and the Don*, Harlan portrays the combination as a foreign corporate sovereign, who has infiltrated the Nation: "It is the combination of these large and powerful corporations, covering vast sections of territory [. . .], and acting *as one body* [. . .], that constitutes the alleged evil [. . .]" (*Northern Securities v. United States* 339, emphasis in the original). In this passage, Harlan evokes the image of rival corporate bodies and of centralized power threatening the republic that is reminiscent of the fears over corporate conspiracy from the 1830s. Quoting from an earlier case, Harlan makes explicit that the combination is an aggregate of individuals that can threaten the social body: "*There is a potency in numbers when combined which the law cannot overlook*, where injury is the consequence" (*Northern Securities v. United States* 341, emphasis in the original).

In his dissenting opinion, Justice Wendell Holmes Jr. criticizes Harlan. In his view, Harlan's interpretation of the Sherman Act and of the role of combinations in the market threatens the associational foundations of US society. He argues that the Act should not be construed "to mean the universal disintegration of society into single men, each at war with all the rest, or even the prevention of all further combinations for a common end" (*Northern Securities v. United States* 407). Holmes's dissent is based on an understanding of combinations as cooperative in nature. He adds that Harlan's interpretation, if sustained, "would make eternal the *bellum omnium contra omnes* and disintegrate society so far as it could into individual atoms. If that were [the Act's] intent, I should regard calling such a law [. . .] an attempt to reconstruct society" (*Northern Securities v. United States* 411). If taken to its logical conclusion, the policy of unrestricted competition that Harlan pursues would mean the dissolution of the social contract on which society is based. Because nobody can truly be pursuing this goal, Holmes argues, they must admit that combinations are an essential component of a society based on contract and cooperation.

But as we have seen, Harlan does not only see conspiracy in an act of combining against others. He is also troubled by an absence of substance. As Harlan's use of figurative language shows, the corporation as empty container cannot pass as legal person. In fact, in his concurring opinion, Justice Brewer takes extra care to make this point: "A corporation [. . .] is not endowed with the inalienable rights of a natural person. It is an artificial person, created and existing only for the convenient transaction of business" (*Northern Securities* v. *United States* 363). As artificial person, one might add, it is dependent on the state's power to grant it existence. During the last two decades of the nineteenth century, it was the presence or absence of the state in the creation of the business organization that distinguished trusts and corporations. As we have seen, this difference gave rise to fears of business conspiracies to monopolize markets which also evoked republican fears of the corruption of the polity and the emergence of rivaling corporate bodies. But in order to conceive of these entities as single units and thus bodies capable of unified action, lawyers like Eddy had to transform the trusts' "discordant elements" (Cook 218) into a corporate body that retained its ability to contain multiple constituents and simultaneously harmonized and unified them. Organic metaphors not only lent themselves to an image of coherent growth, but also legitimized the corporate form as pre-legal and natural. As Justice Harlan's words suggest, such figurative shifts did not conceal the emptiness of the corporate person, which was threatening to become an endless chain of signifiers, a "combination of combinations," as lawyers and economists sought ways to express corporate agency in keeping with the corporations' pluralist foundation and against the specter of conspiracy. The representational challenge was not theirs alone, however. Any journalists intent on investigating the role of corporations in politics and society likewise had to find ways to represent the corporate form to their readers. Depending on their motives and their medium—text or image—journalists responded to this challenge in different yet interrelated ways.

III. Imagining the Standard Oil Company

In the public perception, the emergence of the "Trust Problem" as a political, legal, and economic issue in the late 1880s seemed shrouded in mystery. Between 1888 and 1892, a series of "dramatic" lawsuits had brought the trust form to the public's attention but thrown little light on the details of the arrangement (Sklar 98). "The 'trust' is the sphinx of corporations, except that it is not a corporation at all," writes *The Nation* in May 1887, and it elaborates that the trust

> may own and control many corporations, but it is bound by no law. There are no limitations upon it, not even those of time and space. Neither the public nor the shareholders can call it to account. It has no fixed abode, no place of meeting [. . .]. It may dissipate the capital confided to it without danger to anybody except the confiding investors. It may oppress the public without fear of the State because there is nothing for the State to lay hold

of. Although it calls itself a trust, it is as far as possible from being such. There is a body of law applicable to trusts, but there is no law applicable to "the trust." It should be called a Confidence, since it has no similitude to anything known to the law as a trust. (380)

The public turned to newspapers and periodicals to learn more about big business, in particular through a new form of investigative journalism that was published by magazines like *McClure's* and which Theodore Roosevelt famously described as "muckraking." Writers like Lincoln J. Steffens, Ray Stannard Baker, and Ida M. Tarbell investigated the wrongdoings of political machines and monopolies in their articles. Their journalistic prose adapted established anti-monopoly rhetoric as they revealed to their readers the invisible workings and intangible powers of large industrial combinations.

In this regard it can be said that the journalism of the time was motivated by the aim to expose and to make visible, in other words, to permanently fix what seemed to have neither "fixed abode" nor specific legal shape. This also included the visual art in the magazines, specifically the satirical cartoons and caricatures that took on trusts and "Robber Barons." The 1896 cover of *Puck*, for instance, shows Puck—a plump boy, modeled after the sprite of Shakespeare's *Midsummer Night's Dream*—opening a curtain and pointing at two men sitting in front of an open safe full of money bags, as if lifting the corporate veil, while the caption reads, "The True Inwardness of It." Journalistic prose and magazine art thus jointly shaped the popular imaginary on trusts and combinations in the late nineteenth century. As we will see, metonymy and personification emerged as privileged rhetorical devices by which journalists and cartoonists met the representational challenge that the trusts and combinations posed.

Trusts and "Robber Barons"

In order that their readers could see what seemed otherwise invisible or inaccessible, the magazines had to find ways to represent the trusts. This was particularly important given the period's appetite for images, which had been whetted by the development of new technologies for reproducing original drawings, cartoons, and photographs. In fact, advances in printing and low prices for paper accelerated the growth of magazines and newspapers during the last two decades of the nineteenth century. What the "cheap technique known as the halftone" did for magazines like *McClure's* (Mott, *IV* 5), "chromolithography" did for satirical magazines like *Puck* and *Judge*, which "were two of the first magazines in the country to publish in color as well as black and white" (John 8). Illustrations were not entirely uncontroversial among publishers, since they seemed to cater to an illiterate clientele. Nonetheless, newspapers and weekly magazines regularly included political cartoons, with satire magazines often featuring lavish center spreads. *Puck* and *Judge* were the two most successful satirical magazines of the era. *Puck* had been founded in 1877 by Joseph Ferdinand Keppler, the magazine's chief cartoonist until his death in 1894, and his business partner Adolf Schwarzmann. It had begun as a German-language publication in September 1876, but its success quickly led its editors to publish it in English as well. "By the late 1880s, the Democratic *Puck* claimed a weekly circulation of nearly 90,000. Each issue had three color cartoons: one each on the front and back covers and a two-page spread in the middle" (Culbertson 281). During this period, the magazine's political influence was at its height, in particular in the presidential campaigns of 1880 and 1884. In 1881 a group of former *Puck* employees, among them James A. Wales, founded the magazine's rival, *Judge*. "The new venture seldom matched its longer established rival in verbal wit and imaginative satire, but it often outshone *Puck* in cartoon art" (Grant 111). Under the artistic leadership of Bernhard Gillam, Eugene Zimmerman, and Grant Hamilton, the magazine would eventually eclipse even *Puck* (Culbertson 281). Like its rival, it featured three large color illustrations per issue as well as "a resident comic overseer—'The Judge,' a smirking Falstaffian figure" (Grant 111). While both *Judge* and *Puck* were based in New York City, the West Coast's center of publishing was San Francisco. It was here that Bret Harte and Ambrose Bierce worked as writers and editors for magazines like the *Golden Era*, the *Overland Monthly*, and the *Wasp*.[14] The latter was an illustrated satirical magazine that had been founded in 1876 and which published not only Harte and Bierce but also Mark Twain's work. In 1879, Bierce became the magazine's chief editor and for the next five years the magazine "stung busily here, there, and everywhere" (Mott, *III* 57).

In cartoons and caricatures as well as in written sketches and portraits, journalists depicted and criticized the rise of large organizations. Doing so, they also needed to find ways to convey the position and power of the individuals representing them. Cartoonists drew on a wide variety of "sources, including the Bible, Shakespeare, classical literature, mythology, fables, art, sports, and other contexts and allusions that would have been understood

---

[14] While the former two magazines are prominent examples of California's publishing scene, Frank Luther Mott compares the *Wasp* more explicitly to the *News-Letter* and the *Argonaut*, magazines that were representative of "[t]he urban journal of society news and miscellany" (*III* 77). "The *Wasp* was the illustrated weekly of the trio, and sold for five dollars a year while the others were priced at four. These three and the *Wave*, a fourth urban weekly, had about the same circulation [between 1885 and 1905]—fourteen to eighteen thousand" (Mott, *III* 106).

by even moderately educated readers" (Culbertson 287). In representing the trusts, which were a regular topic throughout the 1890s and early 1900s, the dominant figurative mode of these cartoons was metonymy, followed closely by personification. In 1900, for instance, two of *Puck*'s covers featured cartoons depicting the "ice trust," the American Ice Company incorporated in 1899, "which briefly but spectacularly succeeded in gaining monopoly control over the New York City ice supply" (Hemenway 189). In one cartoon, New York mayor Robert Van Wyck is depicted as Julius Caesar, swimming for his life among a sea of ice blocks labeled "Ice Trust," while help appears to arrive in the shape of a life preserver labeled "Tammany Machine Power." In another, Tammany "Boss" Richard Croker, dressed as a laborer, is carrying a block of ice while pursued by an angry mob.[15] In both cartoons, the commodity thus synecdochically signified the trust, but that was not always the case.

Entrepreneurs and business magnates like Andrew Carnegie, J. P. Morgan, and John D. Rockefeller often featured in these pictures. While they can also be read synecdochically, their presence underscored a different aspect of the trusts. For instance, in anti-monopolist rhetoric, these men—together with the likes of Jay Gould and Cornelius and William H. Vanderbilt—were "robber barons," an epithet that originated with Charles Francis Adams Jr. and emphasized the abuse of the privileges granted by the public (John 3–4).[16] In this regard, it also evokes the Jacksonian anti-monopoly tradition, of course, though with an added emphasis on the kind of quasi-sovereign power wielded through the corporation. This is particularly evident in a cartoon that was published in *Puck* in 1904: the same year that the Supreme Court decided the *Northern Securities* case, and the year in which Ida M. Tarbell's "The History of the Standard Oil Company" was in its last installment. The cartoon by John S. Pughe showed John D. Rockefeller as "The King of the Combinations" (Fig. 4.1).

"The King of the Combinations" is a two-page spread, and the entire left (or upper) half of the cartoon is taken up by the king's crown, so big it reaches

---

[15] The caricature is called "Caesar Up to Date," and was drawn by S. D. Erhart. While the "ice trust" was a short and local affair, it illustrates a case of trust-based monopoly for a staple. "Ice was more a necessity than a luxury in 1900. It was virtually essential for the preservation of foods, and doctors had already documented the relationship between infant mortality and drastic heat or ice shortages—times when it was difficult for the poor to preserve milk. [. . .] Wrote the *Times*: 'To corner ice is very much like cornering air and water'" (Hemenway 159).

[16] This is particularly evident in the case of railroads, to which Adams was referring. For an analysis of the "robber barons" in political cartoons see Richard John's excellent "Robber Baron Redux: Antimonopoly Reconsidered."

all the way up to the clouds. Rockefeller's body, small in comparison to his head, is dressed in a courtier's outfit: hose and stuffed breeches. An ermine cape covers his shoulders and is decked with dollar signs; a chain around his neck proclaims his name. He stands on a Standard Oil barrel and the landscape that surrounds him, overshadowed by his crown, is barren, save some oil wells in the distance. What is most noticeable here is scale: the head and particularly the crown are huge in comparison to the body, and in addition the crown contains whole train wagons and oil barrels representing the different branches of the petroleum industry that the Standard Oil Company has integrated. They are the crown jewels: the Lehigh Valley Railroad, the St. Paul Railroad, and so forth.

The cartoon is an example of how artists used scale as yet another mode to portray industrial power and specifically monopoly. In representations of the conflict between labor and industry, giants often argue over the heads of smaller figures that represent the general population. In a *Puck* cartoon by Udo J. Keppler titled "Between Two of a Kind" (1902), for example, a small figure kneels between two angry-looking giants labeled "Commercial Trust" and "Labor Trust." The "Customer" has raised his hand in a begging gesture. In this image, labor unions appear on an equal footing with the bosses in terms of power, though the origins of their power are identified as much more physical: a club labeled "Strike" refers to the coercion that the strike represented legally, and to the physical violence that too often accompanied strikes. While the union's representative could be both a union boss and a simple laborer, the commercial trust was embodied in capitalist figures with top hats, black coats and striped pants, often barely covering bulging bellies.[17] Despite the relevance of scale as a metaphor in anti-trust cartoons, Richard John argues that it was not the size of the combinations that turned the public against them, but special privilege and corruption.

That is why it is significant that "The King of Combinations" does not explicitly suggest that Rockefeller has gained his position through fraud, which was often the topic of other trust cartoons featuring monarchs. In Pughe's "The Kind of Anti-Trust Legislation That Is Needed" (1902), for example, Uncle Sam shines a light on a surprised king whose crown bears the inscription "Trusts" and who sits on a throne of locked cash books, ledgers, and journals. It is a reference to the difficulties that the courts had in getting access to the trusts' books, and simultaneously an illustration of William Cook's "'dark-lantern' affair[s]" (223). None of this is present in "The King

---

[17] For a particularly grotesque rendition of the capitalist as human money bag see Keppler's famous "Bosses of the Senate" (January 23, 1889).

of Combinations." Instead, Rockefeller, arms akimbo, meets the reader's gaze frontally—a posture that suggests self-confidence. A sovereign whose huge crown overshadows the landscape surrounding him, the figure evokes Justice Harlan's fear of a territory "at the mercy of" a foreign corporation. What is more, by making him a "king," "combinations" become his subjects, as if Rockefeller's rise portends an age of industrial feudalism and political incorporation.

The Standard Oil Company and the Oil Men

At one point, Ida M. Tarbell tells her readers that

> there is probably not a public character in the United States whose private life is more completely concealed than is that of John D. Rockefeller. The same cloak is drawn over it as over his business life, and up to this time the law has never forced back the cloak as it has repeatedly from his business life. ("Character Study II" 387)

In other words, while the law may lift the corporate veil, unmasking the person requires the journalist. By the time Tarbell started writing about the Standard Oil Company, she had already built a reputation, specifically so on two biographical pieces published in *McClure's Magazine* in 1894 and 1896.[18] The first was a series on the life of Napoleon Bonaparte, on the strength of which "McClure's [*sic*] circulation doubled"; the second a series on the life of Abraham Lincoln, which was even more successful and secured Tarbell a permanent position at the magazine (Sicius 111). Both had been written on assignment, and *The History of the Standard Oil Company* likewise came as an assignment, yet with a personal connection that made her particularly suited in the eyes of the *McClure's* staff. Her father had been a member of the Petroleum Producers' Union in Pennsylvania, and therefore Tarbell had had first-hand experience of the Standard Oil Company's impact on small producers (Weinberg 206).[19]

Considered alongside cartoons and caricatures, Tarbell's *The History of the Standard Oil Company* and her subsequent "Character Study" of Rockefeller dovetail with the visual rhetoric described above. Both publications include images that accompany and illustrate the text. The *History* was first published

---

[18] *McClure's Magazine* was a monthly that was published from 1893 to 1929. The literary contributors to *McClure's* included Frank Norris as well as "Stevenson, Kipling, Howells, Gladstone, Conan Doyle, Edward Everett Hale" (Mott, *IV* 7–8).

[19] I will predominantly use the name Standard Oil Company because Tarbell's *History* covers the period from the company's incorporation in Ohio, its transfer into a trust and subsequently into a holding company.

in *McClure's Magazine* as a series of nineteen installments between November 1902 and October 1904 and republished as a two-volume book in November 1904. In *McClure's*, the influence that the popular demand for images had on journalism is particularly evident. Each issue included a

> few pages devoted to what were called "Human Documents," each of them a series of three to six portraits of some famous man taken at different ages. [. . .] [T]he passion of readers of the mid-nineties for portraits of the great and near-great would be hard to overstate [. . .]. (Mott, *IV* 590)

When Tarbell published *The History of the Standard Oil Company* it also featured numerous photographs depicting members of the company and of its competitors, such as the members of the Producers' Union. To the portraits Tarbell added images of teamsters, oil wells, and pipelines, which—just like the faces in the photographs—make manifest what can be described as the *History*'s dominant figurative mode: metonymy. While most often used as a kind of shorthand that would in and of itself be of obvious value to journalistic writing, in this case metonymy and synecdoche may also have been the most immediate solution for the problem of the trusts' immateriality and elusiveness. Both materialize the combination, give it substance, and make it tangible.

In telling the story of the conflict between the Standard Oil Company and its competitors, Tarbell's master narrative is that of the frontier as it had been formulated by, for example, Frederick Jackson Turner in "The Significance of the Frontier in American History" (1893) and Theodore Roosevelt in *The Winning of the West* (1885–94). While Turner had claimed that the frontier was closed, in reality new "bonanza frontier[s]," such as wheat farming in California, continued to open up and thus also appeared to further validate the myth of the frontier (Slotkin 18). Tarbell's *History* registers the transformation of "the political, economic and social conditions under which these new 'frontiers' [developed]" (Slotkin 31). As Richard Slotkin puts it, "Individual entrepreneurs and settlers on the new frontiers of the industrial and railroad eras had to contend (on increasingly disadvantageous terms) with large capitalist enterprises for control of the new resources" (31). The dominant arc of the *History* is the story of how the Standard Oil Company achieved monopoly position in the petroleum industry through a series of quasi-feudal wars over territory and transportation. Part of this plot, moreover, is the story of American civilization itself: the emergence of social and industrial organizations on the petroleum frontier, and the transition from one successful American character to another.

The conflict that drives the narrative is between the Standard Oil Company and the petroleum producers, who will repeatedly establish unions to defend their business against the Standard's intrusions into their territory. Despite stories of individual lives and fortunes, these men feature mostly as a group, and throughout the two volumes Tarbell refers to them as "the oil men," "men of the oil country," or simply "the Oil Regions." They are identified through their relationship with the resource over which the conflict is carried out, and like this resource, the men appear easily set on fire. Over and over again, Tarbell emphasizes their ability to think and decide fast, to recognize "chance[s]" (*History I* 8, 11) and to be "[w]ide awake to actualities" (*History I* 15). Moreover, they had to have "a great persistency in undertakings" (*History I* 8), since they labored under difficult conditions. In this way, Tarbell develops a portrait of a certain type of character that had found a prominent formulation in Turner's thesis. In the *History*, the petroleum industry features as an unchartered territory and a wilderness that is full of potential as well as of danger, and whose exploitation requires a pioneer spirit: "young, vigorous, resourceful, indifferent to difficulties" (Tarbell 21). But unlike Turner's asocial pioneers, "the oil men" do not move on. Despite their pronounced individualism and despite numerous conflicts, such as with the teamsters, the men not only develop a thriving industry, but they also establish towns; in fact, both processes appear related in Tarbell's description: "Out of this poverty and disorder they had developed in ten years a social organization as good as their commercial" (*History I* 35).

The velocity with which they have established both an industry and a community is noteworthy, since relationships to time play a significant role in Tarbell's characterizations. The men recognize chances quickly, decide quickly, and are overall keen on fast results. Many of them engage in land speculation; or, as Tarbell puts it, "it took a dash of the gambler" to succeed in the business (*History I* 32).[20] Moreover, their success makes "the oil men" arrogant, and early on they display their own desire for monopoly position: "The men of the oil country loudly declared that they meant to refine for the world. They boasted of an oil kingdom which eventually should handle the entire business [. . .]" (Tarbell, *History I* 52). Their "boastful ambition" is diametrically opposed to John D. Rockefeller's quiet and methodological personality, which on first sight appears as an example of the ascetic self-discipline of the antebellum character ethic as it applied to the early entrepreneurial capitalists, the captains of industry (Tarbell, *History I* 67).[21]

Though not nearly as exhaustively as in her "Character Study," Tarbell devotes several paragraphs throughout the *History* to describing Rockefeller's

[20] She will specify later that "[t]he Oil Region had [. . .] one fatal weakness—its passion for speculation" (*History II* 254).

[21] See Halttunen 205–6.

family background and character. The crucial moment in his story is his experience of poverty as a child, the dubious morality of his father, and his Franklinesque devotion to systematic frugality and industry. He even keeps a "ledger" (Tarbell, *History I* 41). These lead him first to a partnership business as a commission merchant in Cleveland and then, in 1870, to the incorporation of the Standard Oil Company of Ohio. Tarbell emphasizes the systematic difference in entrepreneurship that follows from these character differences, such as when, for instance, Rockefeller's aversion to waste motivates him to use every product of the petroleum refining process, which consequently increases his profits. But despite the relevance of his industry and his frugality (which, at other times, she calls stinginess), Tarbell repeatedly emphasizes the superior significance of other character traits for his business: secrecy, patience, and persuasiveness. Especially the first of these features prominently in the *History* as one of "Mr. Rockefeller's chief business principles—'Silence is golden'" (*History I* 68). He is a visionary, but in contrast to "the oil men," his perseverance is coupled with patience and foresight. Rockefeller is not a gambler but a strategist, who plays the game of kings: "He was a brooding, cautious, secretive man, seeing all the possible dangers as well as all the possible opportunities in things, and he studied, as a player at chess, all the combinations which might imperil his supremacy" (*History I* 51).

Though Rockefeller is central to her *History*, in the war narrative, the struggle over the petroleum industry is not conducted by individuals but by groups. While the Standard faces opposition from several actors—among them "the railroad kings" and the independent refiners—the producers, or rather, "the oil men," present its most prominent antagonist in the *History*. Between 1872 and 1880 they form several Producers' Unions to destroy the Standard's control over the transportation and distribution of petroleum. In a chapter titled "The Oil War of 1872," Tarbell recounts how "the people of the Oil Regions" learn of the "conspiracy" of refiners and railroads, "how all oildom rushed to the streets" in protest (*History I* 71), and how they decide to form "[t]he Petroleum Producers' Union [. . .] to grapple with the 'Monster'" (*History I* 85), as Rockefeller's first secret combination is popularly called. Engaged in a narrative of feudal wars over territory, Tarbell portrays the combination's forays almost as epically as Justice Harlan had in the *Northern Securities* case when he imagined the invasion of a territory by a holding company. In 1880, the Union has a realistic chance to oust the Standard. But as Tarbell explains, the producers lack "loyalty to the agency [they] had established" (*History I* 118), and the Union dissolves after a false compromise with the Standard. While Tarbell praises the Union's democratic spirit, she makes clear that it is the character of the individuals that compose it that bring about its failure: "Mr. Rockefeller knew the producers, knew how feeble their staying qualities in anything but the putting down of oil wells [. . .]" (*History I* 260). The Union is a "loose and easily discouraged organization," and "the impatience and instability of the prosecuting body and the compactness [is no match for the] resolution and watchfulness of the defendants" (Tarbell, *History I* 260).

Like the "discordant elements" (218) of which Cook warns his readers, "the oil men" remain disparate individuals, unable to "work[. . .] in harmony" for an extended period, and therefore are unable to fully pursue their strategy against the Standard (Tarbell, *History I* 256). At first, Tarbell suggests that it is a lack of competent leaders that weakens the Union; yet when they have finally found them, the Union members desert their leaders at a critical moment: "Their power, their means, were derived from this body [of producers], and this body for many months had been giving them feeble support" (*History I* 257). The very qualities that had made "the oil men" successful pioneer-businessmen appear to make it impossible for them to submit their individual ambitions to the interest of the Union. Yet Tarbell seems to say that it is this quality that is necessary for success in the business. Here her narrative about the warfare in the petroleum industry contains another about the transition from one successful type of businessman to another. While the producers present a rugged frontier individualism, they are also representative of proprietary capitalism. "With many of them the resistance was due simply to their love for their business and their unwillingness to share its control with outsiders" (Tarbell, *History II* 155).

The Union's dissolute condition is developed in contrast to "the compactness and harmony of the Standard organization" (Tarbell, *History II* 254). Like the Union, the Standard consists of capable individuals, yet their individualism is described quite differently.

> The combination, in 1870, of the various companies with which he was connected had brought together a group of remarkable men [. . .]. Indeed nothing could have stopped the Standard Oil Company in 1870 [. . .] but an entire change in the nature of the members of the firm, and they were not the kind of material which changes. (Tarbell, *History I* 50–1)

Notice how the "remarkable men" turn into the "material" that constitutes the Standard, a metaphor that recurs: "No dead wood is taken into the concern" (Tarbell, *History II* 254). In his testimony for the Hepburn Commission in 1879, from which Tarbell quotes, W. H. Vanderbilt underscores the fact that to deal with the Standard is to deal with its combined elements: "They would never have got into the position they now are without a great deal of ability—and one man would hardly have been able to do it; it is a combination of men" (qtd. in Tarbell, *History II* 253). Vanderbilt not only emphasizes the fact that the Standard is a combination of men, but also underscores that the company's success would not have been possible for a single individual to achieve. This crucial insight is backed up by Tarbell: "However sweeping Mr. Rockefeller's commercial vision, however steady his purpose [. . .], he would never have gone far had he not drawn men into his concern who understood what he was after and knew how to work for it" (*History II* 251). Through contrast with the producers, these men, whose names and short business biographies Tarbell provides, emerge from her narrative as representatives of a different kind of individualism; one that can be "integrated" into a larger system. Tarbell refers to this aspect as "harmony."

The terms "harmony" and "harmonious" appear throughout the *History*. The most eloquent use of the terms is found in H. H. Roger's testimony before the Hepburn Commission, testimony that Tarbell calls "a masterpiece of good-natured evasion" (*History II* 130). For Howard Horwitz, harmony here signifies upon the Standard's transcendence of individual agency: "it was sheer form, a symbolic locus of the powers of the market" (184). But the term's historical origins suggest that it had a more concrete and more managerial meaning.

Q. You said that substantially 95 per cent. of the refiners were in the Standard arrangement?

A. I said 90 to 95 per cent. I thought were in harmony.

Q. When you speak of their being in harmony with the Standard, what do you mean by that?

A. I mean just what harmony implies.

Q. Do you mean that they have an arrangement with the Standard?

A. If I am in harmony with my wife, I presume I am at peace with her, and am working with her.

Q. You are married to her, and you have a contract with her?

A. Yes, sir.

Q. Is that what you mean?

A. Well, some people live in harmony without being married.

(Tarbell, *History II* 362)

"Being in harmony" thus implies a union of interests, which enables the combination to endure and its members to cooperate. Moreover, in the antebellum period, political economist and advisor to President Lincoln Henry

C. Carey had made the "harmony of interests" the centerpiece of his work, in which he argued (against the European position advanced by Smith and Ricardo), "that the free growth of market relations would result in the break-down of class distinctions" (Sklansky 80). Not quite Howard Horwitz's transcendence of individual agency,[22] harmony here refers to an orchestration of what may have been and may even continue to be disparate interests and thereby to avoid the kind of "discordant elements" (218) that Cook identifies as the primary reason for the failure of combinations. Hence, Rockefeller's relation to the combination is rather like that of a clockmaker to the workings of a clock: he possesses the ability "to bring men [. . .] to work harmoniously" together (Tarbell, *History II* 234).

But at times, the compactness of the Standard body in Tarbell's narrative is so great that it becomes an actor of its own, even when Tarbell casts it in the role of tool.

> But this huge bulk, blackened by commercial sin, has always been strong in all great business qualities—in energy, in intelligence, in dauntlessness. It has always been rich in youth as well as greed, in brains as well as unscrupulousness. If it has played its great game with contemptuous indifference to fair play, and to nice legal points of view, it has played it with consummate ability, daring and address. [. . .] [T]he Standard Oil Trust has always been something besides a fine piece of brigandage, with the fate of brigandage before it, that it has been a thing with life and future. (Tarbell, *History II* 231–2)

More than just a tool or a device, the trust is given a subjectivity in this passage, "a thing with life and future" that will not have served its purpose after the conquest is over, as brigandage would, but that will last.[23]

---

[22] In his well-argued chapter on Emerson, Rockefeller, and the Standard Oil, Howard Horwitz also argues that Roger's use of the term "harmony" here can be juxtaposed with Cook's "discordant elements" (184), but he also suggests that it signifies upon a form of impersonal, transcendent agency (185–6).

[23] In her analysis of Tarbell's "The New Place for Women in Industry," Martha Banta has pointed out that Tarbell has a gendered view of time. "Real boys are perceived as having ambition. They possess a future history into which they evolve as they pass from one stage of growth to the next. [. . .] [Women] have a long way to go up the evolutionary ladder. It is strongly implied that they are at an historical impasse; no advancement is in sight" (Banta 164).

As in the quote above, in such passages Tarbell tends to mix organic and inorganic metaphors.

> [B]y a marvelous genius in organisation Mr. Rockefeller had devised a machine with a head whose thinking was felt from the seat of power in New York City to the humblest pipe-line patrol on Oil Creek. This head controlled each one of the scattered plants with absolute precision. (Tarbell, *History II* 233)

In this passage, we find both the metaphor of the organization as body and the metaphor of the business as machine or man-made device. The head is identified as the "nine trustees [in whose 'hands'] the entire business was placed in 1882" and who are at the top of a pyramid of unprecedented knowledge management (Tarbell, *History II* 232). Thoughts, of course, are immaterial and can therefore not be felt, but Tarbell depicts the impact of the Standard Oil Company as if it were reaching across the states to touch the pipeline control on Oil Creek—clearly, a power that is superhuman. As its "president," Rockefeller is depicted as part of the combination and sometimes he is truly identical with it, as in the following passage, in which Tarbell imagines Rockefeller's response to a new competitor: "If these refineries operated *outside of him*, they might disturb his system [. . .]" (*History II* 13, my emphasis). Similar to some of Justice Harlan's remarks in the *Northern Securities* case, Tarbell is stacking metaphors here: Rockefeller is the Standard, which is the entirety of the refining industry at this point, which in turn is a container with an inside and an outside.

Tarbell often transfers Rockefeller's character traits onto his "creation" (*History II* 232), in particular when she calls the Standard secretive. But metaphorical transfers can work both ways. In fact, a reverse transfer occurs in which Rockefeller is given attributes that originate in the company proper: omniscience and, to some degree, omnipresence. "Mr. Rockefeller[,] [. . .] this man, whom nobody ever saw and who never talked, knew everything— even unexpected and trivial things—and those who saw the effect of this knowledge and did not see how he could obtain it, regarded him as little short of an omniscient being" (Tarbell, *History I* 65). Tarbell attributes this "popular dread" partly to Rockefeller's secretive manner, "the atmosphere of mystery" that he created (*History II* 64).[24] While Tarbell brushes off this tendency

---

[24] The origin of his knowledge, however, lies in the fact that the Standard has its own "secret bureau for securing information" (Tarbell, *History II* 35). In the chapter "Cutting to Kill," Tarbell explains in detail the company's "news-gathering" strategies and how this is just one example of the Standard's implementation of scientific management. She provides copies of

to mystify Rockefeller, rejecting any "occult" interpretations (*History II* 65), by the end of the *History* she is herself engaged in these mystifications, such as when she calls Rockefeller a "silent, patient, all-seeing man" (*History II* 232) and describes the trustees' skill as "almost preternatural" (*History II* 230). This reverse flow of attributes—from the Standard to Rockefeller—has very real implications, as Tarbell's account of one of the Union's fights against the Standard makes evident. Having brought suit against the railroads and the pipelines in 1880, the Union could have persisted in this course and fought them out. Instead, "they interrupted their work by bringing their spectacular suit for conspiracy" (Tarbell, *History I* 242) and as a result give the witnesses in the other suit an opportunity to plead the Fifth Amendment. While this is another example of the Union's impatience, it is also conditioned by their attitude toward Rockefeller: "The Union was so much more eager to punish Mr. Rockefeller than it was to punish the railroads [. . .]" (Tarbell, *History I* 244); not a particular railroad president, but the railroads, while it is not the Standard they want to punish but Mr. Rockefeller himself.

The bidirectional flow between the two entities, Rockefeller and the Standard, renders Rockefeller often machine-like. While the Standard grows more human in the course of the *History*, Rockefeller becomes less and less so. This is particularly evident in the "Character Study" that Tarbell published in *McClure's* in 1905, in which she recounts his upbringing, his rise from rags to riches, and his unscrupulous business practices. The "Study" is driven by her observation of what she calls Rockefeller's "hypocrisy" and her sense that it is the public's "*duty*" to know more about a man whom many deem a role model (Tarbell, "Character Study I" 227). Tarbell's obsession with Rockefeller's true character and her mission to educate those who may strive to emulate him are reminiscent of the antebellum cultural imaginary, with its belief in the sentimental "cult of sincerity" and its fear of the masked individual or commercial Machiavelli. But what she calls Rockefeller's "hypocrisy" alerts us to the qualities that make him a transitional figure, halfway between entrepreneurial and corporate capitalism ("Character Study II" 396).

While the *History* begins with a quote from Emerson, the two installments of the "Character Study" begin with quotes from Machiavelli's *Prince* which deal with concealment and duplicity. Tarbell's insistence that Rockefeller is "a hypocrite" because his private and his public persona are not identical is

---

the "report cards" that employees were filling out, all the way down to the local agents, and drawings of the command structures within the company that explain how information is sorted and channeled efficiently. In this way, she identifies what will become one of the central features of the representation of corporations (omniscience) as well as the foundation of modern corporations' power.

reminiscent of Cooper's criticism of the gap between Senator Gradenigo's private and public selves ("Character Study II" 395); but in Tarbell's characterization there is even a hint of the schizophrenic.

> [I]t may be that Mr. Rockefeller is one of those double natures that puzzle the psychologist. A man whose soul is built like a ship in air-tight compartments to use the familiar figure—one devoted to business, one to religion and charity, one to simple living and one to nobody knows what. But between these compartments there are no doors. [. . .] Each is a solitary unit. It is an uncanny explanation, but it may be a true one. (Tarbell, "Character Study II" 395)

Tarbell's "uncanny explanation"—reminiscent of Cook's "intricate machine" and Harlan's nesting dolls—turns Rockefeller into a contraption, one that "is well fitted to baffle investigation," to quote William Cook. In fact, while Tarbell introduces her investigation as necessitated by the public's need to know, her continuous bafflement may be the result of her own creation. Because she has turned him into an "intricate machine" for business, Tarbell expects Rockefeller to function solely on the principle of profit maximization. In trying to "harmonize [. . .] the man with a mask and a steel grip" with the "rare 'other self,'" the "quiet, modest, church-going gentleman" (Tarbell, "Character Study II" 395), Tarbell's narrative creates these two Rockefellers.

As part of the narrative of economic conquest, Tarbell also repeatedly casts Rockefeller as Napoleon Bonaparte, about whom she had previously written a biography. As with Ruiz de Burton's references to Napoleon, which alluded to him as a symbol of imperialism as much as of unscrupulous greed, Tarbell's comparison emphasizes at least two aspects: his aggressive entrepreneurialism, and also his talent for strategy and planning.

> With all these reflections fresh in mind Mr. Rockefeller again bent over a map of the refining interests of the United States. Here was the world he sighed to conquer. If we may suppose him to have begun his campaign as a great general with whom he has many traits in common—the First Napoleon—to begin his, by studding a map with red-headed pegs marking the points he must capture, Mr. Rockefeller's chart would have shown in and around Boston perhaps three pegs, representing a crude capacity of 3,500 barrels [. . .]. His work was to get control of this multitude of red pegs and to fly above them the flag of what the irreverent call the "holy blue barrel." (Tarbell, *History I* 146)

It is important to note the reference to Napoleon as "the great general" that suggests that Tarbell, unlike Ruiz de Burton, does not mean this comparison as unflattering. Rockefeller's talent for strategy and planning is epitomized by his company, the Standard, which "is as perfectly centralized as the Catholic church or the Napoleonic government" (Tarbell, *History II* 232). According to historians, this latter aspect is also what drew Populists to the figure of Napoleon. Tarbell's own biography of Napoleon had been part of "a Napoleon revival" during the 1890s which made manifest many Americans' hope "for a strong man to deliver the nation from its multiple ills" (Postel 164). As Charles Postel explains, "the Populists [. . .] were drawn less to military valor and patriotic glory than to the example of Napoleon's administrative systems and energized state power" (Postel 164).[25] As Tarbell persistently understands Rockefeller as Napoleon, thus emphasizing his influence and ability as an individual, she also needs to account for "the force of the combination" (*History II* 253), which transcends the individual, yet of which the individual is also part, and prosperously so. Tarbell's depiction of Rockefeller and the Standard is therefore an attempt to reconcile the liberal ideal of self-reliance with the triumph of corporate capitalism.

The Standard Oil Octopus and Centralized Power

Among the tropes that would become most closely associated with the trusts in the popular imaginary of the late nineteenth and early twentieth centuries was the octopus. Tarbell, too, evokes this trope in her prose, such as in the following remark: "Mr. Rockefeller had devised a machine with a head whose thinking was felt from the seat of power in New York City to the humblest pipe-line patrol on Oil Creek" (*History II* 233). In a famous two-page spread in *Puck's* September 1904 issue, the Standard Oil octopus sits on the surface of the globe, the curved horizon visible in the background, and thereby appears even larger than in other cartoons, suggesting that its reach is global. It has already wrapped tentacles around a state house, the US Capitol, as well as around helpless representatives of different industries. Now it seems to move toward the White House, tucked into the lower left corner of the cartoon. The bottom caption reads, "Next!" The octopus's many arms thus

[25] In *The Populist Vision*, Charles Postel discusses other biographies, such as Tom Watson's *The Story of France* (1899) and *Napoleon* (1908). In cartoons of this period, though, public figures appear as Napoleon in different contexts. Twice, for instance, *Puck* features Napoleon figures sitting on a rock in exile and abandoned by their friends, and each time the context is Wall Street and financial investments; see Frederick Burr Opper, 1885, "The 'Little Napoleon of Wall Street' in Exile"; Keppler, 1904, "A Napoleon of 'High Finance.'" In 1895, a sullen "Napoleon McKinley," worshiped only by "Southern Friends," watches as Columbia—cast in the role of the heroine of George du Maurier's novel *Trilby* (1894)—is cheered by crowds, with the bottom caption reading, "Say, what's the matter with those blooming jays? Don't they know there's a Napoleonic revival now going on?" (Louis Dalrymple, "The Neglected Idol.")

correspond to the Standard's far reach, the fact that its "thinking was felt from the seat of power in New York City to the humblest pipe-line patrol on Oil Creek." Of course, the octopus, like the many-headed beasts that were also used to depict trusts, drew on Jacksonian anti-monopoly rhetoric. In 1888, for instance, William Allen Rogers drew a cartoon for *Harper's Weekly* titled "The Trustworthy Beast" that pictures such a many-headed creature[26] along-side Andrew Carnegie, who is stating that "[t]he public may regard trusts or combinations with serene confidence." In the cartoon, the bovine animal features five visible heads, with captions on the horns that identify each head: Oil Trust, Sugar Trust, Salt Trust, Lumber Trust, and Steel Trust. Carnegie himself is shown, true to life, as introducing the beast to a skeptical-looking Uncle Sam.

At the same time, as noted at the beginning of this chapter, the *Wasp's* 1882 Chinese octopus image suggests that the octopus metaphor also lent itself to evoking non-individualist subjects. In this respect, it is significant that Keller modified his depiction of the Mussel Slough incident from a two-headed giant, as in "The Ogre of Mussel Slough" (March 12, 1882) to a single-headed octopus. In "The Curse of California" (August 19, 1882), Stanford and Leland are depicted inside the head of an octopus, itself labeled "Railroad Monopoly" (Fig. 5.1). As a result, Leland and Crocker lose some of their representative function in favor of the abstract concept of "monop-oly" personified directly in the octopus. Published by James Swinnerton in the San Francisco *Examiner* on December 14, 1896, another cartoon that is related to the Mussel Slough incident shows Collis P. Huntington as an octopus. Swinnerton has given it Huntington's bearded face and his name is imprinted on his forehead, while the tentacles clutch figures representing the manufacturer, the farmer, the merchant, and the orange raiser, as well as the San Francisco State House and slips of paper representing the honest vote and the subsidized press. The caption reads, "This Is The Monster California Must Destroy Now If Ever" (repr. in Lewis).[27] As in the cartoon "Next!," which depicts the Standard Oil Company, there is only one head. While the image of the octopus has mostly been interpreted as portraying the company's far-reaching influence and great strength, Tarbell's emphasis on Rockefeller's

---

[26] The year before, *Harper's* had published a similar cartoon, possibly by Rogers as well, in which several such beasts had represented individual trusts: "Nothing but Feed and Fight," *Harper's Weekly*, December 3, 1887.

[27] In *The Cartoon History of California Politics* (1978), Ed Salzman and Ann Leigh Brown point out that the octopus makes a twentieth-century return in Californian cartoons. In 1960, the *San Francisco Chronicle* published a caricature by Robert Bastian that criticized "[Pat] Brown's proposal for a massive water project" (113).

managerial skills and the Standard's organizational structure suggests that it can also be read as an image of centralization.

IV. *The Octopus* and the End of Individualism

As scholars often point out, it is likely that young Frank Norris never saw Keller's cartoons. It was probably not until 1886, when he moved to San Francisco, that Norris began to learn about California's difficult relationship with the Southern Pacific Railroad Company: first as a citizen and then, between 1896 and 1898, as a reporter for the San Francisco *Wave*. But the octopus was such a common symbol for trusts and monopolies that it is hard to see how Norris could have avoided encountering some representation of it even before then. As Glen Love and David Carpenter point out, a statement in a letter he wrote to a friend suggests that Norris "had decided upon the title of the novel before beginning his research" (Love 5). Once he had begun the latter, moreover, it is likely that he came across Swinnerton's cartoon of Huntington, particularly as Norris personally interviewed Huntington. In addition to questioning his source for the octopus, literary scholars have suggested that other metaphors, such as the wheat and the railroad, are more important. For instance, Colleen Lye has shown that the trust and the wheat share important characteristics, and Adam H. Wood has even argued that the railroad and the wheat are the novel's real protagonists.

At the same time, the octopus does connect the novel most directly to the contemporary anti-monopoly discourse and presents its strongest claim to the status of reform fiction, as June Howard has pointed out. Referring to the first chapter's ending, which features a train running over a flock of sheep in the night, she explains, "[t]his image, used repeatedly in the novel, is one of the crucial elements that enables readers to interpret *The Octopus* as an unequivocal denunciation of the Southern Pacific and the trusts, and therefore as an unequivocal reform novel" (Howard 120). Not everybody agrees with this view, however, as readers and critics have struggled to reconcile the novel's purported reform agenda with the fate of the individuals who fight the corporation and the interpretation of their destruction provided by the homodiegetic narrator at the end of the novel. Leaving California on a ship bound for India, Presley famously declares, "[g]reed, cruelty, selfishness, and inhumanity are short-lived; the individual suffers, but the race goes on" (Norris, *The Octopus* 1098). The final section of this chapter addresses this paradoxical position and proposes to read *The Octopus* not as a critique but as a celebration of corporate capitalism.

The events on which the *The Octopus* is based occurred in May 1880, during Charles Crocker's presidency of the railroad. The farms in Mussel Slough, located in the San Joaquin Valley, had been part of one of the first commercial agricultural ventures in California. As George L. Henderson explains, in the 1870s an almost seamless transition occurred in California between gold mining and, once the mines had given out, "bonanza farming." Crucial to this development was transportation, and accordingly, it was when the Southern Pacific Railroad, under Leland Stanford and Charles Crocker, extended the line that the boom began. Before the Southern Pacific Railroad's claims to the land had even cleared, however, squatters moved in. They took advantage of the fact that the company's ownership of the land was not yet settled and began what Henderson calls "an economy of squatter capitalism," based on "the speculative values of the railroad lands" (128). "When the railroad's claims were finally confirmed, a large faction of squatters, including a militia, organized into a Settlers' Grand League to thwart attempts to dislodge them" (Henderson 128). In 1878, the railroad gave the squatters the opportunity to buy their land. While the settlers insisted on prices based on the "previous government prices and would even pay for the land at current prices, minus the value of improvements" (Henderson 130), the railroad offered prices that were consistent with the value that the settlers' speculative economy was trading on. In a California Supreme Court ruling in 1878, the court upheld the railroad's claim. After a failed compromise brokered by Stanford in early 1880, the situation escalated. On May 11, "outside purchasers" arrived with a US Marshal to take possession of their land. During a discussion between representatives of the two groups, a misunderstanding led to a shooting in which five farmers and two railroad agents were killed. In the aftermath, "Mussel Slough came to be venerated by farm, labor, and anti-monopoly civic groups as a site of anti-railroad martyrdom" (Henderson 130).

Scholars suggest that Norris must have been attracted by the dramatic quality of the material and the opportunity that it provided for him to write about the American West. "The Mussel Slough incident was [. . .] Norris's almost inevitable choice," maintains Donald Pizer, "for it combined in one sensational event the nucleus of a story about California wheat growers and the Southern Pacific with a chance to explore the larger problem of industrial monopoly in America" (*Norris* 120). In addition to Ruiz de Burton's *The Squatter and the Don* (1885), whose title alludes to the event, at least two novelistic treatments existed prior to Norris's novel, though there seems to be no evidence that Norris was aware of them: William Chambers Morrow's *Blood-Money* (1882), and Josiah Royce's *The Feud of Oakfield Creek* (1887).[28]

---

[28] Royce used two historical events as material for his novel. In addition to Mussel Slough he drew on a conflict "in Contra Costa County between a rich San Francisco lawyer holding title and settlers claiming to live on public land" (Thomas, *New Historicism* 138). For further reading see McKee, Brown, Conlogue, and Beers.

In Royce's novel, the conflict is carried out on a personal level between two former friends: Alonzo Eldon, the railroad's president, and Alf Escott, who represents the squatters. The novel suggests that "the settlers have no legal rights whatever, and that they have all the moral rights you please" (Royce 184).[29]

In addition to these literary fictions, John R. Robinson had published a nonfiction account of corruption in the practices of the Big Four in 1894 that may have served as a source for Norris.[30] This text uses the octopus in its title: "The Octopus: A History of the Construction, Conspiracies, Extortions, Robberies, and Villainous Acts of the Central Pacific, Southern Pacific of Kentucky, Union Pacific, and Other Subsidized Railroads" (1894). While not concerned with the Mussel Slough incident, Robinson's "The Octopus" makes the case for shareholders' rights, the "interests" to which Royce's Eldon refers when he justifies his actions. Written with the intention of informing the public about the fraudulent and corrupt practices of a monopoly, Robinson's account quotes from witness testimonies and newspaper reports, provides financial documents, and throughout adds personal commentary on the railroad agents' conduct, in particular the Big Four. Robinson had a personal motive in uncovering the railroads' misdeeds: he claimed to have been defrauded into selling his railroad stock below value by his own lawyer, who was secretly working for the road. In contrast to Royce's and even Robinson's work, Norris's depiction of the corporation is much more ambivalent.

Norris designed *The Octopus* as the first novel in a trilogy "around the subject of Wheat" (qtd. in Pizer, *Norris* 113). He told William Dean Howells in a letter that the project would comprise, "[f]irst, a study of California (the producer), second, a study of Chicago (the distributor)[,] third, a study of Europe (the consumer) and in each to keep the idea of this huge, Niagara of wheat rolling from West to East" (qtd. in Pizer, *Norris* 113). In the final pages of this chapter, I want to show how Norris responded to the representational challenge of the corporate form by drawing on and further developing the popular imaginary that I have outlined so far; how he designed the central conflict as one between two combinations in which the individual members

---

[29] Josiah Royce's view of California was much more critical than Norris's, and he had laid it out in detail in *California: From the Conquest in 1846 to the Second Vigilance Committee*, a history he had published in 1886. Moreover, Royce's pragmatist philosophy strongly went against the grain of radical self-reliance and rugged individualism. His 1908 work on ethics, *The Philosophy of Loyalty*, for instance, emphasizes the priority of community and communication and makes them the basis of an individual moral life. For a discussion of Royce's novel and his philosophy, see F. G. Robinson, "Josiah Royce's *California*."

[30] Love and Carpenter suggest that Robinson's "exposé" served as a source for Norris (2).

are of secondary importance, and how that shapes his representation of individual and collective agency. How, in fact, the ability to subdue individual ambition emerges as a prerequisite for economic success. Instead of Howard's "unequivocal denunciation of the Southern Pacific and the trusts" (120), I argue that we should read *The Octopus* as an exploration of what Christopher Newfield has called "corporate individualism" and as a vision of an incorporated American empire (5).

The corporation in *The Octopus* is introduced metonymically: piece by piece, or rather, sign by sign. The first of these is, of course, the locomotive as well as the actual roads or lines; the second is its representatives, such as S. Behrman.[31] Moreover, the locomotive's "steam whistle" accompanies Presley's bicycle ride across the countryside at the beginning of chapter 1, and its slaughter of a flock of sheep closes the exposition (Norris, *The Octopus* 579).

> [A]bruptly Presley saw again, in his imagination, the galloping monster, the terror of steel and steam, with its single eye, cyclopean, red, shooting from horizon to horizon; but saw it now as the symbol of a vast power, huge, terrible, flinging the echo of its thunder over all the reaches of the valley, leaving blood and destruction in its path; the leviathan, with tentacles of steel clutching into the soil, the soulless Force, the iron-hearted Power, the monster, the Colossus, the Octopus. (Norris, *The Octopus* 617)

Colleen Lye has suggested that Norris's use of mixed metaphors in his descriptions of the railroad may originate in the trusts' "elusive representability" ("American Naturalism" 87). But as we have seen, the simultaneous use of organic and mechanic metaphors in representations of trusts during this era was common and signified upon different aspects of combinations, such as industrial growth, competition, and control.[32] Moreover, central to these first encounters with the corporation in the novel are its focalizer, Presley, whose perspective orients large parts of the novel and complements the heterodiegetic narrator that takes over when Presley is absent from events. Presley's style as focalizer is very visual: as in the passage above, he is continuously engaged in seeing, interpreting, and imagining. But while this emphasis on visuality is reminiscent of Cooper's *The Bravo*, for example, and of Tarbell's probing gaze in her work on the Standard Oil, neither Presley nor

---

[31] S. Behrman enters and exits the plot via synecdoche. We first learn of him when Presley reads a newly erected sign, and the last thing we see of him is his hand sticking out from under the avalanche of wheat that has buried him.

[32] In her survey of organic and inorganic metaphors in German constitutional law, Laura Muenkler explains that mechanical and organic metaphors were not mutually exclusive until the Romantic period (193).

the heterodiegetic voice are interested in exposure or revelation, but in the relationship between the many and the one.

Presley's visions of the California countryside open and close the novel, yet in between, his perception of it has transformed. His initial view from the hillside provides a nostalgic and romantic image of the land that is interrupted in classical fashion by the machine, which signifies upon progress and the impact of industrialization on nature. The romanticizing hilltop view also provides the reader with an opportunity to adjust Presley's guiding perspective as narrative center, and it also foreshadows Presley's visual and economic education in the course of the novel: "Presley occupies a very specific social and economic position. His desire in the opening chapter of the novel to marginalize economic and political constraint to epic mythos only identifies the prerogative of that position" (R. J. Ellis 21). By the end of the novel, Presley has come to recognize that "the larger view" to which he also aspired in his art must include an economic perception of the landscape that surrounds him (Norris, *The Octopus* 1097). For James Dorson, the novel's continuous shift between micro- and macro-visions of events, between individuals and aggregates, reflects Norris's aesthetic approximation of a "statistical vision" (63), which Dorson relates to the role of empirical data in contemporary debates over railroad rates and monopolies. Brook Thomas has similarly commented on the novel's response to the challenge of representing not just individual but "group reality." Rejecting Benn Michaels's interpretation of corporate personality as central to the logic of naturalism itself, Thomas writes:

> If there is a "logic" to naturalism, and especially the work of Norris, [. . .] it is related to the difficult effort to express the rising influence of all sorts of associations within American culture (including labor unions, ethnic groups, and professional organization, as well as corporations) in a genre that demands individual characterization. (*New Historicism* 149)

The difficulty is exacerbated by Norris's investment in the frontier myth (an effort that finds its counterpart in Presley's attempt to write a Poem of the West), with its emphasis on the individual. As we saw in *The History of the Standard Oil Company*, such old-fashioned frontier individualism is ultimately incompatible with corporate liberalism. Accordingly, *The Octopus* not only closes with the poet's larger vision of society, but also with the vision of a new kind of corporate individual that has submitted to "a massive (yet benevolent) administrative power which is private and out of one's control" (Newfield 63).

Throughout the novel, however, administrative, technocratic visions of the land are represented by maps. *The Octopus* contains three "maps-in-prose," which establish claims of ownership to the land as well as reinforcing the novel's portrayal of "space [as] contested and subjective" (Berte 209, 210). As Leigh A. L. Berte has argued, these maps are also "narratives of force," representing the political, economic, and social forces that shape the novel's naturalist geography (208). The first map, which hangs in Magnus Derrick's office, shows Los Muertos (Norris, *The Octopus* 619); the second hangs behind the railroad agent's desk in his office in Bonneville (Norris, *The Octopus* 730); the third map is "a commissioner's official railway map of the State of California" and represents the entire network of railway tracks that run through the state (Norris, *The Octopus* 805). As the narrative moves outward—from Presley's and the farmers' local concerns to the state-wide and, through association with trade, ultimately global reach of the corporation—the maps take the reader to ever higher planes of vision and abstraction. All three, however, express not only "claims of ownership," as Berte argues, but also attempts at organization.

In Tarbell's depiction of Rockefeller bending over a map like Napoleon, it is ultimately not conquest but organization that matters. As I argued earlier, Tarbell's emphasis on Napoleon's and, by extension, Rockefeller's abilities to organize and centralize territory resonates with late nineteenth-century visions of economic leadership as described by Alfred D. Chandler: "[t]o unite [. . .] men and offices into a smooth working organization" ("Industrial Corporation" 83).[33] As a result, organization in itself becomes a virtue and loses some of its specifically economic or political connotations. Instead, it establishes a homology between political and economic incorporation in which the corporate and the national body become near identical. In the following passage, which describes the "commissioner's official railway map of the State of California," this incorporation is imagined in terms of a grotesque literalization of the process:

> The whole map was gridironed by a vast, complicated network of red lines marked P. and S. W. R. R. [. . .] The map was white, and it seemed as if all the color which should have gone to vivify the various counties, towns, and cities marked upon it had been absorbed by that huge, sprawling organism, with its ruddy arteries converging to a central point. It was as though the State had been sucked white and colorless, and against this pallid background the red arteries of the monster stood out, swollen with life-blood,

[33] Following Chandler's lead, Olivier Zunz's *Making America Corporate, 1870–1920* (1990) is a study of precisely this type of personality, epitomized by the mid-level executive: "For empire building was dependent on bureaucracy building, and the ultimate success of bureaucratic rules depended on the imposition of new values, shared, and, to a large extent, created by this new managerial stratum" (7). Also see Robert Wiebe for the influence of "bureaucratic thought" on ideas of leadership and democracy, in particular 160–2.

reaching out to infinity, gorged to bursting; an excrescence, a gigantic parasite fattening upon the life-blood of an entire commonwealth. (Norris, *The
Octopus* 805–6)

The image of the railroad as a "parasite" feeding on the "commonwealth"
also evokes the octopus, with a head ("a central point") and arms ("ruddy
arteries"). But while the depiction's grotesqueness is clearly meant to repulse
the reader, it is rooted in the same organic metaphors that are employed in the
description of Magnus Derrick's office and the map of Los Muertos.

> The office was the nerve-centre of the entire ten thousand acres of Los
> Muertos, but its appearance and furnishings were not in the least sugges-
> tive of a farm. [. . .] A great map of Los Muertos with every water-course,
> depression, and elevation, together with indications of the varying depths
> of the clays and loams in the soil, accurately plotted, hung against the wall
> between the windows [. . .]. (Norris, *The Octopus* 619)

Like Rockefeller and "the oil men," the railroad and the farmers are
engaged in a war over national territory and its resources. Through the maps,
moreover, the novel places a similar emphasis on the role of organization and,
as we will see, management in this conflict as does Tarbell's *History*, for example. As a result, it becomes clear that contrary to interpretations of the novel
as reformist, it does not pitch an evil corporation against a virtuous group of
farmers, nor invading squatters and corporations against a hybrid Californian
elite in the making, as in the case of Ruiz de Burton's *The Squatter and the
Don*. Rather it explores the conditions necessary for organization, whether
economic or social.

Hence, Norris's depiction of the farmers warrants a closer look as well.
As has often been noted, the wheat farmers in *The Octopus* are very unlike
the squatters of Mussel Slough.[34] The methods by which most of the farmers
work their farms are those of large-scale businesses: centralization of management and investment in new technologies. For instance, even before the
farmers have made their first appearance, we learn that Magnus Derrick wants
to farm Los Muertos without tenants. What this must mean for the tenant
farmers is only hinted at, since the only farmer in the novel is the German
Hooven, who pleads his case, having worked on the farm for seven years, and
is eventually allowed to stay. But even as Hooven returns to his work with

---

[34] For example, by Donald Pizer: "Norris included a few tenant farmers and railroad workers
among these victims, but for the most part they are capitalists who have large investments
in land and equipment and who are competing with the railroad for the riches of the land"
(*Norris* 120).

"the watering-tank" (Norris, *The Octopus* 580), Presley observes Magnus Derrick's son "setting out the automatic sprinkler" (Norris, *The Octopus* 582), which, we must assume, will eventually replace men like Hooven. Support for this reading can be found in June Howard's observation on how the farmers consistently exclude working-class men like Hooven from their decision-making processes:

> Hooven is asked to leave the meeting at which the league is organized, for he is not a landowner but a tenant. The small farmer and former engineer Dyke is asked to leave [. . .]. But Presley and his friend the mystical shepherd Vanamee, who however improbably is also college-educated, are permitted to remain as observers; there is no question but that a class distinction is what is at stake. (Norris, *The Octopus* 121)

Connecting Norris's disregard for the common people to his aim of writing an "Epic of the Wheat," Adam H. Wood has argued that "[w]hat we find in the novel is [. . .] a distinctly 'whitewashed' American story. That is, once the workers [. . .] are erased from the novel, the image of the wheat can begin to take on new prominence" (114). In other words, just as railroads build themselves, so does wheat grow without the need for human labor.

In this respect, the novel shares another parallel with Tarbell's *History*: the absence of labor unions. Just as Tarbell's narrative focuses almost exclusively on the capitalists and their combinations, so does Norris's retelling of the conflict refuse the tenant farmers and workers any form of agency, let alone organization. Annixter's disgust and rejection of the unions' and the novel's characterization of the communist Caraher as scheming and violent only serve to further elevate the cause of the farmers (Norris, *The Octopus* 713). The conflict that the novel portrays thus ensues between two organizations, the corporation and the league of farmers. What is striking is that the league is also characterized in terms of a combination: from its conspiratorial nature to its individualistic (and therefore unstable) foundations.

Reminiscent of Ida Tarbell's "oil men," the farmers are portrayed as rugged individualists, and their pronounced individuality resists sustained integration into a social whole. Their individuality is associated with that of the frontier spirit. Magnus Derrick, for instance, is described as a speculator with a background in mining.

> At the very bottom, when all was said and done, Magnus remained the Forty-niner. Deep down in his heart the spirit of the Adventurer yet persisted. [. . .] For all his public spirit, for all his championship of justice and truth, his respect for law, Magnus remained the gambler, willing to play for colossal stakes, to hazard a fortune on the chance of winning a

million. [. . .] It was in this frame of mind that Magnus and the multitude of other ranchers of whom he was a type, farmed their ranches. They had no love for their land. They were not attached to the soil. They worked their ranches as a quarter of a century before they had worked their mines. (Norris, *The Octopus* 813–14)

Unlike Tarbell's "oil men," the farmers do not draw their identity from the land, and their interest in it is temporary. Moreover, their gamble is based on a resource that is firmly established in the novel as a food of the people: wheat. In other words, their gamble endangers the sustenance and livelihood of those whose epic battle they are supposedly fighting. When Magnus conceives of his plan to cut out the middlemen and deal with markets directly, it is another instance in which his individualist entrepreneurialism precludes his participation in global networks of force or at least, results in an inability to submit to them.

While the League could have provided a moment of solidarity and unity, it is marred by self-interest and ambition. The agreement to act together against the railroad that is formed during the meeting on Los Muertos is portrayed as partly motivated by a desire for revenge on S. Behrman. But more importantly, it is clearly characterized as a combination in restraint of trade. In order to get better transportation rates, the group intends to bribe the members of the "Railroad Commission" (Norris, *The Octopus* 660). At first their combination only includes a small number of farmers, who enter it to reduce the grain rates by having their own candidates elected for the Commission. After the publication of the land prices, which could mean the loss of their farms for them, one of the farmers proposes to found a "League," which would include all the farmers in the region.

"*Organisation*," he shouted, "that must be our watch-word. The curse of the ranchers is that they fritter away their strength. Now, we must stand together, now, *now*. Here's the crisis, here's the moment. Shall we meet it? *I call for the League.* [. . .] Every one of us here to join it, to form the beginnings of a vast organisation, banded together to death, if needs be, for the protection of our rights and homes." (Norris, *The Octopus* 797, emphasis in the original)

Yet in a moment of dire need—when the original group of "conspirators" finds out that they are about to be evicted (Norris, *The Octopus* 719)—they cannot assemble the League's members to support them. Ultimately, the League lacks "loyalty" (Norris, *The Octopus* 942), and after the shooting, once Magnus has resigned, "they got quarreling among themselves," and the League dissolves (Norris, *The Octopus* 1027). Their individualistic personalities

appear to make the farmers ill-suited for collective action, and the novel's portrayal of the League's disintegration evokes William Cook's argument that it is
the nature of trusts and combinations to disintegrate: "Hence it is that most
of the trusts now existing, being merely contract agreements to act together,
will be broken up by the acts of the members themselves, who will secretly
or openly violate their contract" (236). As we have seen, it requires a form of
management and containment to create the harmony of interest that would
characterize a corporate body.[35]

Their "political manager," Magnus Derrick, is unable to fulfill this role
(Norris, *The Octopus* 664). Magnus is not just defined by his willingness to
take great risks, to "gamble," but also by his political "ambition," which has
earned him the nickname "the Governor" (Norris, *The Octopus* 723). A man
of integrity, he initially hesitates to become party to the scheme of bribery
that the others have proposed, but vanity and ambition are the character flaws
that doom Magnus. Looking at his son Harran, "full of the promise of the
future years," he sees also "himself":

> His blue eyes looked straight into his father's with what Magnus could *fancy*
> a glance of appeal. Magnus could see that expression in the faces of the
> others very plainly. They looked to him as their natural leader, [. . .] and
> in them all he saw many types. They—these men around his table on that
> night of the first rain of a coming season—seemed to stand in his imagi-
> nation for many others—all the farmers, ranchers, and wheat growers of
> the great San Joaquin. Their words were the words of a whole community;
> their distress, the distress of an entire State, harried beyond the bounds of
> endurance, driven to the wall, coerced, exploited, harassed to the limits of
> exasperation. (Norris, *The Octopus* 668, my emphasis)

Not only are the farmers representative types, but Magnus is presented as
a *type*, too. His public exposure takes place on the stage of an opera house and
one of the final glimpses the reader gets of Magnus is him sitting in a dress-
ing room, where the "miserable sham" comes to an end (Norris, *The Octopus*
1023). Yet it was that very atmosphere in which the organization of farmers
was first founded: "Suddenly Osterman leaped to his feet [. . .]. Like the hero
of a melodrama, he took stage with a great sweeping gesture. '*Organisation*,'
he shouted, 'that must be our watch-word'" (Norris, *The Octopus* 797). This

---

[35] Descriptions of the League not only echo that of the corporation in *The Octopus*, but they
also evoke the many-headed beast of the *demos*: "It was the uprising of The People [. . .]. It
was the blind fury of insurrection, the brute, many-tongued, red-eyed, bellowing for guidance, baring its teeth, unsheathing its claws [. . .]" (Norris, *The Octopus* 800).

association of Magnus's kind of leadership and the League's combination with melodrama, emotions, and with vanity stand in contrast to the corporation's president, Shelgrim.

Much has been written about the novel's depiction of Shelgrim, and in particular about Presley's meeting with him: how Presley arrives with the intention of confronting Shelgrim with his responsibility for the horrible events in the Valley, and how he leaves confused as to the conflict's cause and effect. Donald Pizer and other critics have pointed out that Shelgrim's physique resembles that of C. P. Huntington: from the long gray beard to the skullcap. Based on the fact that Presley's acceptance of Shelgrim's view presents a "complete reversal of his earlier convictions," Pizer has also read this scene as an ironic depiction of the rhetorical power and persuasiveness of men like Huntington or, for that matter, J. D. Rockefeller ("Conclusion" 137). Yet the passage does not in itself provide any clues that it should be read ironically, and as to Presley's convictions, they have been completely reversed before. While he is repulsed by workers and tenant farmers at the beginning of the novel, he passionately represents their cause in his poem and even travels to San Francisco to help Hooven's family after his death. Therefore, we can also read this scene as part of Presley's ongoing struggle to adjust his categories of perception; as part of his economic education, which appears at its height during his meeting with Shelgrim, the railroad's president. More importantly, however, the novel's ambivalent depiction of Shelgrim and the corporation is a result of its exploration of organization and (collective) agency.

As in the description of the railroad map, centralization at first serves as part of a discourse of conspiracy in which the protagonist must finally confront and reveal the source of agency behind the tragic events. The corporate headquarters in San Francisco are described as

> the stronghold of the enemy—the centre of all that vast ramifying system of arteries that drained the life-blood of the State; the nucleus of the web in which so many lives, so many fortunes, so many destinies had been enmeshed. From this place—*so he told himself*—had emanated that policy of extortion, oppression and injustice [. . .]. (Norris, *The Octopus* 1031, my emphasis)

Norris is careful to distinguish between the narrator's and Presley's perspective in this passage, and therefore doubt infiltrates the scene from the beginning: "so he told himself." Like the contemporary readership's, Presley's perception is shaped by anti-monopoly rhetoric, such as the octopus. At first admiring the mental and physical energy with which Shelgrim goes about his work, Presley quickly corrects himself: "But the next instant Presley set his teeth. 'It is an ogre's vitality,' he said to himself" (Norris, *The Octopus* 1033).

Throughout the scene, Presley struggles to reconcile his idea of Shelgrim with the man sitting in front of him. In contrast to Magnus, whose first act by which the reader learns about him is the dismissal of the tenant farmers, Shelgrim is introduced by an act of charity. When one of his managers suggests firing a man who has repeatedly appeared at work drunk, Shelgrim considers the man's situation as a husband and a father of three and decides to double his pay. As the narrator is careful to let us know, "Presley had not time to readjust his perspective to this new point of view of the President of the P. and S. W." before being left alone with him (Norris, *The Octopus* 1034). In the following description, Shelgrim literally turns into an octopus; yet while prior octopus metaphors were highly negative, such as the blood-sucking parasite depicted in the railway map, Shelgrim the octopus is evidently an image of superhuman efficiency, reminiscent of the image of centralization in Tarbell's *History*.

> Shelgrim did not move his body. His arms moved, and his head, but the great bulk of the man remained immobile in its place, and [. . .] Presley began to conceive the odd idea that Shelgrim had, as it were, placed his body in the chair to rest, while his head and brain and hands went on working independently. (Norris, *The Octopus* 1035)

Like an octopus, Shelgrim appears to consist only of a head and arms that work independently of the body. Like the Chinese laborer depicted in the *Wasp*, this productivity has an alien quality to it that suggests an almost superhuman power in Shelgrim—as if he himself was not just one, but many. In this way, the novel establishes a sense of conspiracy familiar from the legal discourse on combinations: Shelgrim is not the source of the corporation's agency, he is its agent, acting for it. But in addition, some critics have suggested that Shelgrim's "skullcap" alludes to racial stereotypes and the antisemitic discourse on Jewish world conspiracies such as can be found in anti-monopoly texts such as Ignatius L. Donnelly's *Cesar's Column* (1891).[36] Yet skullcaps were worn by both Collis Huntington and John Rockefeller, neither of whom was Jewish. Moreover, Shelgrim is not portrayed as physically repulsive in the way that S. Behrman is for Presley. The ambivalence in Shelgrim's depiction evidently originates in the novel's ambivalence over corporate agency itself.

This ambivalence becomes evident when Presley charges Shelgrim with being responsible for the railroad, with being its "head," and therefore in control. In his response, Shelgrim famously describes the market as a force field

---

[36] See Lye, *Asia* 63–75.

that follows natural laws and inevitably moves toward growth, thus abdicating any responsibility for the events in the Valley.

> "But—but," faltered Presley, "you are the head, you control the road."

> "You are a very young man. Control the road! Can I stop it? I can go into bankruptcy if you like. But otherwise if I run my road, as a business proposition, I can do nothing. I can not control it. It is a force born out of certain conditions, and I—no man—can stop it or control it. Can your Mr. Derrick stop the Wheat growing? He can burn his crop, or he can give it away, or sell it for a cent a bushel—just as I could go into bankruptcy—but otherwise his Wheat must grow. Can any one stop the Wheat? Well, then no more can I stop the Road." (Norris, *The Octopus* 1037)

In this passage, Shelgrim incorporates agency at the same time that he denies it. From a human octopus he turns into the empty container that his name has been designating all along: a grim shell.[37] Devoid of self, Shelgrim incorporates the agencies of others, such as those of the railroad's shareholders and, ultimately, even of the Chinese laborers that build the railroad, but this agency has been completely abstracted and reduced to "forces." While Presley will later revise his acceptance of this explanation by pointing out that, despite the role of impersonal forces, more harm has been done to the farmers than to the railroad, the image of Shelgrim as agent and container of forces is not itself questioned. This is even more evident when compared to the scene in *The Squatter and the Don* in which Stanford freely admits to acting in his own self-interest.[38]

Following a logic similar to that which underwrites Justice Harlan's discussion of the holding company in the *Northern Securities* case, Norris has created in Shelgrim a figure of speech. A mere executor of these forces, Shelgrim is presented as an agent in a legal sense and not as a principal; as president of the railroad, he is acting for others, in the interest of shareholders, for instance, and not for himself. In *American Literary Realism and the Promise of Contract*, Brook Thomas connects this concept of agency with that of naturalism. Drawing on the work of Mark Seltzer, who argues that the impersonal forces that affect the actors of naturalist fictions render the

---

[37] This passage is a frequent object of literary discussion. On the naturalization of the market see, for example, Wood, and also Collins. David A. Zimmerman reads the novel's portrait of the market as field of invisible forces in terms of the era's fascination with mesmerism.

[38] "I do not aspire to anything more than taking care of my business," Stanford tells his visitors, and adds, "if I don't cause distress, someone else will" (Ruiz de Burton, *S&D* 62).

distinction between bodies and machines problematic and reduce all actors to "middlemen" (qtd. in Thomas, *Realism* 274), Thomas explains:

> The naturalist sense of agency, in other words, betrays a similarity with the corporate sense of agency, although it lacks its organicism. Both are at odds with the promise of contract and the sense of agency suggested by the realists. (*Realism* 274)

The danger of acting for oneself and not for others, or, to put it differently, not in harmony with the forces of the naturalist universe, is also portrayed in *The Pit* (1902), the second novel in Norris's Wheat Trilogy.[39] It deals with wheat speculators in Chicago and in particular with Curtis Jadwin, a self-made man of humble beginnings, who loses his entire wealth by speculating on wheat prices. Gradually, his success in the "pit," where the wheat is traded, edges him on, and he begins to build an excessive corner in wheat (Norris, *The Pit* 197). By doing so he not only contributes to rising wheat prices, but also to hunger and starvation in Europe. Yet, as Donald Pizer notes, Jadwin refuses to see the consequences of his actions, even after he has lost his entire fortune. It falls to his wife, Laura, to care for him at the end of the novel. While many critics have found the marriage plot's lack of integration into Jadwin's story problematic, it gives room to Laura's emotional transformation,[40] in which she learns to subdue the self and to eschew self-interest: "Self, self. Had she been selfish from the very first? What real interest had she taken in her husband's work?" (Norris, *The Pit* 404). Like *The Pit*, *The Octopus* suggests that in order to achieve greatness, one must be able to subdue the self, and in order to act in this world, one must act for others. Despite his title as "political manager," Magnus is unable to integrate the "discordant elements" of the League. In order to be able to do that, the novel suggests, he would have to be more than an individual. One must become an empty container, a grim shell: the representation of a representation.

At the end of *The Octopus*, the corporation is a manifestation of the higher forces that work for the good of all—which, considering the novel's general prioritization of white characters, is the good of the Anglo-Saxon race. But the theme of the subordination of self-interest should not be mistaken for classical republicanism, for example, in which—as discussed in this study's

---

[39] James Dorson reads S. Behrman as "anticipating Jadwin's hubris in *The Pit* (1903)" and emphasizes the contrast between Behrman's selfish and Shelgrim's transcendent personality (56).

[40] The similarity between Magnus and Jadwin has been noted by critics before, but in fact Laura is also connected to Magnus, since they both are said to have a penchant for "the grand manner" (Norris, *The Octopus* 628).

early chapters—virtue consisted in supporting the general interest and corporations were condemned because they served special interests.[41] Shelgrim
is not subordinating his self-interest to the common good, but to corporate
profit. Richard Slotkin aptly summarizes the economic pressures and social
transformations demanding such a personality at the turn of the nineteenth
century: "The health of the new corporate order required the willing subordination [. . .] of private ambition to corporate necessity" (18). Norris is
fascinated with this kind of personality: one who is an agent and serves an
impersonal, powerful collective interest. The fact that it seems to mirror the
classical republican virtue of subordination of self-interest only highlights
the degree to which civic (political) and economic sphere have merged for
Norris. What he portrays here, to paraphrase Christopher Newfield, is the
administrative-bureaucratic kind of corporate individualism.[42]

[41] Based on J. G. A. Pocock's work on the classical republican tradition, you could perhaps
argue that the novel's closing scene does in fact evoke a republican vision. Referring to
Henry Nash Smith's work on myths and symbols in American culture, he writes, "Among
the constants in the literature of American mythology [. . .] is the repetition of prophecies
that the fee-simple empire would not only perpetuate the virtue of a farming yeomanry,
but generate a commerce designed to exceed continental limits and, by opening up the
markets of Asia, bring about the liberation of the most ancient of human societies." He
adds, "The liberation of Asia [. . .] is part of a vision of America as 'redeemer nation'; and
the reason is plainly that it would break the closed circle in which Berkeley had confined
America and would transform the closing fifth act of his *translatio* into a truly millennial
Fifth Monarchy" (542). Also note that Herbert Croly's *The Promise of American Life* (1909)
is a conscious return to the positions of Alexander Hamilton and Thomas Jefferson, with a
preference for the former.

[42] Writing about Emerson and the antebellum corporation, in particular its public and private dimensions, Christopher Newfield notes, "Such a structure had at least the potential
to negotiate the conflicting demands of personal and collective agency, private and public
power, by adapting the more isolated 'possessive' self of classical liberalism to mass culture
while claiming to sustain this possessive self" (68). Ideologically still committed to this
possessive individualism, in practice, corporate liberalism "could depart from a laissez faire
individualism that hampered capital accumulation, not to mention mass governance, for
a corporate model" (Newfield 68). This "particular liberal rhetoric," in which, as Newfield
writes, "the more a person is corporate, the more that person is individual," also informs
Walter Benn Michaels's reading of *The Octopus* and Howard Horwitz's study of Emerson,
Rockefeller, and the Standard Oil, which Newfield criticizes (69).

Conclusion:
Frankenstein in a Gray Flannel Suit

A corporation is an artificial being, invisible, intangible, and existing only in contemplation of law. (*Dartmouth* v. *Woodward*, 1819)

Such is the Frankenstein monster which States have created by their corporation laws. (*Liggett Co.* v. *Lee*, 1933)

In early 1933, a case about Florida chain stores reached the US Supreme Court and prompted Justice Louis D. Brandeis to write a particularly literary condemnation of corporations. The case, which had reached the Court on appeal, concerned a Florida statute requiring the owners of chain stores to pay higher licensing fees. The details were complex, including not just the Equal Protection and Due Process Clause of the Fourteenth Amendment, but also the Commerce Clause of the Constitution. But the bottom line was that the state of Florida was exacting higher fees from single owners—whether corporations or natural persons—that were operating multiple stores across county lines, as opposed to individually owned and operated small stores or cooperatives. More than a dozen corporations, incorporated in Florida as well as in other states, had sued and demanded equal treatment as persons within the meaning of the Fourteenth Amendment—to which, as the Court agreed, they were principally entitled: "Corporations are as much entitled to the equal protection of the laws guaranteed by the Fourteenth Amendment as are natural persons" (*Liggett Co.* v. *Lee* 536). The natural entity theory and the so-called fiction theory of corporate personhood had been more or less accepted by the Court since at least *Southern Railway Co.* v. *Greene* (1909), though it had not replaced the older models. While the Court ultimately did not find a violation of the Fourteenth Amendment, it did hold certain provisions in the statute "unreasonable" and returned the case to Florida for a new trial.

In Justice Brandeis's opinion, not only had the Court missed the point of the statute but there was another, more pressing reason why the statute should be sustained: the fact that the Court was no longer dealing with a rich individual owning many stores, as opposed to a less well-off individual owning only one, as had been the case in the past. Instead, he pointed out, "[the] plaintiffs [in this case] are all corporations" (*Liggett Co.* v. *Lee* 543). The point of "Anti-Chain Store Laws," Brandeis explained, "is to protect the individual, independently-owned, retail stores from the competition of the chain stores" (*Liggett Co.* v. *Lee* 541). Moreover, Brandeis added, the states had history on their side when they tried to restrict the size of corporations. He pointed out that incorporation had been a carefully guarded instrument for the better part of American history precisely because "[t]here was a sense of some insidious menace inherent in large aggregations of capital, particularly when held by corporations" (*Liggett Co.* v. *Lee* 549). It was only because some states (such as New Jersey) had resigned and had begun to exploit the trend toward industrial combination that American society had arrived at a point at which "[t]he prevalence of the corporation [. . .] has led men of this generation to act, at times, as if the privilege of doing business in corporate form were inherent in the citizen; and has led them to accept the evils attendant upon the free and unrestricted use of the corporate mechanism as if these evils were the inescapable price of civilized life [. . .]" (*Liggett Co.* v. *Lee* 548). As a result, corporations had grown to giant proportions, both in terms of capitalization and of the scope of their activities and powers.

It was precisely the sheer size of industrial corporations in the first decades of the twentieth century, critics observed, that gave these enterprises an unprecedented "social significance" (Berle and Means 7). This corporate system, Brandeis declared in 1933, presented "the negation of industrial democracy" and contributed directly to the depression: "Such is the Frankenstein monster which States have created by their corporation laws" (*Liggett Co.* v. *Lee* 567). In fact, in *The Modern Corporation and Private Property* (1932), which Brandeis referenced in his footnotes, Adolf Berle and Gardiner Means (a lawyer and a sociologist) argued that, on account of their size and their use of an open market for their securities, modern corporations "assume[d] obligations towards the investing public which transform[ed] [the corporation] from a legal method clothing the rule of a few individuals into an institution" (6). They had become "quasi-public corporations" (Berle and Means 28), owned by an anonymous multitude of shareholders and operated by small groups of managers without classical interest in the property they were managing (Berle and Means 5). The meaning of their size and the extent to which they occupied a "dominant position" (Berle and Means 28) in the US economy, Berle and Means admitted, was hard to grasp. From their professional perspective, it was only through "the tool of statistics [. . .] [that] we grasp the picture of our economic life as a whole" (Berle and Means 28). In addition to these statistics, they also provided a more narrative account of quasi-public corporations' role and influence on American society, such as in their sketch of the life of the average American individual.

In this sketch, Berle and Means point out how ubiquitous corporations have become, how their goods and services—by way of metonymy, one could add—render them omnipresent, though often unnoticed. "The great companies," Berle and Means write, "form the very framework of American industry. The individual must come in contact with them almost constantly. He may own an interest in one or more of them, he may be employed by one of them, but above all he is continually accepting their service" (19). In great detail, Berle and Means illustrate this ubiquity: how the average American citizen travels on a railway system that is owned by corporations, in trains that are built by corporations, or how he drives an automobile built and fueled by corporations.

> Perhaps, on the other hand, the individual stays in his own home in com-
> parative isolation and privacy. What do the two hundred largest companies
> mean to him there? [. . .] The newspaper which comes to his door may be
> printed on International Paper Company paper [. . .]; his shoes may be one
> of the International Shoe Company's makes; and although his suit may
> not be made of American Woolen Company cloth, it has doubtless been
> stitched on a Singer sewing machine. (Berle and Means 27)

In this way, Berle and Means suggested in 1932, industrial corporations were reaching into every American home and had, in fact, assumed the roles previously assigned only to "major social institution[s]" (1). Drawing on narratives and tropes that should be familiar to the reader of this study by now, they compared this new "'corporate system'" to an older "feudal system," warned of the "concentration" of wealth that it presented, and drew attention to how it was changing older conceptions of private property that had for a long time provided the ideological foundations of American society (Berle and Means 1, 2). In a 1967 preface to the revised edition, Adolf Berle would call the system that this "silent" revolution had produced "Collective Capitalism" (vii, viii).

Between the Frankenstein monster of corporate jurisprudence and the Singer sewing machines of industrial capitalism, the corporation emerges as a larger-than-life collective entity in US culture at the beginning of the twentieth century. Yet this unprecedented scale would increasingly pose a social and cultural problem for these companies.

> The pure size of many corporations—their number of employees, the mag-
> nitude of their production, their capital resources, their national scope in

distribution, and their capacity for political influence—persuaded many Americans, classic economic theory notwithstanding, that the nexus of social institutions within which they lived had been radically transformed. The traditional potency of the family, the church, and the local community suddenly seemed dwarfed by the sway of the giant corporations. This momentous shift in the balance of social forces created a crisis of legitimacy for the large corporations. (Marchand 2)

According to Roland Marchand, the large corporations embraced their status as institutions (rather than mere organizations), through which they hoped to "enhanc[e] [their] moral and social legitimacy" (4). In fact, as Marchand has shown in *Creating the Corporate Soul* (1998), during these decades, this quest for legitimacy would contribute to the professionalization of the narrativization of corporate power, producing a field of its own: public relations.

As this study has repeatedly shown, scale and in particular the relationship between the one and the many (or the sum and its parts), as well as, more specifically, the corporate collective's place within or in relation to the republic and the nation, present recurring themes for the narrativization of the corporation and corporate agency throughout the nineteenth century. While the courts had begun to accept the natural entity theory and, by extension, the separate legal being of the corporate person, for the popular imaginary in the first half of the twentieth century, the corporation would continue to play a role as collective entity: as one of the institutions that they inhabited and that defined social reality. By the 1950s, the corporate cubicle came to symbolize the massification and deindividualization that threatened the American individual, such as in the sociological studies of David Riesman (*The Lonely Crowd*, 1950) and William H. Whyte (*The Organization Man*, 1956) and in the literary fictions of Richard Yates (*Revolutionary Road*, 1962) and Sloan Wilson.

In fact, the titular commodity of Wilson's best-selling *The Man in the Gray Flannel Suit* (1955) could easily have been "made of American Woolen Company cloth, [and] stitched on a Singer sewing machine" (Berle and Means 27). For Wilson's novel, it serves as the central symbol of the corporate "rat race"—which the protagonist eventually refuses to join—and of the deindividualizing effect of corporate work that is only comparable, in the novel, to that other powerful corporate body in US culture, the military (Wilson 4). Arriving at the United Broadcasting Corporation, at which he is applying for a job at the beginning of the novel, the protagonist observes an employee:

> Mr. Everett's office was a cubicle with walls of opaque glass brick, only about three times as big as a priest's confessional. Everett himself was a man

about Tom's age and was also dressed in a gray flannel suit. The uniform of the day, Tom thought. (Wilson 8)

Nor is it a coincidence (given the observations of Berle and Mean) that, when Tom finally decides to quit the job and thereby the rat race forever, he turns to the staple of nineteenth-century liberal capitalism: real estate.

While corporations thus remain relevant as collective entities in the popular imaginary of the twentieth century, the professional narrativization of corporate power, what we call *corporate storytelling* today, would also increasingly strive to individualize the corporation. Because to do so is to reinscribe the legal person into the cultural imaginary in a manner that is not trivial. *Individualizing* and *personalizing* the corporation ultimately provides cultural legitimacy to the claim of single legal personhood that is the basis for the courts' decisions in cases such as *Citizens United* v. *Federal Election Commission* (2010). In this respect, (auto)biography plays a central role among the genres of corporate storytelling, as recent scholarship has noted.[1]

We can glimpse the connection between life writing and corporate personhood in Wilson's novel, too. As part of the job application process, Tom is asked to write his "autobiography" (Wilson 11). "Explain yourself to me," the interviewer tells him. "Tell me what kind of person you are. Explain why we should hire you" (Wilson 11). As Lisa Siraganian has observed, "The relationship between the corporation and Tom is thus predicated not on the corporation exploiting his cheap labor, but on the corporation acquiring and learning from Tom's personal story of underachievement" (103). In the course of the twentieth century, the popular (auto)biographies of CEOs and company founders would play a major role in the public's perception of corporate businesses and brands, but also, I would argue, in the naturalization of the legal fiction of corporate personhood. As Purnima Bose and Laura E. Lyons have observed in the introduction to a special issue of the journal *Biography*, "Life Writing and Corporate Personhood" (2014), "Corporate personhood [. . .] has acquired a social life in contemporary popular and political discourse by creating powerful personas in the forms of advertising emblems and celebrity CEOs" (ix). And the more the public identifies these exceptional individuals with companies they lead, the more self-evident seems the logic by which corporations claim legal individuality and personhood. As the revolutionary origins of the Frankenstein trope remind us, however, corporations are always *the many*, even when disguised as *the one*.

---

[1] See, for example, Bose and Lyons, "Life Writing and Corporate Personhood" (2014).

Bibliography

Acuña, Rodolfo. *Occupied America: A History of Chicanos*. Pearson Longman, 2004.

Adams, Henry. *Democracy: An American Novel*. Penguin Books, 2008.

Alexander, Gregory S. *Commodity & Propriety: Competing Visions of Property in American Legal Thought, 1776–1970*. University of Chicago Press, 1997.

Angell, Joseph K., and Samuel Ames. *A Treatise on the Law of Private Corporations Aggregate*. Arno Press, 1832.

Anon. "Trusts and Confidence," *The Nation*, 5 May 1887, pp. 380–1.

Antelyes, Peter. *Tales of Adventurous Enterprise: Washington Irving and the Poetics of Western Expansion*. Columbia University Press, 1990.

Aranda, José F. Jr. "Contradictory Impulses: María Amparo Ruiz de Burton, Resistance Theory, and the Politics of Chicano/a Studies." *American Literature*, vol. 70, no. 3, 1998, pp. 551–79.

—. "Returning California to the People: Vigilantism in *The Squatter and the Don*." *María Amparo Ruiz de Burton: Critical and Pedagogical Perspectives*, edited by Amelia María de la Luz Montes and Anne Elizabeth Goldman. University of Nebraska Press, 2004, pp. 11–26.

Austin, William. "Martha Gardner; or, Moral Re-action." *American Monthly Magazine*, December 1837, pp. 565–74.

Avi-Yonah, Reuven S., and Dganit Sivan, "A Historical Perspective on Corporate Form and Real Entity." *The Firm as an Entity: Implications for Economics, Accounting and the Law*, edited by Yuri Biondi, Arnaldo Canziani, and Thierry Kirat. Routledge, 2007, pp. 153–83.

Bain, David Howard. *Empire Express: Building the First Transcontinental Railroad*. Penguin Books, 2000.

Balleisen, Edward J. *Navigating Failure: Bankruptcy and Commercial Society in Antebellum America*. University of North Carolina Press, 2001.

Banta, Martha. *Taylored Lives: Narrative Productions in the Age of Taylor, Veblen, and Ford*. University of Chicago Press, 1993.

Barkan, Joshua. *Corporate Sovereignty: Law and Government Under Capitalism*. University of Minnesota Press, 2013.

Barrett, Ross. *Rendering Violence: Riots, Strikes, and Upheaval in Nineteenth-Century American Art*. University of California Press, 2014.

Barry, J. Neilson, "Documents. Washington Irving and Astoria." *The Washington Historical Quarterly*, vol. 18, no. 2, April 1927, pp. 132–9.

Baym, Nina. *The Shape of Hawthorne's Career*. Cornell University Press, 1976.

Beard, Charles A., and Mary Beard. *The Rise of American Civilization*. Macmillan, 1927.

Beers, Terry. *Gunfight at Mussel Slough: Evolution of a Western Myth*. Santa Clara University Press, 2004.

Benn Michaels, Walter. *The Gold Standard and the Logic of Naturalism*. University of California Press, 1987.

Bergmann, Johannes Dietrich. "The Original Confidence Man." *American Quarterly*, vol. 21, no. 3, 1969, pp. 560–77.

Berlant, Lauren. *The Anatomy of National Fantasy: Hawthorne, Utopia, and Everyday Life*. University of Chicago Press, 1991.

Berle, Adolf A., and Gardiner C. Means. *The Modern Corporation and Private Property*. Rev. ed. Harcourt, Brace and World, 1967.

Berte, Leigh Ann Litwiller. "Mapping 'The Octopus': Frank Norris' Naturalist Geography." *American Literary Realism*, vol. 37, no. 3, Spring 2005, pp. 202–24.

Black's Law Dictionary: Definitions of the Terms and Phrases of American and English Jurisprudence, Ancient and Modern, edited by Henry Campbell Black, Joseph R. Nolan, and Jacqueline M. Nolan-Haley. 6th ed. West, 1990.

Blumenberg, Hans. *Work on Myth*, translated by Robert Wallace. MIT Press, 1988.

Böckenförde, Ernst-Wolfgang. "Organ, Organismus, Organisation, politischer Körper." *Geschichtliche Grundbegriffe*, edited by Otto Brunner, Werner Conze, and Reinhart Koselleck, vol. 4. 2nd ed. Klett-Cotta, 1997, pp. 519–622.

Bose, Purnima, and Laura E. Lyons. "Life Writing and Corporate Personhood." *Biography–an Interdisciplinary Quarterly*, vol. 37, no. 1, 2014, pp. v–xxii.

Bouvier, John. *A Law Dictionary: adapted to the Constitution and laws of the United States of America, and of the several states of the American union, with references to the civil and other systems of foreign law*. 2 vols. T. & J. W. Johnson, 1839.

—. *A Law Dictionary: adapted to the Constitution and laws of the United States of America, and of the several states of the American union, with references to the civil and other systems of foreign law*. 2 vols. J. B. Lippincott & Company, 1892.

Bryant, John. *Melville and Repose: The Rhetoric of Humor in the American Renaissance*. Oxford University Press, 1993.

Bunyan, John. *The Pilgrim's Progress*, edited by N. H. Keeble. Oxford University Press, 1998.

Butterfield, Kevin. *The Making of Tocqueville's America: Law and Association in the Early United States*. University of Chicago Press, 2015.

Carey, Mathew, ed. *Debates and Proceedings of the General Assembly of Pennsylvania*. Seddon and Pritchard, 1786.

Chandler, Alfred D. "The Large Industrial Corporation and the Making of the Modern American Economy." *Institutions in Modern America: Innovation in Structure and Process*, edited by Stephen E. Ambrose. Johns Hopkins University Press, 1967, pp. 71–101.

—. *The Visible Hand: The Managerial Revolution in American Business*. Belknap Press, 1977.

—. *Strategy and Structure: Chapters in the History of the American Industrial Enterprise*. Beard Books, 2003.

Cheng, Anne Anlin. "Ornament and Law." *New Directions in Law and Literature*, edited by Elisabeth Anker and Bernadette Meyler. Oxford University Press, 2017, pp. 229–51.

Cheng, Thomas K. "The Corporate Veil Doctrine Revisited: A Comparative Study of the English and the US Corporate Veil Doctrines." *International and Comparative Law Review*, vol. 34, 2011, pp. 329–412.

Chesnutt, Charles W. "The Partners." *The Short Fiction of Charles W. Chesnutt*, edited by Sylvia Lyons Render. Howard University Press, 1981, pp. 70–2.

—. *A Business Career*. University Press of Mississippi, 2005.

Clarke, M. St. Clair, and D. A. Hall, eds. *Legislative and Documentary History of the Bank of the United States: Including the Original Bank of North America*, vol. 2. Gales and Seaton, 1832.

Cohen, Lara Langer. *The Fabrication of American Literature: Fraudulence and Antebellum Print Culture*. University of Pennsylvania Press, 2012.

Coke, Sir Edward. *The Reports of Sir Edward Coke, Knt.: In Thirteen Parts. A New Ed., With Additional Notes and References, and With Abstracts of the Principal Points*. London: J. Butterworth and Son, 1826.

Collins, Peter E. "Nature, the Individual, and the Market in Norris and Dreiser." *Twentieth-Century Literature*, vol. 58, no. 4, Winter 2012, pp. 556–82.

Conlogue, William. "Farmers' Rhetoric of Defense: California Settlers versus the Southern Pacific Railroad." *California History*, vol. 78, no. 1, 1999, pp. 40–55.

Cook, William W. *The Corporation Problem*. New York: G. P. Putnam's Sons, 1891.

Cooper, James Fenimore. *The Bravo*, edited by Donald A. Ringe. Twayne Publishers, 1963.

—. *The American Democrat and Other Political Writings*. Regnery Publishing, 2000.

Culbertson, Tom. "The Golden Age of American Political Cartoons." *The Journal of the Gilded Age and Progressive Era*, vol. 7, no. 3, July 2008, pp. 276–95.

Davis, Joseph Stancliffe. *Essays in the Earlier History of American Corporations*. Harvard University Press, 1917.

Dayan, Colin. *The Law Is a White Dog: How Legal Rituals Make and Unmake Persons*. Princeton University Press, 2011.

De Forest, John William. *Honest John Vane*. Monument Edition. Bald Eagle Press, 1960.

—. *Miss Ravenel's Conversion from Secession to Loyalty*, edited by Gary Scharnhorst. Penguin Books, 2000.

Debates and Proceedings of the Constitutional Convention of the State of California, convened at the city of Sacramento, Saturday, September 28, 1878. E. B. Wills and P. K. Stockton, official stenographers. 3 vols. Sacramento: State Office, J. D. Young, Supt. State printing, 1880–1.

Dorfman, Joseph. *The Economic Mind in American Civilization, 1865–1918*, vol. 3. New Viking Press, 1949.

Dorson, James. "Rates, Romance, and Regulated Monopoly in Frank Norris's *The Octopus*." *Studies in American Naturalism*, vol. 12, no. 1, Summer 2017, pp. 50–69.

Eddy, Arthur J. *The Law of Combinations*. Callaghan & Co., 1901.

Elder, Marjorie J. *Nathaniel Hawthorne, Transcendental Symbolist*. Ohio University Press, 1969.

Ellis, Reuben J. "'A Little Turn Through the Country': Presley's Bicycle Ride in Frank Norris's *The Octopus*." *Journal of American Culture*, vol. 17, no. 3, 1994, pp. 17–22.

Ellis, Richard E. *Aggressive Nationalism: McCulloch v. Maryland and the Foundation of Federal Authority in the Young Republic*. Oxford University Press, 2007.

Fehrenbacher, Don E. "Roger B. Taney and the Sectional Crisis." *The Journal of Southern History*, vol. 43, no. 4, 1977, pp. 555–66.

—. *The Dred Scott Case: Its Significance in American Law and Politics*. Oxford University Press, 2001.

Feidelson, Charles. *Symbolism and American Literature*. University of Chicago Press, 1953.

Ferguson, Robert A. *Reading the Early Republic*. Harvard University Press, 2006.

Fiedler, Leslie A. *Love and Death in the American Novel*. Dalkey Archive Press, 1960.

Field, Henry. *Blood Is Thicker than Water: A Few Days Among Our Southern Brethren*. New York: George Munro, 1886.

Fluck, Winfried. *Das Kulturelle Imaginäre: Eine Funktionsgeschichte des Amerikanischen Romans, 1790–1900*. Suhrkamp, 1997.

Fludernik, Monika. "Collective Minds in Fact and Fiction: Intermental Thought and Group Consciousness in Early Modern Narrative." *Poetics Today: International Journal for Theory and Analysis of Literature and Communication*, vol. 35, no. 4, 2015, pp. 689–730.

Freund, Ernst. *The Legal Nature of Corporations*. University of Chicago Press, 1897.

Gearey, Adam. "'We Want to Live': Metaphor and Ethical Life in F. W. Maitland's Jurisprudence of the Trust." *Journal of Law and Society*, vol. 43, no. 1, 2016, pp. 105–22.

Gierke, Otto Friedrich von. *Political Theories of the Middle Age*, translated by Frederic William Maitland. Cambridge University Press, 1900.

—. *Community in Historical Perspective*, translated by Anthony Black. Cambridge University Press, 1990.

Goforth, Carol. "A Corporation Has No Soul, and Doesn't Go to Church: Relating the Doctrine of Piercing the Veil to *Burwell v. Hobby Lobby*." *South Carolina Law Review*, vol. 67, no. 1, 2015, pp. 73–97.

Grady, Henry Woodfin. "The New South." *The Complete Orations and Speeches of Henry W. Grady*, edited by Edwin Du Bois Shurter. Hinds, Noble & Eldredge, 1910.

Graham, Howard J. *Everyman's Constitution: Historical Essays on the Fourteenth Amendment, the "Conspiracy Theory," and American Constitutionalism*. The State Historical Society of Wisconsin, 2013.

Grant, Thomas. "Judge." *American Humor Magazines and Comic Periodicals*, edited by David E. E. Sloane. Greenwood Press, 1987.

Greiman, Jennifer. "Theatricality, Strangeness, and the Aesthetics of Plurality in *The Confidence-Man*." *Melville and Aesthetics*, edited by Geoffrey Sanborn and Samuel Otter. Palgrave Macmillan, 2011, pp. 173–92.

Hall, Peter Dobkin. *The Organization of American Culture, 1700–1900: Private Institutions, Elites, and the Origins of American Nationality*. New York University Press, 1982.

Halttunen, Karen. *Confidence Men and Painted Women: A Study of Middle-Class Culture in America, 1830–1870*. Yale University Press, 1982.

Hammond, Bray. *Banks and Politics in America: From the Revolution to the Civil War*. Princeton University Press, 1957.

Handlin, Oscar, and Mary Flug Handlin. "Origins of the American Business Corporation." *The Journal of Economic History*, vol. 5, no. 1, 1945, pp. 1–23.

Hartz, Louis. *The Liberal Tradition in America*. Harcourt, Brace & World, 1955.

Hawthorne, Nathaniel. "The Celestial Railroad." *The United States Democratic Review*, May 1843, pp. 515–23.

—. *The House of the Seven Gables*. Modern Library, 2001.

Hays, Samuel P. *The Response to Industrialism, 1885–1914*. Chicago University Press, 1957.

Helfman, Tara. "Transatlantic Influences on American Corporate Jurisprudence: Theorizing the Corporation in the United States." *Indiana Journal of Global Legal Studies*, vol. 23, 2016, pp. 383–424.

Hemenway, David. *Prices and Choices: Microeconomic Vignettes*. Ballinger Publishing Co., 1977.

Henderson, George L. *California and the Fictions of Capital*. Oxford University Press, 1999.

Hill, Christopher. *Change and Continuity in Seventeenth-Century England*. Yale University Press, 1991.

Hilt, Eric. "Early American Corporations and the State." *Corporations and American Democracy*, edited by Naomi R. Lamoreaux and William J. Novak. Harvard University Press, 2017.

Hobbes, Thomas. *Leviathan*, edited by Richard Tuck. Cambridge University Press, 1996.

Horwitz, Howard. *By the Law of Nature: Form and Value in Nineteenth-Century America*. Oxford University Press, 1991.

Horwitz, Morton J. *The Transformation of American Law: 1780–1860*. Harvard University Press, 1977.

—. *The Transformation of American Law, 1870–1960: The Crisis of Legal Orthodoxy*. Oxford University Press, 1994.

Hovenkamp, Herbert. *Enterprise and American Law, 1836–1937*. Harvard University Press, 1991.

—. *The Opening of American Law: Neoclassical Legal Thought, 1870–1970*. Oxford University Press, 2015.

Howard, June. *Form and History in American Literary Naturalism*. University of North Carolina Press, 1985.

Hunt, Lynn, and Jack Censer. "Imaging the French Revolution: Depictions of the French Revolutionary Crowd." *The American Historical Review*, vol. 110, no. 1, February 2005, pp. 38–45.

Hurst, James Willard. *The Legitimacy of the Business Corporation in the Law of the United States, 1780–1970*. University Press of Virginia, 1970.

Ihalainen, Pasi. "Towards an Immortal Political Body: The State Machine in Eighteenth-Century English Political Discourse." *Contributions to the History of Concepts*, vol. 5, no. 1, 2009, pp. 4–47.

Irving, Washington. *Astoria. Three Western Narratives*, edited by James P. Ronda. Literary Classics of the United States, 2004.

Iser, Wolfgang. *The Fictive and the Imaginary: Charting Literary Anthropology*. John Hopkins University Press, 1993.

Jaros, Peter. "The Faculties of Law: Robert Montgomery Bird's *Sheppard Lee* as Legal Fiction." *J19: The Journal of Nineteenth-Century Americanists*, vol. 3, no. 2, Fall 2015, pp. 307–35.

—. "Irving's *Astoria* and the Forms of Enterprise." *American Literary History*, vol. 30, no. 1, Spring 2018, pp. 1–28.

John, Richard R. "Robber Barons Redux: Antimonopoly Reconsidered." *Enterprise & Society*, vol. 13, no. 1, 2012, pp. 1–38.

Kantorowicz, Ernst Hartwig. *The King's Two Bodies: A Study in Mediaeval Political Theology*. Princeton University Press, 1957.

Kaplan, Edward. *The Bank of the United States and the American Economy*. Greenwood Press, 1999.

Kendall, Amos. "Anecdotes of General Jackson." *The United States Democratic Review*, September 1842, pp. 272–4.

Knight, Peter. *Reading the Market: Genres of Financial Capitalism in Gilded Age America*. Johns Hopkins University Press, 2016.

Kokkinakis, Yannis. "The "Many-Headed Monster" and Its Critics in Revolutionary America. *Review of History and Political Science*, vol. 3, no. 1, June 2015, pp. 81–94.

Kutler, Stanley I. *Privilege and Creative Destruction: The Charles River Bridge Case*. Lippincott, 1971.

Kyd, Stewart. *Treatise on the Law of Corporations*. London: Butterworth, 1793.

Lamoreaux, Naomi R. "Partnerships, Corporations, and the Limits of Contractual Freedom in US History: An Essay in Economics, Law, and Culture." *Constructing Corporate America: History, Politics, Culture*, edited by Kenneth Lipartito. Oxford University Press, 2004, pp. 29–65.

Lamoreaux, Naomi R., and William Novak, eds. *Corporations and American Democracy*. Harvard University Press, 2017.

Larson, John Lauritz. *Market Revolution in America: Liberty, Ambition, and the Eclipse of the Common Good*. Cambridge University Press, 2009.

Laski, Harold J. "The Personality of Associations." *Harvard Law Review*, vol. 29, no. 4, 1916, pp. 404–26.

LeMenager, Stephanie. "Trading Stories: Washington Irving and the Global West." *American Literary History*, vol. 15, no. 4, 2003, pp. 683–708.

Letwin, William. *Law and Economic Policy in America: The Evolution of the Sherman Antitrust Act*. Random House, 1965.

Leverenz, David. *Paternalism Incorporated: Fables of American Fatherhood, 1865–1940*. Cornell University Press, 2004.

Levine, Robert S. *Conspiracy and Romance: Studies in Brockden Brown, Cooper, Hawthorne, and Melville*. Cambridge University Press, 1989.

Levy, Leo B. "Naturalism in the Making: De Forest's *Honest John Vane*." *New England Quarterly: A Historical Review of New England Life and Letters*, vol. 37, no. 1, 1964, pp. 89–98.

Lewis, Oscar. *The Big Four*. Knopf, 1941.

Linebaugh, Peter, and Marcus Rediker. *The Many-Headed Hydra: Sailors, Slaves, Commoners, and the Hidden History of the Revolutionary Atlantic*. Beacon Press, 2013.

Lipartito, Kenneth. "The Utopian Corporation." *Constructing Corporate America: History, Politics, Culture*, edited by Kenneth Lipartito. Oxford University Press, 2004, pp. 94–119.

Livingston, James. *Pragmatism and the Political Economy of Cultural Revolution, 1850–1940*. University of North Carolina Press, 1994.

Love, Glen A., and David A. Carpenter. "The Other Octopus." *American Literary Realism, 1870–1910*, vol. 14, no. 1, Spring 1981, pp. 1–5.

Loveland, Ann C. "James Fenimore Cooper and the American Mission." *American Quarterly*, vol. 21, no. 2, 1969, pp. 244–58.

Lustig, R. Jeffrey. "Private Rights and Public Purposes: California's Second Constitution Reconsidered." *California History*, vol. 87, no. 3, 2010, pp. 46–70.

Lye, Colleen. "American Naturalism and Asiatic Racial Form: Frank Norris's *The Octopus* and Moran of the 'Lady Letty.'" *Representations*, vol. 84, no. 1, 2003, pp. 73–99.

—. *America's Asia: Racial Form and American Literature, 1893–1945*. Princeton University Press, 2005.

Maier, Pauline. "The Revolutionary Origins of the American Corporation." *The William and Mary Quarterly*, vol. 50, no. 1, January 1993, pp. 51–84.

Malkmus, Bernhard. "The Birth of the Modern Pícaro out of the Spirit of Self-Reliance: Herman Melville's 'The Confidence-Man.'" *Amerikastudien/American Studies*, vol. 54, no.4, pp. 603–20.

Marchand, Roland. *Creating the Corporate Soul: The Rise of Public Relations and Corporate Imagery in American Big Business*. University of California Press, 2000.

Mark, Gregory A. "The Personification of the Business Corporation in American Law." *University of Chicago Law Review*, vol. 54, 1987, pp. 1441–83.

McCarthy, Kathleen D. *American Creed: Philanthropy and the Rise of Civil Society, 1700–1865*. University of Chicago Press, 2005.

McKee, Irving. "Notable Memorials to Mussel Slough." *Pacific Historical Review*, vol. 12, 1948, pp. 19–27.

McNally, David. *Monsters of the Market: Zombies, Vampires, and Global Capitalism*. Haymarket Books, 2012.

Mellor, Anne. "English Women Writers and the French Revolution." *Rebel Daughters: Women and the French Revolution*, edited by Sara E. Melzer and Leslie W. Rabine. Oxford University Press, 1992.

Melville, Herman. *The Confidence-Man: His Masquerade*, edited by Hershel Parker and Mark Niemeyer, 2nd ed. W. W. Norton, 2006.

Meyers, Marvin. *The Jacksonian Persuasion: Politics and Belief*. Stanford University Press, 1957.

Michaels, Walter Benn. *The Gold Standard and the Logic of Naturalism*. University of California Press, 1987.

Mihm, Stephen. *A Nation of Counterfeiters: Capitalists, Con Men, and the Making of the United States*. Harvard University Press, 2007.

—. "The Fog of War: Jackson, Biddle and the Destruction of the Bank of the United States." *A Companion to the Era of Andrew Jackson*, edited by Sean P. Adams. Wiley-Blackwell, 2013, pp. 349–75.

Morrow, William Chamber. *Blood-Money*. San Francisco: Walker & Co., 1882.

Mott, Frank L. *A History of American Magazines*, vols. III & IV. Harvard University Press, 1957.

Muenkler, Laura. "Metaphern im Recht: Zur Bedeutung organischer Vorstellungen von Staat und Recht." *Der Staat*, vol. 55, 2016, pp. 181–211.

Murphy, Brian Phillips. "The Market Revolution." *A Companion to the Era of Andrew Jackson*, edited by Sean P. Adams. Wiley-Blackwell, 2013, pp. 93–110.

Nevins, Allan. *Study in Power: John D. Rockefeller, Industrialist and Philanthropist*, vol. 1. Scribner, 1953.

Newfield, Christopher. *The Emerson Effect: Individualism and Submission in America*. University of Chicago Press, 1996.

Newmyer, R. Kent. *Supreme Court Justice Joseph Story: Statesman of the Old Republic*. University of North Carolina Press, 1986.

Norris, Frank. *The Pit*. Doubleday, Page & Co., 1903.

—. *The Octopus. Frank Norris: Novels and Essays*, edited by Donald Pizer. Literary Classics of the United States, 1986.

Novak, William J. *The People's Welfare: Law and Regulation in Nineteenth-Century America*. University of North Carolina Press, 1996.

Palmeri, Frank. *Satire in Narrative: Petronius, Swift, Gibbon, Melville, and Pynchon*. University of Texas Press, 1990.

Patrides, C. A. "'The Beast with Many Heads': Renaissance Views on the Multitude." *Shakespeare Quarterly*, vol. 16, no. 2, Spring 1965, pp. 241–6.

Pavlovskis-Petit, Zoja. "Irony and Satire." *A Companion to Satire*, edited by Ruben Quintero. Blackwell Publishing, 2007.

Pérez, Vincent. "Remembering the Hacienda: Land and Community in Californio Narratives." *María Amparo Ruiz de Burton: Critical and Pedagogical Perspectives*, edited by Amelia María de la Luz Montes and Anne Elizabeth Goldman. University of Nebraska Press, 2004, pp. 27–55.

Pfister, Joel. *Individuality Incorporated: Indians and the Multicultural Modern*. Duke University Press, 2004.

Pitt, Leonard. *Decline of the Californios: A Social History of the Spanish-Speaking Californians, 1846–1890*. University of California Press, 1966.

Pizer, Donald. *The Novels of Frank Norris*. Indiana University Press, 1966.

—. "Collis P. Huntington, William S. Rainsford, and the Conclusion of Frank Norris's The Octopus." *Studies in American Naturalism*, vol. 5, no. 2, 2011, pp. 133–50.

Plato. *The Republic of Plato*, translated by Allan Bloom. Basic Books, 1991.

Pocock, J. G. A. *The Machiavellian Moment: Florentine Political Thought and the Atlantic Republican Tradition*. Princeton University Press, 2016.

Porter, Kenneth W. *John Jacob Astor, Business Man*. Harvard University Press, 1931.

Post-Lauria, Sheila. *Correspondent Colorings: Melville in the Marketplace*. University of Massachusetts Press, 1996.

Postel, Charles. *The Populist Vision*. Oxford University Press, 2007.

Pudaloff, Ross J. "Cooper's Genres and American Problems." *ELH*, vol. 50, no. 4, 1983, pp. 711–27.

Raab, Josef. "The Imagined Inter-American Community of María Amparo Ruiz de Burton." *Amerikastudien/American Studies*, vol. 53, no. 1, 2008, pp. 77–95.

Ramirez, Pablo A. "American Imperialism in the Age of Contract: Herbert Spencer and the Defeat of Contractual Capitalism in Ruiz de Burton's *The Squatter and the Don*." *ESQ: A Journal of the American Renaissance*, vol. 57, no. 4, 2011, pp. 427–55.

Remini, Robert V. *Andrew Jackson and the Bank War: A Study in the Growth of Presidential Power*. W. W. Norton, 1967.

—, ed. *The Age of Jackson*. Harper & Row, 1972.

Reynolds, David S. *Beneath the American Renaissance: The Subversive Imagination in the Age of Emerson and Melville.* Harvard University Press, 1989.

Reynolds, Larry J. "Hawthorne's Labors in Concord." *The Cambridge Companion to Nathaniel Hawthorne,* edited by Richard H. Millington. Cambridge University Press, 2004, pp. 10–34.

Richardson, James D. *A Compilation of the Messages and Papers of the Presidents,* vol. III. Bureau of National Literature, 1917.

Riesman, David. *The Lonely Crowd: A Study of the Changing American Character.* Yale University Press, 1950.

Ritter, Gretchen. *Goldbugs and Greenbacks: The Antimonopoly Tradition and the Politics of Finance in America, 1865–1896.* Cambridge University Press, 1999.

Rivera, John-Michael. *The Emergence of Mexican America: Recovering Stories of Mexican Peoplehood in US Culture.* New York University Press, 2006.

Robinson, Forrest G. "Josiah Royce's California." *Western American Literature,* vol. 36, no. 4, 2002, pp. 343–58.

Robinson, John R. *The Octopus: A History of the Construction, Conspiracies, Extortions, Robberies, and Villainous Acts of the Central Pacific, Southern Pacific of Kentucky, Union Pacific, and Other Subsidized Railroads.* San Francisco, 1894.

Rolston, Arthur. "Capital, Corporations, and Their Discontents in Making California's Constitutions, 1849–1911." *Pacific Historical Review,* vol. 80, no. 4, 2011, pp. 521–56.

Ronda, James P. "Chronology." *Three Western Narratives* by Washington Irving. Literary Classics of the United States, 2004.

Royce, Josiah. *California: From the Conquest in 1846 to the Second Vigilance Committee in San Francisco. A Study of American Character.* Boston and New York: Houghton, Mifflin and Co., 1886.

——. *The Feud of Oakfield Creek: A Novel of California Life.* Boston and New York: Houghton, Mifflin and Co., 1887.

Ruiz de Burton, María Amparo. *Conflicts of Interest: The Letters of María Amparo Ruiz de Burton,* edited and with an introduction by Rosaura Sánchez and Beatrice Pita. Arte Público Press, 2001.

——. *The Squatter and the Don,* edited and with an introduction by Jennifer M. Acker. Modern Library, 2004.

——. *Who Would Have Thought It?,* edited by Amelia María de la Luz Montes. Penguin Books, 2009.

Salzman, Ed, and Ann Leigh Brown. *The Cartoon History of California Politics.* California Journal Press, 1978.

Saxton, Alexander. *The Indispensable Enemy: Labor and the Anti-Chinese Movement in California.* University of California Press, 1995.

Scheiber, Harry N. "Race, Radicalism, and Reform: Historical Perspective on the 1879 California Constitution." *Hastings Constitutional Law Quarterly,* vol. 17, no. 1, Fall 1989, pp. 35–80.

Secor, Robert. "Puck." *American Humor Magazines and Comic Periodicals,* edited by David E. E. Sloane. Greenwood Press, 1987.

Sedgwick, Theodore. *What Is a Monopoly? Or, Some Considerations upon the Subject of Corporations and Currency.* New York State, 1835.

Sellers, Charles. *The Market Revolution: Jacksonian America, 1815–1846.* Oxford University Press, 1991.

Seybold, Matthew. "Quite an Original Failure: Melville's Imagined Reader in *The Confidence-Man*." *Reception: Texts, Readers, Audiences, History*, vol. 8, 2016, pp. 73–92.

Sicius, Francis J. *The Progressive Era: A Reference Guide*. ABC-CLIO, 2015.

Siraganian, Lisa. "Theorizing Corporate Intentionality in Contemporary American Fiction." *Law & Literature*, vol. 27, no. 1, 2015, pp. 99–123.

—. *Modernism and the Meaning of Corporate Persons*. Oxford University Press, 2020.

Sklansky, Jeffrey P. *The Soul's Economy: Market Society and Selfhood in American Thought, 1820–1920*. University of North Carolina Press, 2002.

Sklar, Martin J. *The Corporate Reconstruction of American Capitalism, 1890–1916*. Cambridge University Press, 1988.

Slotkin, Richard. *Gunfighter Nation: The Myth of the Frontier in Twentieth-Century America*. Macmillan, 1992.

Smith, Adam, and Andrew S. Skinner. *The Wealth of Nations*. Penguin Books, 1999.

Smith, Stacey L. *Freedom's Frontier: California and the Struggle over Unfree Labor, Emancipation, and Reconstruction*. The University of North Carolina Press, 2013.

Speir, Ian. "Corporations, the Original Understanding, and the Problem of Power." *The Georgetown Journal of Law & Public Policy*, vol. 10, 2012, pp. 115–83.

Stephens, Beth. "Are Corporations People? Corporate Personhood under the Constitution and International Law." *Rutgers Law Journal*, vol. 44, no. 1, 2013, pp. 1–38.

Stern, Philip J. *The Company-State: Corporate Sovereignty and the Early Modern Foundation of the British Empire in India*. Oxford University Press, 2011.

Stolleis, Michael. *Das Auge des Gesetzes: Geschichte einer Metapher*. Beck, 2004.

Story, Joseph. *Commentaries on the Law of Agency: As a Branch of Commercial and Maritime Jurisprudence, with Occasional Illustrations from the Civil and Foreign Law*. 2nd ed., revised and enlarged. Boston: Charles C. Little & James Brown, 1844.

—. *The Life and Letters of Joseph Story*, edited by William Wetmore Story. 2 vols. Houghton and Haywood, 1851.

Stout, Daniel. *Corporate Romanticism: Liberalism, Justice, and the Novel*. Fordham University Press, 2017.

Swisher, Carl B. *The History of the Supreme Court: The Taney Period, 1836–1864*. Cambridge University Press, 2010.

Tarbell, Ida Minerva. *The History of the Standard Oil Company*. 2 vols. McClure, Phillips & Co., 1904.

—. "John D. Rockefeller: A Character Study, Part I." *McClure's Magazine*, July 1905, pp. 227–49.

—. "John D. Rockefeller: A Character Study, Part II." *McClure's Magazine*, August 1905, pp. 386–97.

Taylor, Welford D., ed. *The Newsprint Mask: The Tradition of the Fictional Journalist in America*. Iowa State University Press, 1991.

Thomas, Brook. *Cross-Examinations of Law and Literature: Cooper, Hawthorne, Stowe, and Melville*. Cambridge University Press, 1990.

—. *The New Historicism: And Other Old-Fashioned Topics*. Princeton University Press, 1991.

—. *American Literary Realism and the Failed Promise of Contract*. University of California Press, 1998.

—. *The Literature of Reconstruction: Not in Plain Black and White*. The Johns Hopkins University Press, 2017.

Trachtenberg, Alan. *The Incorporation of America: Culture and Society in the Gilded Age*. 25th anniversary ed. Hill and Wang, 2007.

Trimpi, Helen P. *Melville's Confidence Men and American Politics in the 1850s*. Archon Books, 1987.

Turner, Henry S. *The Corporate Commonwealth: Pluralism and Political Fictions in England, 1516–1651*. University of Chicago Press, 2016.

Twain, Mark, and Charles Dudley Warner. *The Gilded Age*, edited by Augustus Hoppin. Modern Library, 2006.

United States Congress. *Register of Debates in Congress*, vol. 13. Gales and Seaton, 1837.

Vann Woodward, C. V. *Reunion and Reaction: The Compromise of 1877 and the End of Reconstruction*. Oxford University Press, 1991.

Wadlington, Warwick. *The Confidence Game in American Literature*. Princeton University Press, 1975.

Walter, John. *Crowds and Popular Politics in Early Modern England*. Manchester University Press, 2014.

Warford, Elisa. "'An Eloquent and Impassioned Plea': The Rhetoric of Ruiz de Burton's *The Squatter and the Don*." *Western American Literature*, vol. 44, no. 1, 2009, pp. 5–21.

Warner, Susan, and Jane Tompkins. *The Wide, Wide World*. The Feminist Press at CUNY, 1993.

Watson, David. "Lawless Intervals: Washington Irving's Astoria and the Procession of Empire." *American Studies in Scandinavia*, vol. 42, no. 1, 2010, pp. 5–24.

Weinberg, Steve. *Taking on the Trust: The Epic Battle of Ida Tarbell and John D. Rockefeller*. W. W. Norton, 2008.

Weinstein, Cindy. *The Literature of Labor and the Labors of Literature: Allegory in Nineteenth-Century American Fiction*. Cambridge University Press, 1995.

White, Richard. *Railroaded: The Transcontinentals and the Making of Modern America*. W. W. Norton, 2011.

White, T. H., ed. *The Book of Beasts: Being a Translation from a Latin Bestiary of the Twelfth Century*. Dover, 1984.

Whyte, William H. *The Organization Man*. Doubleday, 1956.

Wiebe, Robert H. *The Search for Order, 1877–1920*. Hill and Wang, 1967.

Wilson, Sloan. *The Man in the Gray Flannel Suit*. Da Capo Press, 2002.

Winkler, Adam. *We the Corporations: How American Businesses won their Civil Rights*. Liveright Publishing, 2018.

Wood, Adam H. "'The Signs and Symbols of the West': Frank Norris, *The Octopus*, and the Naturalization of Market Capitalism." *Twisted from the Ordinary: Essays on American Literary Naturalism*, edited by Mary E. Papke. University of Tennessee Press, 2003, pp. 107–27.

Wood, Gordon S. *The Creation of the American Republic, 1776–1787*. University of North Carolina Press, 1998.

Wormser, I. Maurice. "Piercing the Veil of Corporate Entity." *Columbia Law Review*, vol. 12, no. 6, 1912, pp. 496–519.

Wright, Robert E. *Corporation Nation*. University of Pennsylvania Press, 2014.

Yates, Richard. *Revolutionary Road*. Dell, 1961.

Zimmerman, David A. "Frank Norris, Market Panic, and the Mesmeric Sublime." *American Literature*, vol. 75, no. 1, 2003, pp. 61–90.

Zunz, Olivier. *Making America Corporate: 1870–1920*. University of Chicago Press, 1992.

Cartoons and Caricatures

Anon. "King Andrew the First." New York, 1833. Library of Congress, Washington, DC.

Anon. "Nothing but Feed and Fight." *Harper's Weekly* (December 3, 1887). Library of Congress, Washington, DC.

Bisbee, Ezra. "Political Quixotism." New York, 1833. Library of Congress, Washington, DC.

Dalrymple, Louis. "The Neglected Idol." Cover, *Puck's Magazine*, vol. 37, no. 946 (April 24, 1895). Library of Congress, Washington, DC.

Ehrhart, S. D. "Caesar Up to Date." Cover, *Puck's Magazine*, vol. 47, no. 16 (June 27, 1900). Library of Congress, Washington, DC.

Keller, G. Frederick. "The Ogre of Mussel Slough." *The Wasp*, vol. 6, no. 241 (March 12, 1881). California State Library, Sacramento, CA.

Keller, G. Frederick. "What Shall We Do With Our Boys?" *The Wasp*, 8 (January to June 1882). The Bancroft Library, University of California, Berkeley.

Keller, G. Frederick. "The Curse of California." *The Wasp*, 9, no. 316 (August 19, 1882). The Bancroft Library, University of California, Berkeley.

Keppler, Udo J. "The True Inwardness of It." Cover, *Puck's Magazine*, vol. 40, no. 1025 (October 28, 1896). Library of Congress, Washington, DC.

Keppler, Udo J. "Between Two of a Kind." Centerfold, *Puck's Magazine*, vol. 51 (June 11, 1902). Library of Congress, Washington, DC.

Keppler, Udo J. "A Napoleon of 'High Finance.'" Cover, *Puck's Magazine*, vol. 55, no. 1410 (March 9, 1904). Library of Congress, Washington, DC.

Keppler, Udo J. "Next!" *Puck's Magazine*, vol. 56, no. 1436 (September 7, 1904). Library of Congress, Washington, DC.

Keppler, Udo J. and J. Ottmann. "Bosses of the Senate." *Puck's Magazine*, vol. 24, no. 620 (January 23, 1889). Library of Congress, Washington, DC.

Opper, Frederick Burr. "The 'Little Napoleon of Wall Street' in Exile." *Puck's Magazine*, vol. 18, no. 450 (October 21, 1885). Library of Congress, Washington, DC.

Pughe, John S. "The King of Combinations." *Puck's Magazine*, vol. 49, no. 1251 (February 27, 1901). Library of Congress, Washington, DC.

Pughe, John S. "The Kind of Anti-Trust Legislation That Is Needed." *Puck's Magazine* (February 5, 1902). Library of Congress, Washington, DC.

Robinson, Henry R. "General Jackson Slaying the Many-Headed Monster." 1836. Library of Congress, Washington, DC.

Rogers, William Allen. "The Trustworthy Beast." *Harper's Weekly*, vol. 32, no. 1661 (October 20, 1888). The George Peabody Library, The Sheridan Libraries, Johns Hopkins University.

Court Cases

Abrams v. United States. 250 U.S. 616 (1919).

Bank of Augusta v. Earle. 38 U.S. 519 (1839).

Bank of the United States v. Deveaux. 9 U.S. 61 (1809).
Charles River Bridge v. Warren Bridge. 36 U.S. 420 (1837).
Citizens United v. Federal Election Commission. 58 U.S. 310 (2010).
Commonwealth v. Alger. 61 Mass. 53 (1851).
Commonwealth v. Hunt. 45 Mass. 111 (1842).
Dred Scott v. Sanford. 60 U.S. 393 (1857).
Fletcher v. Peck. 10 U.S. 87 (1810).
Gibbons v. Ogden. 22 U.S. 1 (1824).
Hale v. Henkel. 201 U.S. 43 (1906).
In re Ah Chong. 2 Fed. 733 (C.C.D. Cal. 1880).
In re Tiburcio Parrott, 1 Fed. 481 (C.C.D. Cal. 1880).
Louisville Rail-road Co. v. Letson. 43 U.S. 497 (1844).
Liggett Co. v. Lee. 288 U.S. 517 (1933).
Marshall v. Baltimore & Ohio Railroad Company. 57 U.S. 314 (1853).
Mayor and Commonality v. Wood. 88 Eng. Rep. 1592 (1702).
McCulloch v. Maryland. 17 U.S. 316 (1819).
Munn v. Illinois. 94 U.S. 113 (1877).
Northern Securities Company v. United States. 193 U.S. 197 (1904).
Plessy v. Ferguson. 163 U.S. 537 (1896).
Richardson v. Christian H. Buhl and Russel A. Alger. 77 Mich. 632 (1889).
Rundle v. Delaware & Raritan Canal Company. 55 U.S. 80 (1852).
San Bernardino County v. Southern Pacific Railroad Company. 118 U.S. 417 (1886).
San Mateo County v. Southern Pacific R. Co. 116 U.S. 138 (1885).
Santa Clara County v. Southern Pacific Railroad Company. 118 U.S. 394 (1886).
Slaughter-House Cases. 83 U.S. 36 (1873).
Southern Railway Co. v. Greene. 216 U.S. 400 (1910).
State v. Nebraska Distilling Co. 29 Neb. 700 (1890).
State v. Standard Oil Co. 49 Ohio St. 137 (1892).
Stokes v. Saltonstall. 38 U.S. 13 (1839).
Strawbridge v. Curtiss. 7 U.S. 267 (1806).
The People v. The North Sugar Refining Co. 121 N.Y. 582 (1890).
Thorpe v. Rutland & Burlington R. R. Co. 27 Vt. 140 (1854).
Trustees of Dartmouth College v. Woodward. 17 U.S. 518 (1819).
United States v. Trans-Missouri Freight Association. 166 U.S. 290 (1897).
Wabash, St. Louis & Pacific Railway Company v. Illinois. 118 U.S. 557 (1886).

Index